THE SUBLIME, TERROR AND HUMAN DIFFERENCE

Christine Battersby is a leading thinker in the field of philosophy, gender studies and visual and literary aesthetics. In this important new work, she undertakes a thought-provoking exploration of the nature of the sublime, one of the most important topics in contemporary debates about modernity, politics and art. Through a close and compelling examination of terror, transcendence and the 'other' in the writings of key European philosophers, Battersby articulates a radical 'female sublime'.

A central feature of *The Sublime, Terror and Human Difference* is its engagement with recent debates around '9/11', race and Islam. Battersby shows how, since the eighteenth century, the pleasures of the sublime have been described in terms of the transcendence of terror. Linked to the 'feminine', the sublime was closed off to flesh-and-blood women, to 'Orientals' and to other supposedly 'inferior' human types. Engaging with Kant, Burke, the German Romantics, Nietzsche, Derrida, Lyotard, Irigaray and Arendt, as well as with women writers and artists, Battersby traces the history of these exclusions, while finding resources within the history of western culture for thinking *human* differences afresh.

This exceptional book will be of interest to students of continental philosophy, aesthetics, gender studies, literary theory, visual culture, and race and social theory.

Christine Battersby is Reader in Philosophy at the University of Warwick. She is author of *Gender and Genius: Towards a Feminist Aesthetics* and *The Phenomenal Woman: Feminist Metaphysics and the Patterns of Identity*.

'Battersby's new study offers challenging arguments backed up by detailed textual analysis; her treatment of Kant is a real *tour de force*, and the writing is
clear and vivid. The examination is especially deep on the subjects of gender,
the female, and the feminine in relation to the concept of the sublime.'

Carolyn Korsmeyer, University at Buffalo, USA

'... a rich and insightful treatment of the aesthetics and the politics of the
sublime. It is impressive not only for its historical range and philosophical
perspicuity, but likewise for its thoughtful treatment of questions of race, gender
and the event of 9/11. Philosophers, political theorists, and students of cultural
studies alike will benefit from Battersby's original and nuanced intervention.'

Robert Gooding-Willliams, The University of Chicago, USA

'Christine Battersby's deep understanding of the history of the idea of the sublime has enabled her to present a new account of it that is sensitive to multicultural and especially feminist concerns. This wonderfully informative and
stimulating study deserves a wide readership.'

Robert Bernasconi, The University of Memphis, USA

THE SUBLIME, TERROR AND HUMAN DIFFERENCE

Christine Battersby

Routledge
Taylor & Francis Group

LONDON AND NEW YORK

First published 2007
by Routledge
2 Park Square, Milton Park, Abingdon, OX14 4RN

Simultaneously published in the USA and Canada
by Routledge
270 Madison Ave, New York, NY 10016

Routledge is an imprint of the Taylor & Francis Group, an informa business

© 2007 Christine Battersby

Typeset in Goudy by Taylor & Francis Books
Printed and bound in Great Britain by
TJ International Ltd, Padstow, Cornwall

British Library Cataloguing in Publication Data
A catalogue record for this book is available from the British Library

Library of Congress Cataloging in Publication Data
A catalog record for this book has been requested

ISBN 10: 0-415-14810–3 (hbk)
ISBN 10: 0-415-14811–1 (pbk)
ISBN 10: 0-203-94561–1 (ebk)

ISBN 13: 978-0-415-14810-8 (hbk)
ISBN 13: 978-0-415-14811-5 (pbk)
ISBN 13: 978-0-203-94561-2 (ebk)

CONTENTS

ACKNOWLEDGEMENTS

I would like to thank the Arts and Humanities Research Council for funding the completion of this project, as well as the University of Warwick for Study Leave. Chapter 2 and portions of Chapters 3, 5, 6 and 7 have been previously published in *Postcolonial Studies* (*Forum Terror*, 2003); *Feminism and Tradition in Aesthetics* (eds Peggy Z. Brand and Carolyn Korsmeyer); *Political Gender* (eds Sally Ledger, Josephine McDonagh and Jane Spencer) and *Antinomies* (Mead Gallery, University of Warwick). I am indebted to the editors of these various volumes for their feedback, as well as to all those who asked questions during or after the numerous seminars, conference papers and lectures where I tried out this material. For funding to travel to overseas venues, I am grateful to The British Council and The Australia Council.

Sincere thanks are also due to my colleague, Keith Ansell Pearson, for his detailed, helpful and generous comments on the section on Nietzsche. I am also grateful to all those current and former graduate students at Warwick—especially Rachel Jones and Janice Richardson—who pushed me to think further about Kant and the sublime. Finally, I would like to thank the Routledge team, most especially Tony Bruce and Amanda Lucas, for all their help with the production of this book.

Arts & Humanities
Research Council

NOTES ON THE TEXTS AND ABBREVIATIONS

Corr.	I have generally tried to give an in-text reference to an existing translation into English; *corr.* indicates where I have made corrections to the cited text.

Kant, Immanuel

All in-text references to Kant's writings follow the standard format of the volume and page in the German Akademie edition (*KGS* below); where Akademie numerals are not noted in the cited English translation, the page number in the translation is also supplied.

A	1781 ed. of *CPR* (see below).
Anth.	(1798/1800) *Anthropology from a Pragmatic Point of View*, trans. Victor Lyle Dowdell, Southern Illinois University Press, 1996.
B	1787 ed. of *CPR* (see below).
CPJ	(1790) *Critique of the Power of Judgment*, trans. Paul Guyer and Eric Matthews, Cambridge University Press, 2000. Abbreviated to *CPJ*. Unless otherwise noted, numerals refer to the pagination of vol. 5 of *KGS*. The first (unpublished) Introduction is published in vol. 20 of *KGS*, and is marked as appropriate in the text.
CPR	(1781/87) *Critique of Pure Reason*, trans. and ed. Paul Guyer and Allen W. Wood, Cambridge University Press, 1993. Standard references to the 1781 (A) edition and to the 1787 (B) edition are provided. Published in vols. 3 (B ed.) and 4 (A ed.) of *KGS*.
KGS	(1902–) *Gesammelte Schriften*, ed. der Deutschen [formerly Königlich Preussischen] Akademie der Wissenschaften. Walter de Gruyter Verlag.
Obs.	(1764) *Observations on the Feeling of the Beautiful and Sublime*, trans. John Goldthwait, University of California Press, 1960.
RWB	(1793/94) *Religion Within the Boundaries of Mere Reason*, trans. Mary J. Gregor and Robert Anchor in Kant (1996b), *Religion*

and Rational Theology, trans. and ed. Allen W. Wood and George di Giovanni, Cambridge University Press.

Nietzsche, Friedrich

BGE   (1886) *Beyond Good and Evil,* trans. Walter Kaufmann, Vintage, 1966. Referenced by section.

BT   (1872/86) *The Birth of Tragedy,* prefaced by 'Attempt at Self Criticism', in *The Basic Nietzsche,* trans. and ed. Walter Kaufmann, The Modern Library, 2000. Referenced by section.

D   (1881) *Daybreak: thoughts on the prejudices of morality,* eds. Maudemarie Clark and Brian Leiter, trans. R. J. Hollingdale, Cambridge University Press, 1997. Referenced by section.

GM   (1887) *On the Genealogy of Morals* trans. Walter Kaufmann and bound with Nietzsche, Friedrich (1908), *Ecce Homo,* Vintage, 1969. Referenced by section.

GS   (1882/87) *The Gay Science,* trans. and ed. Walter Kaufmann, Vintage, 1974. Referenced by section.

TI   (1888) *Twilight of the Idols,* in *The Portable Nietzsche,* trans. and ed. Walter Kaufmann, The Viking Press, 1968.

Z   (1883–85) *Thus Spoke Zarathustra,* in *The Portable Nietzsche,* trans. and ed. Walter Kaufmann, The Viking Press, 1968.

Schopenhauer, Arthur

WWR   (1819/59) *The World as Will and Representation,* trans. E. F. J. Payne, Dover Publications, 2 vols., 1966.

1

A TERRIBLE PROSPECT

The pleasurable shudder at the sublime has been with us since the late seventeenth century: its focus, intensity and character repeatedly transformed by changing theories and by political and cultural events. The sublime was overwhelming; breath-taking; awe-inspiring; tremendous; terrifying; unrepresentable; revolutionary. But the word was also slippery, denoting a concept that was subject to metamorphosis and flux. Many nineteenth- and twentieth-century philosophers and theorists (especially those belonging to a post-Hegelian tradition) picked out as the most salient characteristic of sublimity the failure of the understanding and reason to capture the infinity that it invoked. Eighteenth-century writers, by contrast, tended to emphasise the way that pleasure mixed with terror in the experience of the sublime. Between these two traditions we find Immanuel Kant, writing at the end of the eighteenth century, who described the sublime in terms of the encounter between an 'I' and that which has the capacity to annihilate it completely. For Kant and many of the Romantics, the 'I' is the victor in this (ennobling) conflict; but for others like Arthur Schopenhauer writing in the middle years of the nineteenth century or Jean-François Lyotard theorising at the end of the twentieth century, the delights of the sublime involve a surrender or displacement of the ego.

In the philosophical frameworks of empiricism and idealism as they developed during the course of the eighteenth century, the term 'sublime' came to refer to a quasi-aesthetic response to nature, to a work of art or to a political or historical event that produces a kind of shock to the human spectator or auditor. In the experience of the sublime the audience or observer was said to derive pleasure from being (temporarily or potentially) overwhelmed by an object or an entity that seemed infinite or vast, powerful or terrible, exceeding the capacities of the human to imaginatively grasp or understand it. Breaking with conscious control and individual personality or preferences, the pleasure-in-pain that was integral to the sublime seemed to take man temporarily beyond the human; but the pleasure was generated by the object—not by a god or by the divine—and opened up a kind of split within the subject before consciousness and reason re-established control. Kant's is one of the most important voices in the history of the sublime, decisively influencing the

Romantics and other later modern and postmodern thinkers. For nineteenth-and twentieth-century philosophers and artists, the destabilisation to the I produced by the sublime was often more than momentary.

Indeed, it was this emphasis on an affect that bypassed conscious reflection and control that was so important to modernist artists as they theorised a response to colour and abstract form in terms of an 'absolute' that became associated with the 'sublime'. The Expressionists, the Futurists, the Surrealists and the Vorticists were amongst the many types of twentieth-century artists who drew on the language and imagery of the sublime to suggest that modernist art derives its energy neither from classical beauty nor from the tastes or preferences of the individualised subject, but from a kind of power that stems from 'modern life' in which space, time and objects have been reconfigured into vortexes, planes, surfaces, colours, patterns of dissonance and speed. Although often refusing the technical label of the 'sublime', modernist European artists and theorists deployed the conceptual framework of sublimity when, like Kasimir Malevich writing in 1916, they advocated a variety of diverse ways to energise art whilst simultaneously 'spitting' on the 'altar' of beauty and the past 'idols' of art (Harrison and Wood 1992: 169). The concept of the sublime was also integral to the changing notion of the avant-garde as mainstream modernism switched its allegiances from Paris to New York at the close of the Second World War when Abstract Expressionist painters like Barnett Newman, Mark Rothko and Clyfford Still explicitly appropriated the language of the sublime for a specifically American and anti-Romantic project to revolutionise art (Guilbaut 1983; Beckley 2001: 8; Golding 2002: 201ff.). As we will see, towards the end of the twentieth century Lyotard's 'postmodern sublime' picked up—and reworked—a tension inherent in the very notion of the avant-garde inherited from modernist visual artists, especially Barnett Newman.

Jean-Luc Nancy has claimed that 'there is no contemporary thought of art and its end which does not, in one manner or other, pay tribute to the thought of the sublime' (Nancy 1993: 26). Analogously, Lyotard finds the 'frame of contemporary aesthetics and aesthetic commentary, built by pre-romanticism and Romanticism' to be 'completely dominated by (and subordinate to) the idea of the sublime' (Lyotard 1986: 8). Thus Lyotard insists that it is 'indispensable to go back through the Analytic of the Sublime from Kant's *Critique of Judgement* in order to get an idea of what is at stake in modernism, in what are called the avant-gardes in painting or in music' (Lyotard 1988a: 135). Even if one were to agree with Mark Cheetham (2001: 102) and say that Nancy and Lyotard are offering over-exaggerated and 'historically inaccurate' claims, it is clear that the question of the sublime has resonance for philosophers, art historians and cultural critics writing today—so much so that the postmodern feminist critic Meaghan Morris has reacted with (ironic) terror to the re-emergence of the sublime in late twentieth-century debates: 'a new Sublime: what a terrible prospect!' (Morris 1988: 214).

Morris' ambivalent response to the sublime is symptomatic, since the links between the sublime, terror and human transcendence might lead one to elaborate on Nancy's claim and add: 'there is no representation of modern political terror which does not, in one manner or other, touch on the idea of the sublime'. Some of these links will be explored in Chapters 2 and 10; but we should not be surprised that the politics and aesthetics of a 'new' sublime might cause anxiety. But the imagery and language of the sublime is also not so easily escaped, even when—as artist and critic Anthony Haden-Guest puts it—'We seem, in fact, more comfortable with work that sidles into the Sublime, as if accidentally' (Haden-Guest 2001: 53).

Published in America in 2001—but written prior to the events of September 11th—Haden-Guest reminds us how the imagery of the sublime did, even then, make visual artists and art critics uneasy. He writes at a moment at which all varieties of the sublime—Romantic, modernist, postmodern—seemed outdated to the fashionable New York art world who were advocating a return to 'extreme' and 'uncontrollable beauty' and hence to a mode of aesthetic pleasure which has often been theorised as antithetical to the sublime (Beckley and Shapiro 1998; Gilbert-Rolfe 1999). But if the sublime could only be approached obliquely (and slightly ironically) in up-market art journals and catalogues, those mounting marketing campaigns seem much more direct. A flyer advertising a new and 'awesome' computer opens with a headline that shouts 'SUBLIME' in large capitals, and continues by quoting a review of the product in *Computer Buyer*, April 2002:

> 'a truly sublime experience', even we were surprised to hear one of our computers being talked of in such terms, but *Computer Buyer* magazine ... went on to say, 'every single feature is pretty much the biggest, fastest or most luxurious you could possibly want'.

What this particular advertisement picks out as the relevant characteristics of the new and 'sublime' computer is its extravagant power and its excessiveness to human imagination, desires or needs. Historically, the pleasures of the sublime were linked to an encounter with something tremendous: an infinite; something indefinitely great, grand or boundless; a longed-for absolute. Starting out as a term within rhetoric, the effect of the sublime was described in terms of a kind of overwhelming compulsion and a reaction so powerful and so inexplicable as to appear irresistible. If the computer marketing team does not know this history, it is nevertheless still employing the term 'sublime' in ways that directly link with this past.

The history of the concept of the sublime is complex, and is generally traced back to Nicolas Boileau's 1674 French translation of a fragmentary ancient text on stylistic greatness in spoken speech. The Greek treatise had been entitled *Peri Hypsous* (*About Elevation*) and was written by an unknown author (conventionally, but probably not accurately, called Longinus) some time between

3

the first and third centuries CE. The author is clearly immersed in Greek culture; but the treatise is addressed to a Roman friend, and includes a single quotation from Genesis as well as mention of the Jews (Longinus 1957: 14). The author's apparent familiarity with the philosophy of the Alexandrian Hebrew philosopher, Philo Judaeus (born about 20 BCE), has led some scholars to speculate that 'Longinus' also lived in Greco-Roman Egypt.

Almost lost in antiquity, 11 manuscripts of *Peri Hypsous* survive, with the tenth-century Paris codex accepted as the oldest and most complete. The first printed edition was that of Francisco Robertello in Basel in 1554, with an influential Latin translation appearing under the title *De Sublimi Genere Dicendi* (*Of the Sublime in Types of Speech*) in Venice in 1555 (Macksey 1997; Saint Girons 1998). The emphasis on spoken language was underplayed in Boileau's French translation of 1674 which was entitled simply *Du Sublime* (*Of the Sublime*), but in the Greek text *hypsous* is a stylistic category, and concerns a type of speech which has such 'irresistible' strength that it induces astonishment (*ekplexis*) and overpowers and transports the hearer. Longinus links this state of elevated transport to the inspired author, and to texts that are themselves 'frenzied', with the 'strong and inspired' impact transmitted directly to the audience from the animated author and text.

Amongst texts on rhetoric, Longinus' treatise is unusual. Conventionally, rhetoric was portrayed as occupying itself with the techniques of convincing and persuading an audience. It was the 'fourth part of logic', and operated either via an appeal to the reason or understanding (producing conviction) or by operating on the specific passions or character of the individual auditor (persuasion). Thus Longinus' apparent concern to produce an emotional affect which is non-individualised is distinctive. So also is his neglect of the classical divisions between the 'High', 'Middle' and 'Plain' styles analysed in exhaustive detail by other Greek and Latin writers on eloquence. Instead, Longinus explores the means whereby an audience might be elevated (gain *hypsous*) or attain '*ekstasis*' (meaning, literally, to 'stand outside' oneself). The mysterious nature of this transport was further emphasised in Boileau's French translation through appeal to an obscure quality—a '*je-ne-sais-quoi*'—as the causal origin of the power that 'sublime' speeches or texts exercised on the spell-bound audience. The overall sense of mystery was also intensified by Boileau's adoption of the French term '*sublime*' to replace '*hypsous*'. As we will see in Chapter 6, this word had rich alchemical connotations and was linked to the purification or sublimation of matter through the process of heating. These associations would be exploited by the German Romantic writers and by Nietzsche and Freud in the nineteenth and twentieth centuries. The complex and highly problematic gender politics of this usage will also become apparent, and in Chapter 9 we will see Nietzsche deliberately exploiting the language of 'sublimation' as he seeks to reconfigure the sublime and render it more material.

Other more technical uses of the term 'sublime' in the seventeenth century included usage in architecture and the building trades where it was employed in relation to chimneys and lintels. In both alchemy and architecture the Latin word *sublimis* is in play, in particular '*sub*' denoting 'under' or 'up to' and *limin* meaning 'threshold'. It is, however, the conventions of rhetoric that Boileau is primarily drawing on in his translation of Longinus. Thus, in other Latin, French and English texts on rhetoric reference had also been made to a 'sublime style', but in ways that were completely at odds with the analysis of *hypsous* provided by Longinus. The non-Longinian 'sublime' style was a synonym for the so-called 'high' or 'lofty' style deemed suitable to describe 'the heroical and mighty actions of kings' (as A. Day puts it in the 'English Secretorie' of 1586). This could not have been more different from Longinian *hypsous* which fits more with the so-called 'low' or 'plain' style than with this highly flowery and gran-diloquent mode of address. However, as we will see, connotations of kingly power and also of masculinity would be carried over from the old-fashioned 'sublime style' to the modern concept of the sublime. Thus, for example, in Edward Benlowes' *Theophilia* (1652) we find an explicit linking between 'Sublime poets' and 'the masculine and refined pleasures of the understanding' which 'trans-cend the feminine and sensual of the eye'. As we will see, analogous gendered metaphors can be found in both Edmund Burke and Immanuel Kant.

Boileau's translation of Longinus generated a kind of mania for a more simple style that produces its effect by means of a magical and ineffable *je-ne-sais-quoi* that transforms language and also its audience. After 1674 and throughout most of the eighteenth century, re-translations of Longinus fol-lowed by the score: not only into English, but also into most other European languages. Most followed Boileau and left out any reference to 'Types of Speech' (*Genere Dicendi*) from the title of the treatise, so that gradually the scope of the sublime was broadened out to include not only speeches, but also images and events—especially as depicted on the stage. By 1721 Tam-worth Reresby was equating the sublime with 'the marvellous' and with that '*which produces a certain admiration mixed with wonder and surprise*' (Reresby 1721: 43). Even earlier, in 1701 and 1704, John Dennis, the English critic and actor-manager, had explicated the sublime in terms of 'enthusiastic' passions that were based on an imitation of nature and then further excited by the subject matter and the poetic technique, specifically claiming that 'ideas producing terror, contribute extremely to the sublime' (Dennis 1701: 32–34; 1704: 37).

Dennis claims that 'the sublime does not so properly persuade us, as it ravi-shes us and transports us, and produces in us a certain admiration, mingled with astonishment and surprise'. Never without passion, 'it gives a noble vigour to a discourse, an invincible force, which commits a pleasing rape on the very soul of the reader' (Dennis 1704: 37). Dennis' sublime thus produces an emo-tional and imaginative effect that seems to bypass the three traditional (Aris-totelian) routes for convincing or persuading an audience by rhetorical means: via an appeal to the reason; through reliance on the specificity of the character of the speaker; by playing on the particularity of the emotions or beliefs of the subject who is being addressed (Aristotle c. 350 BCE; Ijsseling 1976). Although for Dennis the sublime always does involve 'passion', the passion involved is not the 'ordinary passions' of the individual subject. These are set to one side; instead, 'like the artillery of Jove', the 'united force of a writer' takes over the reader and 'thunders, blazes, and strikes at once', generating a specific set of 'enthusiastic' passions that are both violent and irresistible (Dennis 1704: 37).

For Dennis, these enthusiastic passions are linked to a particular set of 'terrible' and 'wonderful' ideas, including 'gods, dæmons, hell, spirits and souls of men, miracles, prodigies, enchantments, witchcrafts, thunder, tempests, raging seas, inundations, torrents, earthquakes, volcanoes, monsters, serpents, lions, tigers, fire, war, pestilence, famine, &c.' (38). What is important about this set of imaginary and real objects is, according to Dennis, the capacity of each of them for generating 'religious terror', an emotion that is said to be distinguished both from ordinary terror and from fear. Ordinary terror is different from fear in that it is 'more sudden', 'less gradual' and involves an element of surprise in the way it registers 'an approaching evil, threatening destruction or very great trouble'; by contrast, 'great enthusiastic terror' is mixed with wonder and borders on astonishment. It is this religious terror that is characteristic of the sublime on Dennis' model, with the degree of terror generated made dependent on the more 'powerful' the object is that induces the terror, and the more likely that object is to hurt the subject—so the greatest, most sublime idea becomes 'the idea of an angry god' (36).

As a playwright and stage manager, Dennis was reputedly the inventor of the sound effect of 'stage thunder' as a dramatic means of evoking the sublime. He was also so taken by the 'sublime' that he earned himself the nickname 'Sir Tremendous Longinus' through the mockery of John Gay, Alexander Pope and other members of the Scriblerus Club. For all his excesses, in terms of the developing history of the sublime Dennis' treatment of the Longinian sublime is symptomatic since, at least until Kant's *Critique of the Power of Judgment* (1790), the aesthetic of the sublime would be torn between several competing tendencies that we find in Dennis: first, the sublime is defined in terms of a particular set of objects or properties that generate enthusiastic terror; second, there is a tendency to assert that whatever generates great and intense terror is also sublime; third, a distinction is made between 'ordinary' passions and those elevated passions that are characteristic of the sublime; and fourth, the sublime is linked with the religious, the numinous, the non-human and the superhuman. This is already an unstable mix, and Dennis compounds this by linking the sublime to 'spirit, or genius in poetry' (Dennis 1701: 33). Importantly, in Germany as well as in Britain, the language of the 'sublime' was deployed to explain how Shakespeare and other 'natural geniuses' could produce such a powerful effect on an audience, despite breaking the rules of neoclassical poetry and art.

Sexing the difference

In mid eighteenth-century Britain the spectator of the sublime was theorised as passive; but so also was the genius himself, so that the genius took on many stereotypically 'feminine' characteristics, including imagination, intuition, strong emotions and frenzy (Battersby 1989). For pre-Romantic writers like Edmund Young (1759), William Duff (1767) or the young Goethe, geniuses like Shakespeare were little more than super-spectators: mirrors that give us access to the region of the sublime. The *maleness* of this feminised spectator was taken for granted, but was spelt out more explicitly in Edmund Burke's classic and influential text, *A Philosophical Enquiry into the Origin of our Ideas of the Beautiful and Sublime* of 1757 (revised 1759).

Burke divides passions into those which are social and are linked to the 'purposes of propagation' and 'generation', and those that are bound up with 'self-preservation', involving pain, danger, terror and reason. The social feelings give rise to the pleasure that we take in beauty; but the enjoyment in the sublime is generated by the ego as it operates in defensive mode. In particular, Burke links the sublime to 'delight': a term which is given a narrow and technical definition involving the 'removal of pain or danger' (1757/59: 36–44). Thus, for Burke, the sublime and the beautiful are modes of affect which function as polar opposites insofar as taste is concerned:

> There is a wide difference between admiration and love. The sublime, which is the cause of the former, always dwells on great objects, and terrible; the latter on small ones, and pleasing; we submit to what we admire, but we love what submits to us; in one case we are forced, in the other we are flattered into compliance.
>
> (Burke: 1757/59: 113)

The 'we' that Burke uses here is sexually specific. According to Burke, it was the beautiful that operates on the (male) observer by a form of flattery; the sublime that threatens to overwhelm the male ego via a form of mental rape that renders him (temporarily) passive, and like his ideal woman who was herself 'beautiful' and not 'sublime'. Burke never made the adjustments to his vocabulary that would have been necessary had he registered that there could be another 'we' (women) who do not simply admire, but also love the sublime.

In Burke's text, the language of sexual power is employed to explain the psychological thrill that comes from the sublime. The latter is exemplified by kings and commanders discharging their terrible strength and destroying all obstacles in their paths, as well as by the grandeur of the Alps (64ff.). By contrast, the 'beautiful'—small, smooth, delicate and graceful—is claimed to be what men (i.e. males) love in the opposite sex (42, 113, 91ff.). Burke characterises beauty as a mental state of relaxation produced by the physical encounter with objects that are small, smooth, without sharp contrasts or angles, and with delicacy of form and colour. It is what 'we'/'men' (males) love in 'the *sex*' (women):

> this mixed passion which we call love, is the *beauty* of the *sex*. Men are carried to the sex in general, as it is the sex, and by the common law of nature; but they are attached to particulars by personal *beauty*.
>
> (Burke: 42)

The sublime, by contrast, was bound up with a 'stretching' of the nerve fibres: with tension and with feelings of terror and infinity generated by power, obscurity, magnitude, difficulty, absences (such as solitude, silence and darkness) and impressions of endlessness (146n; 132ff.).

Via the framework of the Burkean 'beautiful', women—who, during the Renaissance, had been allied to the frenzied, the passionate, the ecstatic and the passively reactive—found themselves deprived of sisterhood with raw Nature. It was, of course, no coincidence that this happened at that time in the history of Europe when passivity and the 'natural' were being revalued and made integral to the sublime. Instinct, madness, the emotional and the capricious remained 'feminine' characteristics and were eulogised; but they were no longer thought of as specifically *female* characteristics (Battersby 1989). Instead, these characteristics were increasingly debarred to women or presented as part of a 'natural' condition that women themselves were unable to transcend. Mary Wollstonecraft was amongst the many women writers who raged against the ways in which the 'sublime' was often explicitly, and nearly always implicitly, gendered as male (Wollstonecraft 1792). Her record of her adventures amongst the wild mountain scenery of Scandinavia was a way of countering the newly emergent gender ideals which confined women to the (distinctly inferior) category of the 'beautiful' (Wollstonecraft 1796).

The British writers on the sublime were influential across Europe, but particularly in Germany. Thus, in his *Observations on the Feeling of the Beautiful and Sublime* of 1764 Kant draws on Burke as he allies woman with the beautiful and the male with the sublime, arguing that a woman 'should show nothing else than a beautiful nature'. Kant allows that the 'fair sex' has 'as much understanding as the men', but insists that woman has 'a *beautiful understanding*, whereas ours should be a *deep understanding*, an expression which signifies identity with the sublime' (*Obs*: 2/229, p. 78).[1] Kant links the 'beautiful' to 'facility' and to apparent ease:

> On the other hand, strivings and surmounted difficulties arouse admiration and belong to the sublime. Deep meditation and a long-sustained reflection are noble but difficult, and do not well befit a person in whom unconstrained charms should show nothing else than a beautiful nature. Laborious learning or a painful pondering, even if a

woman (*Frauenzimmer*) should greatly succeed in it, destroy the merits that are proper to her sex.

(*Obs*: 2/229, p. 78)

'Charm' and 'beauty' are positive virtues for women; but the sublime is ruled out. Kant even claims that a woman 'with a head full of Greek' or one who studies mechanics is 'disgusting', and 'might as well even have a beard' (2/229–30, p. 78). Since Kant will link full personhood and moral autonomy to the sublime in his later writings, it is not just a trivial matter that he refuses women the right to develop their capacities for the sublime.

Like Jean-Jacques Rousseau (his philosophical hero), Kant emphasised the need to civilise woman in order to make her more 'natural', more charming, and an ideal (yet subordinate) companion, mother and wife. However, as we will see in Chapter 3, in Kant's mature philosophy there were significant changes in his account of the beautiful and the sublime, and, as we will also discover, Kant's later, critical writings continued to have a strongly charged sexual subtext insofar as the sublime was concerned. Women (and various racial and ethnic types originating from outside Europe) remain excluded from his account of the 'universals' of reason and of taste, of freedom and personhood that are operational in 'our' (male and European) enjoyment of the sublime.

In the *Critique of the Power of Judgment* (1790), Kant continued to make the distinction between beauty (*die Schönheit*) and the sublime (*das Erhabene*) fundamental to the structure of his text, but now women no longer count as an example of the beautiful in any straightforward way. By 1790 Kant was taking a stand against empiricists such as Burke whose account of mental functioning emphasised passivity, sensibility and affectivity, as well as against accounts such as those of Young or Duff who presented the ideal male—the original genius—as a creature as wild, capricious and irrational as a Renaissance female. In his late writings Kant makes a merely passive response to danger—a block to the appreciation of the sublime which is now described as involving terror and its simultaneous transcendence. Since Kant also insists that women and 'effeminate' ('Oriental') males either cannot, or should not, transcend fear, his *Critique of the Power of Judgment* does, in effect, return to older notions of masculinity that were uncontaminated by the newly re-valued passions and irrationality. This explains why, in 1818, we find Goethe praising Kant for his 'immortal service': of having 'brought us all back from that effeminacy in which we were wallowing' (Cassirer 1918: 270).

There are clear fault-lines in Kant's philosophy of the sublime, especially in relation to sexual difference and race, and these will need to be explored in subsequent chapters. But some of the difficulties in untangling what Kant himself said about the sublime comes from the fact that his own views are too often mediated by Friedrich von Schiller's interpretation of Kant's aesthetics. It would be difficult to overemphasise the influence of Schiller, since, in the history of philosophy, it is Schiller's Kant who has often come to displace what

Kant himself said. Thus, for example, both Hegel and Nietzsche seem to read Kant through spectacles borrowed from Schiller. What is emphasised in this tradition is the defeat of the imagination, and the role of the understanding and reason in relation to the pleasures of the sublime as sensibility opens up the individual to 'the Idea'. There is thus also an emphasis on the potential of the sublime to enable man to transcend the limited framework of the space–time structures which shape our world.

Schiller described the feeling of the sublime as involving a mixture of melancholy and joy, and claimed that this 'mixed feeling' is generated by a sublime object which is itself 'of a dual sort':

> We refer it either to our *power of apprehension* and are defeated in our attempt to form an image of its concept; or we refer it to our *vital power* and view it as a power against which our own dwindles to nothing.
>
> (Schiller 1801: 198)

Importantly, for Schiller the truly moral man is dynamised by this failure. He is 'ravished by the terrifying', and takes 'delight in the sensuously infinite because we are able to think what the senses can no longer apprehend'. With his understanding out of alignment with his senses, 'Nature' uses 'a sensuous means of teaching us that we are more than merely sensuous' (199). Such a man 'abandons the possibility of *explaining* Nature and takes this incomprehensibility itself as a principle of judgment': he is forced by this imaginative and sensory failure to 'apprehend the great and sublime by means of reason' (207, 203). The encounter with the sublime object thus provides evidence that man is a free and autonomous being with a '*spiritual mission*' that is integral to the 'rational vocation' of human nature (211). For Schiller, there is thus a moral and educative dimension to the sublime experience—and, indeed, terror—that pushes man towards a kind of spiritual salvation. If women and various ethnic groupings are refused this capacity for spiritual salvation and moral improvement, then the Kantian–Schillerian type of philosophical framework can be used to justify counting whole classes of humans as non-persons.

Kant was writing during a period in which ideals of human nature and of attainment were in crisis; and this was particularly evident in terms of the way that accounts of the character and merits of women seemed to be at odds with ideals and norms that were presented as valid for all mankind. Although racial stereotypes also had a role to play in this predicament, it was not until the nineteenth and twentieth centuries that the racial and cultural consequences of an aesthetics and politics of the sublime would move into focus. For the German National Socialists there was a deliberate attempt to attach the aesthetics of the 'sublime' to certain superior (primarily Aryan) races or specific non-effeminate, non-degenerate human types (Carter 2004). And in the Soviet Union the 'sublime' of labour and of physical work was also linked to a politics of terror and of transcendence. In Chapters 2 and 10 I will need to consider further whether there is any worthwhile future for the sublime, given this history.

Containing the shock

Although this book cannot hope—and, it should be stressed, does not even attempt—to solve the problems posed by political terror, it is concerned to show how aesthetic debates about the sublime and questions of political theory and value overlap. At stake is the question about what remains when understanding fails and when we are shocked by 'terror', or by an encounter with that which is so strange or shockingly 'other' that our conceptual framework is unable to encompass it. And here it is also necessary to point to a third aesthetic category which emerged late in the eighteenth century, and which involved an attempt to block the power of the 'other' to destabilise the 'I'. Neither fully sublime nor conventionally beautiful, the 'picturesque' involved a tension between man (the perceiver and shaper of his surroundings) and 'wild nature' which was celebrated, but which was positioned as an object of curiosity rather than of power.

I will also touch on the problem of the picturesque in Chapters 2 and 10 in relation to the discussion of the representation of political terror; here I need to note that it started out as a deliberate attempt to block the 'sensuously infinite' and the power of the sublime:

> Infinity is one of the most efficient causes of the sublime ... to give [an object] picturesqueness, you must destroy that cause of its sublimity; for it is on the shape and disposition of its boundaries, that the picturesque must in great measure depend.
>
> (Price 1810: vol. i, 84)

To gain this visual control and 'see' the picturesque, it was customary to view nature through the lens of a *camera obscura*. Although unable to fix the image onto paper, this precursor of the modern camera nonetheless produced a two-dimensional image on a flat ground (supposed equivalent to the retina) from which linear tracings, tonal drawings or paintings were produced. Seen through glass, the shadows become both 'pleasantly coloured' and also 'darker' than in nature. 'The effect is indeed heightened but it is false' (Scharf 1974: 21).

Garden and landscape designers also set out to evoke and contain the sublime, as the full title of Price's 1796 text makes clear: *Essays on the Picturesque (as compared with the Sublime and the Beautiful, for the Purpose of Improving Real Landscape)*. Referred to across Europe as 'The English Garden', the 'picturesque' landscape was designed to mimic the soft hills and 'natural' curves and the English countryside. The gaze of the observer was directed by the construction of (apparently 'natural') artificial lakes; by the 'artless' planting of woods, via sinuous pathways; and by means of strategically positioned (fake) ruins, follies or creeper-covered buildings. Although the resulting vistas were described in language and metaphors that evoked Mother Nature, the apparent roughness, wildness and irregularity was a product of a careful calculation of visual horizons, perspectives and frames (Hussey 1927). Infinity, power and wildness were invoked, but nature was managed, manicured, framed and filtered so as to keep at bay any 'abyss' in understanding. Intermediate between the sublime and the beautiful, the picturesque sets out to reassure us that—even where there is disorder—man is in control, and that nature has been constructed for human delight.

For the traveller or painter touring round England, visual control over the disturbing force of nature was relatively easy. But in the case of the less domesticated landscapes of Asia, Australia, North America and the British Colonies, the aesthetic categories of the sublime and the picturesque were often placed in uneasy conjunction. Australian settlers might have named one of the 'lookouts' in the Blue Mountains 'Sublime Point', and there might also be a tradition of American Landscape Painting that is known as 'The American Sublime', but in general eighteenth- and nineteenth-century colonial artists painted the wilderness in ways that softened or domesticated it so that it became unthreatening and merely 'picturesque'. Strategically placed humans, domestic animals or homesteads softened the scene, and painters adopted perspectives and lighting that toned down the contours and colours in ways that filtered the image through remembered European horizons and tonalities. In these depictions, the aboriginal 'primitives' are generally assimilated into the landscape and become simply a part of the wilderness that the European or colonial traveller presents as 'other' to his own masterful self. Dwarfed by the mountain scenery and by the deserts or wide prairies, the indigenous inhabitants seem merely to enhance the 'picturesque' effect of the overall scene, rather than being positioned themselves as powerful, ominous or sublime.

Race was also very much a feature of the picturesque landscape, and behind the fashion for the picturesque we also find the language of the sublime, in which both the experiencing subject and the sublimities that he encounters are described in racialised terms. Thus, for example, in A *Philosophical Enquiry*, Burke explains that darkness and blackness are natural sensations that are productive of the sublime, illustrating this with the example of a boy who was blind from birth and who, on regaining his sight, accidentally saw a negro woman. The boy was immediately 'struck with great horror at the sight. The horror, in this case, can scarcely be supposed to arise from any association' (1757/59: 144). For Burke, the horror that 'we' (European males) feel at black bodies is entirely natural and is rooted in human nature. Looking at them causes the radial fibres of the eye to contract and the nerves to be strained, since black bodies reflect no light and function 'as vacant spaces among the objects we view'. The absence of light amongst the colours that impact on the eye produces a 'convulsive' motion of the eye and a kind of physiological shock that is 'very violent'. Although custom can in time reconcile us to black objects, the black body is naturally productive of terror and hence an efficient cause of the sublime. As such, it is antithetical to the beautiful which is described as a social passion and linked to what 'we' love (144–49, 38–43).

In Chapters 2 and 4 we will see Kant also describing the enjoyment of the sublime in ways that are racially and ethnically specific, so that the 'Oriental' is denied the capacity to appreciate the sublime; this exclusion occurs even though the religions of Islam and (to a lesser extent) Judaism and are discussed by him in relatively positive terms insofar as the sublime is concerned. As we will see, Kant's restrictions operate rather differently in the case of race and ethnicity than in the case of sexual difference, since Kant indicates that certain racial types have an inability to appreciate the sublime, whereas in the case of women it is a quasi-moral duty for women not to develop their personality, reason and understanding in the direction of the sublime. But these tensions with respect to race have also produced a legacy in the twentieth and twenty-first centuries insofar as the questions of race and religion are concerned. In 'The Muselmann in Auschwitz', an interview with Gil Anidjar on his book *The Jew, the Arab: A History of the Enemy* (2003), Anidjar suggests that the invention of the category of the 'Semite' (including both the Jew and the Arab) during the nineteenth century can be traced back to Hegel, and specifically to Hegel's reading of Kant on the sublime (Anidjar 2004).

As we will see in the next chapter Hegel argues against the ideal of autonomy implicit in Kant's analysis of the sublime, but Anidjar claims that Hegel nevertheless incorporates an understanding of Kant on the sublime into the racial and historical categories employed in his account of the development of Absolute Spirit. For Hegel, Anidjar claims, 'both Jews and Muslims are thoroughly submitted, they are *slaves*. They are slaves to their god', and there is a kind of 'horrifying beauty' about their enslavement. For Anidjar, Kant's account of the 'religions of the sublime' contributes to the invention of the category of the Semite, as well as to the caricature of the *Muselmann* or Muslim as an inferior overly passive type who then becomes the archetypal *political* enemy of the West (as opposed to the Jew who comes to signify the *theological* enemy).

I will come back to Anidjar's complex insights in Chapter 4 as I explore Kant's—extremely depressing—theories of 'race' and ethnicity and read these alongside his analysis of the three monotheistic religions of Judaism, Islam and Christianity. In fact, as we will see, Anidjar reads Kant on Islam through a framework that is more appropriate to the nineteenth and twentieth centuries. Kant's 'Orientalism' is extreme, but does not translate into an anti-Islamic position; instead Kant positions Islam on the side of modernity and, like Voltaire, uses Islam as a strategic weapon to critique certain types of non-rational modes of Christianity that are linked to 'superstition' and fear. Anidjar's emphasis on the role of the sublime in later debates about Islam is nevertheless important, especially in the way it picks up an observation that Primo Levi made about the treatment of prisoners in Auschwitz. Thus Levi records in *If This is a Man*, 'This word *Muselmann*, I do not know why, was used by the old ones of the camp to describe the weak, the inept, those doomed to selection' (Levi 1958: 94n.). Anidjar links some of the most urgent questions of our times—in particular the problem of universalism and the conflation of religious, ethnic and racial categories—back to eighteenth- and nineteenth-century debates relating to autonomy, personhood, transcendence, passivity and the sublime.

Should the sublime have a future?

Although much of this book will be concerned with exploring the eighteenth-century background that continues to haunt contemporary debates relating to an aesthetics of the sublime, there are serious contemporary questions that are posed by its politics. As we will see in the next chapter, 'September 11 2001' is too easily read in terms of the visual vocabulary of the sublime, and in contemporary responses to this event it is also possible to detect the tonalities of Schiller and other post-Kantian philosophers who linked the 'redemption' and 'spiritual mission' of mankind to the mind-defeating incomprehensibility of the sublime, as well as to its attendant terrors. In the portrayal of the collapse of the twin towers of the New York Trade Center as 'Apocalypse Now'—and films and images of it as a kind of 'sublime'—we see a shattered landscape opening up before us: an image so profoundly disturbing as to demand judgement, whilst blocking any easy response that can rely on the 'universals' of human reason or of a 'consensus' of moral or aesthetic response.

Chapter 2 will link the twenty-first-century terror to eighteenth- and nineteenth-century debates concerning the sublime and the French Revolution. And here again questions of sexual and racial difference will be key, since what is at stake is the question of how to think of the individual in relation to the universal. Might it ever be appropriate to sacrifice the individual to some greater good? Can 'terror' ever be justified in terms of 'sublime virtue', along the lines that Robespierre asserted during the time of 'Terror'? How appropriate is it to read Kant's account of the sublime as a defence of Robespierre's view of justice? How do women, non-European races and different religions and ethnicities stand in relation to the 'universal' ideals of freedom and personhood that can be found in Kant's aesthetic texts? Might it be possible to use Kant's aesthetics of the sublime to develop an ideal of non-consensual communities in which difference is respected, as Lyotard suggests?

In Chapter 3 I will show, in detail, how Kant's critical system is fundamentally undermined by his continued refusal to allow women access to the enjoyments of the sublime. In Chapter 4 I will look across Kant's system to see how he deals with issues of ethnicity, non-Christian religions (especially Islam) and race. Although Kant's views on ethnicity and race are less deeply embedded in his system (and often seem simply inconsistent), Kant's refusal to allow all peoples access to the sublime will have serious consequences for those who look to Kant's aesthetics for solutions for moral and political philosophy today. In Chapter 10, I will consider how and why Hannah Arendt turned to Kant's aesthetics to find an answer to mid-twentieth-century terror (especially Auschwitz). Here I will argue that Arendt needed to pay more attention to what Kant said about the sublime, and to the way that he secures ethnic and racial exclusions.

Before getting to this point, however, I will need to explore a curious duality in both Kant and the post-Kantian traditions of writing the sublime: one that relates to the differences between the 'feminine' and the 'female'. This will be the task of Chapters 5 and 6 where we will see that the sublime that leads man's reason and imagination upwards and onwards in Kant and post-Kantian writers is often allocated a feminine (and Egyptian) persona; but that access to this feminised 'other' was barred to flesh-and-blood women who were denied the necessary powers to transcend materiality. Chapter 6 will consider the tactics of three women poets and writers who seem to suggest another model of Other-ness, and whose writings contribute to a tradition of 'the *female* sublime'. The question of the anti-fleshy—and that means anti-female—bias in the aesthetics of the sublime will be addressed extensively in these two chapters, and also in Chapter 7 where I will consider some images produced by contemporary women artists, in order to show further what a *female* sublime involves.

In Chapters 8 and 9 I will explore in some detail Nietzsche's critique of the sublime, showing how this links to his critique of the 'feminine' and an ever-elusive, veiled truth. We will also see how Nietzsche does not simply give up on the language of the sublime, but redescribes it in ways that are more phy-siological, and that involve reconfiguring otherness, identity, truth and value. Nietzsche will be in many ways helpful, but, as we will see in Chapter 9, he remains unable to think the bodily in ways that can adequately register *female* embodiment or the *female* subject position.

Chapter 10 also draws on Nietzsche, as I explore the links between the sublime, 'difference', temporal irruption and the sublime in recent discussions of terror and the 'postmodern sublime'. Here, I will consider the politics of the 'event' and its relation to terror and the sublime, in relation to three thinkers: Lyotard, Derrida and Arendt. As we will see in the next chapter, Lyotard deploys Kant's analysis of the sublime to defend a 'postmodern' politics of dif-ference that privileges respect for discordant voices, rather than an ideal of consensus or 'universal' values based on reason that should ideally remain always and everywhere the same. Lyotard privileges 'dissensus', and turns to Kant's analysis of sublime pleasures to model a framework for political under-standing that is not simply relativist, but which is attentive to 'differends', which he defines in terms of untranslatable elements within incompatible, but nevertheless equally valid, linguistic frameworks. The question of how ade-quate Lyotard's 'postmodern sublime' is for dealing with empirical, human dif-ferences and *historical* change will also need to be considered.

15

The sublime and its 'others'

Throughout, my approach to the sublime will be historical, since I will be arguing that the position of the 'other' that is hidden and that is at stake in the politics of the sublime is one that is first constructed by history itself. I will end by arguing for the need to look within the cultural history of the West for the hidden 'others within', and suggest that the self–other relationship does not have to be thought of always and only in terms of an adversarial relationship. But neither should the 'other' be conceptualised as 'beyond' the temporal or spatial horizons of Western cultures. I will argue that it is important not to simply reproduce the errors of those Romantic and psychoanalytic theorists who supposed that the 'other' that is encountered in the experience of the sublime is simply 'the Other of the same'.

As we will see, the sublime is associated by Romantic writers, such as William Wordsworth, with the ego encountering 'nature' or a 'feminine' other, and then re-establishing control via a return to a self that is confident in its underlying freedom, its mastery of otherness, and in the (male) poet or philosopher's right to speak and be heard. Wordsworth's 1808 poem 'Composed While the Author Was Engaged in Writing a Tract Occasioned by the Convention of Cintra' is one of many examples of his so-called 'egotistical sublime' in which the author first yields to 'mighty Nature' and her 'school sublime', before returning to a triumphant 'I' and 'thoughts no bondage can restrain' (Wordsworth 1888). On the other hand, as we will also see, the language of femininity has been deployed by both Kant and the male Romantics in ways that allowed a variety of male alliances with the sublime—all of which negotiated femininity, but erased (as no more than an echo) the female writers who were contemporaneously expressing their own experiences of the demonic and numinous.

Romanticism grew out of Kantianism, and I therefore find it easy to resist the reading of Kant as a simple defender of reason (and hence as emotionally and imaginatively paralysed) that has been fashionable amongst those feminists and postmodernists who lump Kant in with other 'Enlightenment' thinkers. This is not the Kant that I have been influenced by—and whom I also oppose. There are gaps in the Kantian system: gaps occupied by the 'unrepresentable'; by emotion; sexual desire; and even by a powerful feminine 'Isis' as the construct (and limits) of the imagination. It was in these gaps that Romanticism flowered and in which women Romantics drew breath. But none of this makes the Kantian universe a space in which I, as a feminist philosopher, can move freely. The 'feminine' principle so often advocated by the Romantics is a trap for women, since it treats femininity as 'other', and as excessive to an ego that is normalised as male.

In the last two centuries this (male, Westernised) 'I' that stands in opposition to its 'other' has seemed at times more domineering, but also more and more fragile. Perhaps unsurprisingly, in the twentieth century, writing about the sublime became one of the sites where this tension between the ideals of autonomy and the competing ideals of loss of self was made visible. For Barnett Newman, the American Abstract Expressionist painter, who produced his celebrated defence of the sublime 'The Sublime is Now' during 1948, creating the sublime was a way of asserting selfhood, as well as a way of challenging the classically Greek ideal of beauty and 'European aesthetic philosophies' which had misunderstood—and mislocated—the sublime (Newman 1990: 171). In this short piece Newman asserts that the new American painters—Abstract Expressionist painters—are producing a 'sublime' art that involves 'absolute emotions', and images so universal that their reality will be obvious to all who look at art 'without the nostalgic glasses of history'. These 'self-evident images' are produced 'out of ourselves, out of our own feelings' (173). In Newman's American sublime the universal (the 'self-evident' and the 'absolute') and the subjective coincide. Later, in 1965, Newman would speak of 'the terror of the Self', declaring 'The self, terrible and constant, is for me the subject matter of painting and sculpture' (187).

By contrast, Jean-François Lyotard—certainly the famous theorist of the postmodern sublime—found no self revealed in Newman's 'sublime' canvases when he came to describe them in 'Newman: The Instant' in 1985:

> The message 'speaks' of nothing; it emanates from no one. It is not Newman who is speaking, or who is using painting to show us something. The message (the painting) is the messenger; it 'says': *'Here I am'*, in other words, *'I am yours'* or *'Be mine'*.
>
> (Lyotard 1985: 242)

For Lyotard what is 'terrible' (and wonderful) about the sublime is not the constancy of the self, but its disappearance. He finds in Newman's 'aesthetic of the sublime' both 'delight' and 'terror'; but 'terror' is glossed as 'threatening that language will cease' and Newman's aesthetic becomes not one of constancy or a masterful subjectivity, but one concerned with process or 'becoming', and with what Newman himself called the 'sensation of time' (Lyotard 1985: 245, 246).

As Lyotard puts it elsewhere in a much-quoted statement: the sentiment of the sublime 'takes place' when 'the imagination fails to present an object which might, if only in principle, come to match a concept' (Lyotard 1982: 78). The 'real sublime sentiment' involves, 'an intrinsic combination of pleasure and pain: the pleasure that reason should exceed all presentation, the pain that imagination or sensibility should not be equal to the concept' (81). Whereas for Lyotard the 'modern' sublime involves a gesture of nostalgic reaching towards that which falls outside the horizons of representation, the postmodern sublime celebrates the unpresentable as it 'puts forward the unpresentable in presentation itself' (81). For Lyotard, the postmodern sublime becomes linked with conflict that is both irresolvable and pleasurable. What is 'terrible and constant' in the postmodern sublime is not the ego—as Barnett Newman supposed—but neither should the sublime be described in terms of an ideal state in which all conflict is resolved. Instead, Lyotard's postmodern sublime is a mode of encountering—and celebrating—the incommensurable. For Lyotard it is the longed-for universality of reason that is linked to the 'terror' of modernity—and it is this absolute universality that the post-modern sublime disturbs and disrupts. However, as we will see both in the next chapter and also in Chapter 10, for Lyotard *human* differences are dissolved into the 'inhuman' and also into the language-based disturbances of 'the differend'.

Lyotard died in 1998 and was thus writing before the suicide missions of radical Islamists made debates about multiculturalism the urgent political issue that it has become since 2001. His defence of difference is, however, clearly relevant to today's debates concerning the 'French' and 'English' models of integrating ethnic and religious minorities within the State. Despite being a French citizen, Lyotard's emphasis on the values of dissensus seems by no means 'French'. In particular, in 'What is Postmodernism?' (1982)—written as an appendix to a report on knowledge for the Quebec Government which was entitled *The Postmodern Condition* (1979)—Lyotard provides a theoretical fra-mework for dealing with minority linguistic and cultural groupings in a way that fits more neatly with the so-called 'English' model which privileges respect for difference above the shared values or directives of a unified State. For Lyo-tard, the 'postmodern sublime' involves incommensurable absolutes that cannot be registered within the linguistic and cultural framework of the com-peting cultures. Instead of privileging consensus, he looks for a way of mobi-lising difference.

The overall object of this book will be to explore the usefulness—and the dangers—of the concept of the sublime for dealing with the politics of differ-ence, including sexual, racial and religious difference. The questions it tackles are both important and complex and, as a methodological guide, I have taken Andreas Huyssen's goal of developing a 'postmodernism of resistance' that can register 'the various and multiple forms of otherness as they emerge from dif-ferences in subjectivity, gender and sexuality, race and class, temporal *Ungleichzeitigkeiten* [discontinuities] and spatial geographic locations and dis-locations' (Huyssen 1984: 269–70). In the face of a crisis in judgemental stan-dards as the values of modernity split apart, Huyssen argues for a 'postmodernism of resistance' that seeks to exacerbate tensions in ways that are 'specific and contingent upon the cultural field upon which it operates':

> The point is not to eliminate the productive tension between the political and the aesthetic, between history and the text, between engagement and the mission of art. The point is to heighten that tension, even to rediscover it and to bring it back into focus in the arts as well as in criticism. No matter how troubling it may be, the

landscape of the postmodern surrounds us. It simultaneously delimits and opens our horizons. It's our problem and our hope.

(Huyssen 1984: 271)

Since 1984 when Huyssen wrote these words, the landscape of the twentieth-first century has been transformed by a new kind of 'terror', as well as by a new type of encounter with 'the various and multiple forms of otherness'. And this makes the threats to the aesthetic and political values of modernity much more urgent. If 'postmodern' solutions to the crisis in modernity now seem less satisfactory, looking at the debates around the sublime will certainly help delineate why this might be the case. What needs to be explored is precisely the inability of some 'postmodern'—as well as 'modern'—thinkers to register differences that are not merely conceptual, symbolic or discursive, but also inscribed on the flesh (of the woman, the Jew or the Arab). Since the sublime involves an aesthetics of transcendence, the tension between the sexually and racially specific body and the response of the non-personal, but also not universal, human subject will be one of the sites where the tension between the political and the aesthetic will be revealed.

When artist and critic Anthony Haden-Guest set out 'On the Track of the "S" Word' not long before the Twin Towers attack, he found it hard to see a future for the sublime that was not parodic or ironic. On the one hand, he registered the 'magnificent and complicated cloudscape' seen out of an aircraft window as he flew into Tokyo: 'This cloudscape was here before we were. It will be here after—just as long as there is water on the planet' (Haden-Guest 2001: 54). On the other hand, he also indicated that at the start of the twenty-first century we find ourselves distanced from the sublime by technology and global marketing. 'Nagoya Castle' in Japan remains and can be visited: 'The quotation marks are deserved because the original was incinerated during air raids in 1945'; it is the replica that is visited:

Nowadays, I think, an honest artist would have to be aware of snowmobiles and global warming as well as the fact that there is no landscape so savage, no 'wilderness' so wild, as not to bring a glitter to the developer's eye, except for those places so remote and rugged—okay, so sublime—that they offer lucrative prospects for Extreme Sports promotions.

(Haden-Guest 2001: 55–56)

If the sublime is to be defined primarily in terms of landscape features or the depiction of a certain set of 'sublime' objects, then any 'honest' artist will certainly need to negotiate between presenting the 'impersonal' real and the framed and the faked. But is that all that the 'sublime' means now? What Haden-Guest has lost is that much less mimetic—much more political—sense of the postmodern sublime as a transformative event: 'Does the sublime have a future? Perhaps that unlikely oracle Pat Buchanan expressed it most succinctly. Speaking to a *New York Times* reporter, Buchanan said, "We are unserious people in an unserious time."' (Haden-Guest 2001: 55). Well, both America and the times have become rather more serious since then. Haden-Guest's 'honest' sublime that can't quite take itself seriously is not a robust or committed enough sublime to help us explore the post-apocalyptic landscape of New York, the Second Gulf War or other televised images of political terror. It is Lyotard who is of more help with that task, and it is to him I will turn in the next chapter, along with Burke, Kant and Hegel and the problems and politics of representing the terror–sublime.

2

TERROR, TERRORISM AND
THE SUBLIME

In this chapter I will address the question of the politics of the sublime and its philosophical and historical links with political terror. Although I will look backwards to explore the relationship between terror and the sublime in Edmund Burke, Immanuel Kant and G. W. F. Hegel, it is recent events that I have in mind. The moral and aesthetic problems that emerge when political violence is viewed as 'art' are as important now as when Burke and Kant were writing in the eighteenth century. This can be seen from the outraged response to some comments reputedly made by Karlheinz Stockhausen, the aged avant-garde composer, in the immediate aftermath of September 11 2001.

Stockhausen is reported as having characterised 'what we saw' of the terrorist attack on New York as 'the biggest work of art anywhere, for the whole cosmos': one that must 'from now on completely change your manner of seeing things'. 'Picture what occurred. Five thousand people are concentrated on a performance and are pushed, in one moment, towards resurrection. I could never manage to obtain this result.' Compared to this, 'we're nothing as composers'. These remarks made on the eve of two concerts of new works by Stockhausen at the Hamburg Music Festival—concerts cancelled in the resultant furore—were only made worse when Stockhausen responded to a Press question about his apparent equation of art and atrocity with the following observation:

> 'It's a crime because the people hadn't agreed to it. They didn't come to the "concert." That's clear. And no one told them that it could kill them. What happened there spiritually, this leap from security, from the everyday, from life, that happens sometimes in art as well. Or else it's nothing.'
>
> (Huson 2001)

Stockhausen's first remark is disputed; but the second (less questionable) comment seems no better. It also seems to draw on Schiller's account of sublime art. As we saw in the last chapter, this starts out with man being 'ravished by

21

the terrifying' and then being taken on a '*spiritual mission*' that leaves phenomenal reality behind (Schiller 1801: 199ff.).

Stockhausen's comments are understandable in a way, in that most of us first learned of the New York tragedy through a series of images on a television screen—and hence through a framework of cinematic expectations that blurs the boundary between the 'real' and the 'fictional', and the 'actual' and 'art'. Even many of those in the buildings or the street reported experiencing the attack as if in a film or a play: mediated by a kind of internalised camera lens that distances the self from the horror and tragedy of which it was a part. Our over-familiarity with framed images of apocalypse and tragedy distances us from the force of uncontained power, somewhat in the manner of the historical category of the picturesque since, as we saw in the last chapter, the picturesque involved a framing of the sublime so that the potential disruption of chaos, infinity and raw power was contained by the eye: 'it is on the shape and disposition of its boundaries, that the picturesque must in great measure depend' (Price 1810: vol. i, 84). It is indeed an interesting question whether our easy habits of framing the spectacular through techniques of the eye mean that anything as powerful as the response to the 'sublime' in its eighteenth-century modes is now closed off to us.

However comprehensible Stockhausen's comments might be, they are still offensive in that they seem to ally the terrorist act to performative art—'great art' moreover—and seem to suggest that there is a kind of redemption at work here. 'Great art'—and Stockhausen is drawing on the tradition of the sublime here, so I will say 'sublime art'—is art in which the individual is sacrificed for the sake of the abstract and the spiritual. Sublime art is that which takes a 'leap from security' and pushes the individual beyond the 'everyday' and 'towards resurrection'. What Stockhausen suggests is that the September 11 attacks involved a criminal act, but the primary crime is that people did not choose 'to go to the concert'—that they did not know what would happen. It's not actually said that if the individuals had known it would have been alright, but that seems to be suggested.

I am not seeking here to defend Stockhausen's comments which, if accurately reported (and there is some dispute about this), seem insensitive—'crass' might be a better term—but I am interested in reading them alongside Kant's sublime which has been interpreted by some commentators as performing a similar 'leap' into spirituality and a similar sacrifice of the 'everyday' in the enjoyment of surrendering 'security'. Thus, in his book *Subjects of Terror*, Jonathan Strauss asserts that the Kantian sublime expresses an incompatibility between abstract reason and sensuous imagination, but represents reason as the clear victor:

> it is a moment in which the 'I' identifies with an abstraction and in so doing negates the individual that it had previously been. The sublime moment is thus a self-identification in which an abstract and impersonal

self rejects a sensuously interested and personally interested self. This triumph is felt as terror, which in itself reveals a profound aversion or resistance to this sublimation on the part of an individual.

(Strauss 1998: 36)

Strauss links this sublime moment in Kant with the invention of the guillotine and with Hegel's discussion of The Terror of the French Revolution in his *Phenomenology of Spirit* (1807), so Strauss is clearly aware of the political consequences of this kind of reading. Strauss reads both Kant and Hegel in terms of a 'radically negative model of self-understanding and self-awareness' that 'remains key to contemporary theories of subjectivity' (Strauss: xii).

In direct contrast to Strauss' interpretation of Kant on the sublime is the one that Jean-François Lyotard offers us in his 1982 essay 'Answering the Question: What is Postmodernism?' Although Lyotard's account of Kant on the sublime is not entirely stable (so that in other places Lyotard seems to shift Kant closer to either Burke or Hegel), in this, his most celebrated essay, Lyotard employs the Kantian sublime as a defence against Hegelian 'terror' and against the (Habermasian) type of discourse that links modernity and Enlightenment to the values of consensus. Arguing that any attempt to 'totalize' conflicting language games is Hegelian and is a form of 'transcendental illusion', Lyotard ends this piece with the following remark:

But Kant also knew that the price to pay for such an illusion is terror. The nineteenth and twentieth centuries have given us as much terror as we can take. ... Under the general demand for slackening and for appeasement, we can hear the mutterings of a desire for the return of terror, for the realization of the fantasy to seize reality. The answer is: Let us wage a war on totality; let us be witness to the unpresentable; let us activate the differences and save the honor of the name.

(Lyotard 1982: 81–82)

I will side with Lyotard against Strauss' reading of Kant and argue that Lyotard's Kant provides us with useful resources for thinking a response to 'terror' which neither simply aestheticises that terror (in the manner of Stockhausen) nor homogenises the response to 'terror' by an appeal to a single set of descriptors ('terrorism', 'absolute evil', 'unconditional good' etc.) with which all would concur. The chapter will end, however, by suggesting that Lyotard's own political strategy works by producing new blind spots. Not only does he write out the way that sexual, ethnic, racial and material differences figure in Kant's account of the tensions generated by the sublime, but his liberatory 'postmodern' sublime that preserves the tension between 'individual' and 'universal' is described in ways that are implicitly Eurocentric. Lyotard provides some of the resources that would be required to link the postmodern sublime to a postcolonial sublime; but he himself does not make any such move. In fact, he ends by withdrawing from the realm of the political when he asserts in *Post-modernism Explained*: 'As for a politics of the sublime, there is no such thing. It could only be terror. But there is an aesthetic of the sublime in politics' (Lyotard 1988c: 71).

To contextualise this claim, I need first to explore the links between 'terror' and 'the sublime' in three authors who are foundational to the discourse of the sublime as it developed in Western modernity: Burke, Kant and Hegel. What I will suggest is that there are two sets of related debates concerning the sublime. There is, on the one hand, a dispute between Burke and Kant concerning the relationship between terror and the sublime moment. For the young Burke, terror is a necessary determinant of the sublime, and in a way that leaves obscure the question of the moral status of the 'sublime'—so much so that Burke was, in effect, forced to reject his own account of the sublime when he came to write his *Reflections on the Revolution in France* between 1789 and 1790. Opposed to Burke is Kant for whom terror is a component, but not a necessary determinant, of the sublime, and for whom the experience of the sublime (even the sublime of war) is morally educative in that through the terrible or ungraspable the mind is propelled towards an idea of a higher (hidden) order and the supersensible. In the second set of debates concerning the sublime the issue is whether or not the empirical individual is sacrificed to spirit or the universal in the enjoyment of the sublime; or whether, in the sublime, the universal and the individual, reason and sense, are held together in productive tension. Here the debate is between Lyotard's Kant and the Hegelians, and relates to the question of whether 'terror' could ever be justified by stepping up to a higher level—that of reason or 'spiritual' resurrection.

Burke, the sublime and revolutionary terror

Edmund Burke's *A Philosophical Enquiry into the Origin of Our Ideas of the Sublime and Beautiful* (1757/1759) provides the background to all subsequent debates and did, indeed, help shape the modern taste for the sublime. Within its logic of taste, there is no question but that the events of September 11 2001 would have counted as sublime. As indicated in the last chapter, for Burke passions fall into two primary groups: those linked with society and social interaction generally (linked to the aesthetic response of the 'beautiful') and passions concerning 'self-preservation' which 'turn mostly on *pain* or *danger*' and which generate our enjoyment of the sublime (38).

> Whatever is fitted in any sort to excite the ideas of pain, and danger, that is to say, whatever is in any sort terrible, or is conversant about terrible objects, ... is a source of the *sublime*; that is, it is productive of the strongest emotion which the mind is capable of feeling.
>
> (Burke 1757/59: 39)

There is thus nothing morally educative (or rational) about the sublime as such. Fear 'robs the mind of all its powers of acting and reasoning'. Further-more, whatever is visually terrible is also necessarily sublime, 'whether this cause of terror, be endued with greatness of dimension or not' (57).

Where there is visually 'greatness of dimension', the experience of the sublime is doubly secured. Burke specifically picks out vastness, infinity, 'magnitude' and 'magnificence' in building, as well as the 'artificial infinite' which involves a succession of mental vibrations generated by the uniformity of parts of a building, especially when the building includes simplicity and straight lines, as well as great size (72–78, 139–42). To add in the racial dimension, in the last chapter we also saw Burke maintaining that there is a 'natural' horror linked not only to the idea of darkness, but also with blackness which is kind of *partial darkness*. The horror of darkness is 'mechanically' generated by 'the contraction of the radial fibres of the iris'; the horror at blackness is generated via 'shock', and by the 'convulsive motion' induced in the mind and in vision through sudden changes in tension and relaxation in the muscles of the body (144–47). Burke claims that custom may reconcile us with the 'painful' sight of black objects, but the 'naturalness' of the distress is also emphasised via the story of the young boy who regains his sight and who is immediately struck 'with great horror' at the sight of a negro woman (148, 144). Burke is insistent that the sublime is an offshoot of power, and linked with those who have power over us, 'So that strength, violence, pain and terror, are ideas that rush in upon the mind together' (65). Although Burke does not explicitly link the sublime to the fear that a black body might have power over those whose skin is white, it seems entailed by his account.

In his *Philosophical Enquiry* Burke registers 'sympathy'—or what we would now call 'empathy'—as an important part of the mechanics of terror that generates the sublime. It is by 'sympathy' that we are 'put into the place of another', but this empathetic response can unite with ideas of pleasure, so that 'we have a degree of delight, and that no small one, in the real misfortunes and pains of others', especially when we read about them or see them acted on a stage. We take particular pleasure in reading about the fall, ruin or distress of a great empire. Whereas experiencing terror in real life only produces pain, 'terror is a passion which always produces delight when it does not press too close'. That we do not simply 'shun' terror is explained in terms of the fact that we do not simply turn away from the image of suffering and are, instead, motivated by pity to 'relieve ourselves in relieving those who suffer' (44–46). This binds the spectacle of terror to the pleasures that come through social interaction, and means that the 'pain' or terror mixes with the 'delight' that is linked to the social. But as a consequence of this,

> there is no spectacle we so eagerly pursue, as that of some uncommon and grievous calamity; so that whether the misfortune is before our

eyes, or whether they are turned back to it in history, it always touches with delight.

(Burke 1757/59: 46)

In his *Reflections on the Revolution in France*, composed more than 30 years later, Burke—for the most part silently—draws back from this account of the sublime and its pleasures. Burke's 1790 text predates those excesses of the guillotine that were subsequently branded 'The Terror' (1793–94) and which gave rise to the first recorded use of the term 'terrorist' in 1795. However, Burke's *Reflections* seems prescient in that it implicitly addresses a theme that would be taken up explicitly by Robespierre in his celebrated justification of Terror as a necessary adjunct to the 'sublime sentiment' of public virtue in a speech to the *Committee of Public Safety* (the committee responsible for order in revolutionary France) in 1794:

> Terror is nothing other than justice, prompt, severe, inflexible; it is therefore an emanation of virtue; it is not so much a special principle as it is a consequence of the general principle of democracy applied to our country's most urgent needs.

(February 5 1794)

In *Reflections* Burke quietly drops the analysis of the passions offered in his *Philosophical Enquiry*. In the whole of his *Reflections*, Burke uses the term 'sublime' only three times, and never in a way that makes the sublime a necessary product of terror. Instead, Burke is careful to distinguish the delight that we take in watching tragedies played out on a stage from the feelings evoked by the spectacle of terror and suffering in revolutionary France. Indeed, even on the stage Burke now claims that we cannot take enjoyment in anything as extreme as the downfall of the King and Queen of France: no theatre audience could bear to see this 'real tragedy' portrayed as a 'triumphal day' in which the pros and cons were, as it were, weighed 'in scales hung in a shop of horrors' for the audience's delight (Burke 1790: 132).

Opposing those who argue that royal power must depend for its justification on the will of the people, Burke now argues that the true grounding of the monarchy is 'the peace, quiet, and security of the realm' and the need for '*certainty in the succession* thereof' (68). It is 'tradition' that guarantees the line of succession and hence the protection of the subject, and in a way that leaves the 'choice' of the individual to one side. Burke sidelines the individual subject as he amalgamates the so-called 'social' passions and passions linked with self-preservation and danger: a distinction which provided the basis for his earlier division between the beautiful and the sublime. In *Reflections on the Revolution in France* there is simply no space left for the response of an individual to revolutionary terror as a trigger for the enjoyable feelings of the sublime (62ff.). Now, Burke opposes his own feelings to those of the French revolutionary

26

'madmen' who are disciples of Rousseau and Voltaire. The English 'know' that there are no new discoveries to be made about either morality or government, and that the principles of both are those hallowed by tradition. The English still 'fear God'; 'look up with awe' to kings; treat parliament 'with affection'; show duty, respect and reverence to magistrates, priests and nobility; and this traditionalism is a consequence of the 'real hearts and flesh and blood' beating in English bosoms. It is these 'natural' and 'inbred' sentiments that are the 'active monitors of our duty, the true supporters of all liberal and manly morals' (137).

It is as if Burke has forgotten everything that he had said in his *Philosophical Enquiry* about the origins of our feelings of the sublime. It is therefore hardly surprising that his critics charged him with inconsistency, as well as with an 'unmanly' response—an obvious riposte given Burke's earlier linking of masculine power with the sublime and the feminine with beauty (1757/59: 42, 65, 116). Thus, in the 1790 version of *A Vindication of the Rights of Men*—a text later revised to take account of the subsequent period of Terror—Mary Wollstonecraft suggests that both the English male aristocrats and Burke himself are lacking in manly feelings or manly morals. Arguing vehemently against Burke's characterisation of women as beautiful—'little, smooth, delicate, fair creatures, never designed that they should exercise their reason'—Wollstonecraft suggests that the languid lifestyle of the aristocrat who exercises neither mind nor body has feminised the upper-class British males (Wollstonecraft 1790: 107; Blakemore 1997). They, like their defender Burke, have 'ceased to be men'. Burke has turned his back on the values of sublimity and, according to Wollstonecraft, this is because he has grown weak, along with the aristocratic males (Wollstonecraft: 10, 26ff., 143ff.). Burke's persistent use of the language of 'natural' and time-hallowed 'feelings', together with his failure to use the language of the sublime—or even to explicitly engage with and renounce the analysis of the passions put forward in his earlier *Philosophical Enquiry*—invites and deserves Wollstonecraft's sharp response.

It is as if Burke has registered the political consequences of tying the delight in the sublime to feelings of terror and, in order to block the kind of aestheticised response that Stockhausen provides to the 'spectacle' of much more recent real-life 'terror', simply backs away in silence, abandoning the discourse of the sublime as immoral and unfeeling. Burke's (apparently cowardly) switch of perspective presents us with one aspect of the problematic politics of the sublime, but gives us few clues towards a means of linking political transformation and moral education with a politics of the sublime. For this we need to turn to Kant whose early essay, *Observations on the Feeling of the Beautiful and Sublime* (1764), is conventionally Burkean with respect to gender, but which already gives terror (*Schreck*) a relatively muted role. 'The terrible-sublime' (*das Schreckhaft-Erhabene*) is named as one of the three varieties of the sublime, but terror is certainly not a sufficient cause of sublime feeling, as it was in Burke's *Philosophical Enquiry* (*Obs*: 2/209, p. 55 *corr.*). Instead, in this short essay Kant's focus is on the relationship between virtue and sublimity, rather than on terror, power or fear.

Kant's sublime: between the aesthetic and the moral

The question of the relationship between terror and sublimity is developed more explicitly in Kant's *Critique of the Power of Judgment* (1790), a text written simultaneously with the French Revolution—with (extensive) revisions (that some scholars argue included major changes to the sections on the sublime) made in the latter part of 1789 and into 1790 (Zammito 1992). Given the events in Paris, and Kant's longstanding interest in the moral dimensions of the sublime, it would have been odd if he had not reworked the account of the sublime in this text, his so-called third *Critique*, so as to secure the distinction between the sublime as a kind of moral attainment and what he had earlier named the 'terror-sublime'. It is as if he needs to find a solution to the problems about the relationship between terror and sublimity that Burke had now closed his eyes to, and that Burke sought to mask through an excess of words. Burke's *Reflections* was not translated into German until 1791; but Kant's longstanding admiration for Rousseau and his well-documented support for the French Revolution (Kuehn 2001), together with his suspicion of the rhetoric of inherited 'feelings' and 'natural entrails', means that Burke's own (never explicitly stated) solution would never have had any appeal for Kant.

In the *Critique of the Power of Judgment*, 'terror' (*Schreck*) is carefully distinguished from real fear. Thus Kant tells us that if we were actually afraid, we would not be able to make any judgement about the sublime in nature and that 'it is impossible to find satisfaction in a terror that is seriously intended' (*CPJ*: 261). Although the sublime involves a kind of '*astonishment* bordering on terror' and a kind of 'horror (*Grausen*) and awesome shudder', the observer does not experience 'actual fear' and this is 'in view of the safety in which he knows himself to be' (269). 'Fear' (*Furcht*) is a noun used by Kant more extensively than 'horror', but again he is careful to distinguish his position from that of Burke in the *Philosophical Enquiry*. We are told that to judge nature in terms of the dynamic sublime 'it must be represented as arousing fear'; but Kant then immediately adds that the converse does not hold: 'not every object that arouses fear is found sublime' (260).

In *Subjects of Terror* Strauss argues that Kant is inconsistent when he claims both that actual fear cannot generate the feeling of the sublime and that '"The *sublime* is what pleases immediately by reason of its opposition to the interest of sense"' (Strauss 1998: 10). Strauss 'resolves' this apparent paradox by arguing that in the case of the Kantian sublime what is required is not '*sensible* interest' (the safety of the body) but '*intellectual* interest' (11):

the only way to resolve the apparent antinomy of freedom here, and this is how Hegel will resolve the problem of freedom, [is] to say that ... 'he' who is assured of safety, or the preservation of interest, can only be a 'he' who has identified with the abstract negative principle of moral law: freedom itself.

(Strauss 1998: 12)

In other words, Strauss turns Kant into something like a Stockhausian terrorist, in making Kant say that the sublime moment comes as the individual subject sacrifices his personal interest to the universal. But is this what Kant means? And is this the only way of resolving this antinomy?

Kant asserts that the immediacy of the pleasure in the sublime comes '*through* its resistance to the interest of the senses' (*CPJ*: 267, italics added). This does not imply that physical safety is incompatible with the sublime, nor that what is felt is actual fear. It is Meredith's poor translation of the third *Critique* that has generated Strauss' 'paradox'. Kant does not claim that the sublime pleases '*by reason of* its opposition to the interest of sense', as Meredith puts it, but only that it is *through* conflict that the pleasure arises (Kant 1952: 267, italics added). Kant is not arguing that actual fear is felt in the experience of the sublime, but that in representing the sublimity of the experience, nature has to be represented as fearful (*CPJ*: 260). The sublime involves not fear, but an enjoyment of the threatening: an awareness of potential danger, an attitude of awe or heightened respect (*Achtung*) for that which could overwhelm the ego (257). Elsewhere Kant explicitly differentiates the state of mind involved in *Achtung* from 'feeling' (*Gefühl*) as generally understood, saying that respect is not generated by sense nor reducible to inclination or fear in the manner of first-order feelings (Kant 1785: 4/401n.).

In the *Critique of the Power of Judgment* Kant's claim is that the mind is '*moved*' in its response to the sublime, and he compares this movement or agitation—in ways not dissimilar to Burke—with a kind of 'vibration' which involves 'a rapidly alternating repulsion from and attraction to one and the same object' (*CPJ*: 258). These fluctuations are excessive or rhapsodic (*überschwenglich*) from the point of view of the empirical imagination—a kind of 'abyss' within which the imagination fears to lose itself—and, from the point of view of reason, 'lawful' in that they are bound up with 'reason's idea of the supersensible'. In experiencing the sublime, it is not fear alone that is registered, but fear mixed and modified by reason, and in a way that means the chaotic and irrational is also 'harmonious' with the purposive and orderly (258).

What the sublime involves is what Kant terms a '*negative*' pleasure (as opposed to the '*positive*' pleasure of the beautiful): 'namely a feeling of the deprivation of the freedom of the imagination by itself' (269). This feeling of self-robbery exists alongside that of sacrifice (*Aufopferung*) to higher ends. Reason posits the idea of the supersensible in relation to the sublime, and this gives the mind the feeling that it is being 'purposively determined' through laws that differ from those that structure the imagination's 'empirical use'. The feelings of lawful 'sacrifice' and lawless 'robbery' are experienced together, and Kant's abstract prose reflects the metaphorics of movement which he says the imagination endures in the experience of the sublime. Man's empirical imagination is simultaneously 'thrown down' (*unterworfen*) as it is subjected to the object, and 'offered up' in a kind of sacrifice (*Aufopferung*) to the powers of reason (269 *corr.*). The imagination is agitated as reason and the object impact on it—from above and below, as it were. What causes our enjoyment is precisely this tension or vibration. But it is through the exchange of the empirical power of imagination for the power of the imagination taken over by the supersensible that the 'I' avoids simple subjection or fear, so that the security of the 'I' is not threatened, but strengthened.

In Kant the experience of the sublime is not straightforwardly reactive: the cause of the sublime is the empirical object, but the response is not just to the object but to the thought of a higher order—the supersensible—an idea that is generated as the imagination *robs itself* of its power. The Kantian sublime is bound up with 'awe', and with our response to the infinite or to the indefinitely great: to that which our senses cannot measure, manage or contain without a kind of shock. Where 'terror' and fear are involved, the terror is not so much bound up with external events, as with the initial incapacity of the mind to bring sensory experience, imagination, understanding and reason together and deal with what we see or otherwise sense. In Kant we have not yet entered a discourse in which art objects are sublime; what is sublime is the natural world or, more accurately, the mind of man as he responds to that world and to the feelings that it engenders (*CPJ*: 280). Kant is quite specific on this point, and he also indicates that the sublime is not a purely aesthetic category, but a mixed genre that occupies the borderline between the aesthetic and the moral (265, 271).

An imagined community (of men)

As we have seen, the origins of the modern concept of the sublime lie in an ancient text on rhetoric, *Peri Hypsous*. Whereas the goal of logic or dialectic was to establish truths, rhetoric was concerned with persuading or convincing another person, and motivating action. It was, in other words, concerned with a speaker's power over another. Unlike Plato—who was famously hostile to rhetoric—Aristotle had set about categorising and analysing the modes of its power in *On Rhetoric* (Aristotle c.350 BCE). As well as the use of reason (*logos*) which produces conviction, power might be exercised via persuasive techniques that play on the status or credibility of the speaker (*ethos*) or on the emotions or passions of a particular audience (*pathos*). Aristotelian rhetoric is not hostile to non-rational power, but seeks to fit it into these three broad types. Kant seems to have this tradition of rhetoric in mind when, in the final sections of his *Critique of Pure Reason* (1781/1787), he draws a distinction between merely 'subjective' judgements that are generated by persuasion and 'objective' judgements in which the understanding is convinced by the argument presented. Arguing that the understanding is involved whenever we take something to be true, Kant distinguishes between 'objectively sufficient' grounds that would be 'valid for everyone'—what we call 'conviction'—and 'persuasion' which is rooted only in the particular constitution of the subject:

> Persuasion is a mere semblance, since the ground of the judgment, which lies solely in the subject, is held to be objective. Hence such a judgment has only private validity, and this taking something to be true cannot be communicated.
>
> (*CPR*: A820/B848)

Persuasion works only on the individual psyche, character and emotional dispositions. From the point of view of the subject who believes in a truth, it is not possible to distinguish between persuasion and conviction, says Kant. However, from an external point of view it is nevertheless possible to distinguish between being persuaded and being convinced that something is true. The person who is convinced believes that 'the ground of the agreement of all judgments, regardless of the difference among the subjects, rests on the common ground, namely the object' and this means that there is 'the possibility of communicating it and finding it to be valid for the reason of every human being to take it to be true' (*CPR*: A820/B848). To distinguish between persuasion and conviction, what is needed is a kind of thought 'experiment' involving 'the understanding of others'. Where 'the grounds that are valid for us' are judged to 'have the same effect on the reason of others' there is conviction; where there is a discrepancy between the individual subject and the universal, there is persuasion (A821/B849).

Kant is not writing about the sublime at this point—indeed his mature doctrine of the sublime would not be developed until the *Critique of the Power of Judgment* in 1790. But this passage about persuasion and conviction is nevertheless revealing in terms of the way that the sublime will come to feature in Kant and his successors. Kant insists on the 'universal communicability' of aesthetic judgements, both with respect to beauty and also the sublime (*CPJ*: 295). Aesthetic pleasure is non-conceptual, but nonetheless universally communicable (306). What is universally communicable is 'the satisfaction' or 'the feeling' (249), so much so that taste is defined as: 'the faculty for judging *a priori* the communicability of the feelings that are combined with a given representation (without the mediation of a concept)' (296). Universal communicability is asserted even though, at an empirical level, the pleasure in the sublime is not open to all and is instead culturally and historically specific—so that, for example, the enjoyment of 'sublime' mountain scenery is closed off to the (inadequately educated) Alpine 'peasant' who is actually afraid of the 'icy mountains' (265). Analogously, a prior moral education is said to be required if the response to war is to find it sublime, and is not to be actual fright. Historical preconditions are also presupposed, since Kant claims that a long period of peace 'usually debases the mentality of the populace' and prevents it from experiencing the sublime (263).

Kant expresses contempt for all cringing, ingratiating, abject creatures who have no confidence in their own strengths, and for those who are only concerned with mental ease and pleasure. He compares a concern with mental and emotional ease with the comforting (and corrupting) enjoyment of 'the voluptuaries of the Orient' who sink into 'agreeable exhaustion' after their bodies have been 'kneaded, and all their muscles and joints softly pressed and flexed' (273–74). In his lectures on *Anthropology* (1798/1800) Kant also registers that there are some empirical subjects who should not be educated in such a way as to transcend fear (*Anth*: 7/306). Here he indicates that it is the duty of women to protect the unborn foetus in the womb, and that fear plays an important role in helping them perform this task. But this means that women are debarred from any proper enjoyment of the sublime, and that they fall outside the bounds of the imagined community of rational subjects for whom the sublime is 'universally communicable'.

For Kant, the experience of the sublime involves a kind of thought experiment in which communication and universality play a role; but that is where the similarity with convincing another rhetorically ends, since the man who enjoys the sublime seems to be taken outside the community of shared (intersubjective) concepts. He is united with others only via the supposition that any other (rational) man must share his pleasure since his own satisfaction is produced not by the object, but by the play of his faculties—faculties that others must share. Thus, what is universally communicable in the case of the sublime is not the concept, but the pleasure; and in the case of the sublime, this pleasure is not just non-conceptual (as in the case of beauty and other judgements of taste), it originates in the defeat of the understanding. This pleasure is generated by discord, through conflict and dissonance, as man's senses, imagination and emotions function disharmoniously—trying to grasp an infinity or a power that is too great for comprehension. It is the conflict of the faculties that generates the enjoyment of the sublime—not the object itself—and it is this conflict that also brings into play the Ideas of reason which are epistemologically (but not temporally) subsequent to the conflict.

For Kant the sublime is no longer simply an affect generated by an overwhelming or external force (as it was in the case of Burke), but involves registering and also moving beyond the 'abyss' opening before the mind—with this step back towards order being taken by reason, via the idea of the supersensible, as a response to disharmony and conflict between faculties. Reason is involved from the start; but this is 'reason' used in the technical Kantian sense of something excessive to understanding, and involves the three Ideas—of freedom, God and immortality—that are 'beyond' or 'other' to the space–time framework that is supplied by the senses and organised into a unity via the understanding. Reason does not make the object any more comprehensible to the understanding, but it does serve to universalise the pleasure. And it is this universalising of his pleasure that also makes the experience of the sublime so unlike the 'subjective'—and individualised—response that characterises persuasion on the Kantian account, and means that Kant has escaped the limitations of the rhetorical tradition of thinking about the sublime.

The effect of the sublime is *more* than mere persuasion in that it is not simply subjective; but at the same time it remains *other to* the kind of universality that is linked with the process of convincing another through an appeal to his understanding. The universal element in the pleasure in the sublime attaches to reason, not to the synthetic *a priori* structures of the phenomenal world that are supplied by the understanding. Integral to the Kantian sublime is the notion of an imagined community within which difference is registered and also transcended as the mind is propelled away from the empirical and towards the supersensible—yet the supersensible is not known, but posited as a horizon and as a normative ideal. As Kant puts it in the first (unpublished) Introduction to the *Critique of the Power of Judgment*, 'aesthetic judgments of reflection'—'judgments of taste'—'lay claim to necessity'. It is 'not that everyone does so judge—that would make their explanation a task for empirical psychology—but that everyone *ought* to so judge' (*CPJ*: 20/238–9).

The term 'everyone' here means the paradigm rational man who is—as I argue in more detail in the next chapter—not only 'manly', but male. Through his almost parenthetical remarks on sexual and cultural difference, Kant registers that empirical specificities and embodied difference can mean that whole classes of persons can fall outside the imagined community of rational beings who attain pleasure via the transcendence of fear. His comments on women in particular mean that this is not simply a contingent fact about some human beings, but an important modification to the ideals of disembodied rationality and the transcendence of the merely bodily that his ethics and aesthetics promote.

What Kant does to secure the universal communicability of the 'satisfaction' of the sublime is, in effect, to discuss the response in terms of the paradigm manly (and appropriately educated and racially superior) male who responds to feeling or affect in a '*courageous*' manner, in terms of the 'consciousness of our powers to overcome any resistance' (*CPJ*: 272). Such a man can register that 'Even war, if it is conducted with order and reverence for the rights of civilians, has something sublime about it' (263)—a claim elaborated in the 'Critique of the Teleological Power of Judgment' where we are told that war, although terrible, can also reveal divine purposiveness and provide a moral incentive 'for developing to their highest degree all the talents that serve for culture' (*CPJ*: 433).

The Kantian sublime is generated by sensory, conceptual and imaginative conflict: with gaps opening between our senses and our understanding, imagination or reason as the mind struggles with the infinite, the apparently formless or indefinite—and hence purposeless—shape that confronts it. But as this gap between the faculties opens up, the manly man can regain a sense of order precisely through an act of comparison (or judgement) that makes the space–time ordering imposed by man on the world give way to the idea of a 'higher' or 'supersensible' order that does not have the human 'I' as its source. Confronted by the apparently disorderly, the indefinitely great or apparently infinite, the elite male re-orders the chaos through displacing his own centrality—thereby containing the apparently uncontainable and bringing it within the bounds of reason. But at the same time that the object generates sublime Ideas to reason, it remains a puzzle to sense and an 'abyss' as far as the empirical imagination is concerned.

Through his contact with the uncontainable, the manly man discovers in himself 'a capacity for resistance' which gives 'us' the 'courage to measure ourselves against the apparent all-powerfulness of nature' (CPJ: 261). Whereas in Burke's *Philosophical Enquiry* it was the sublime object that robbed the spectator of his powers as he was overtaken by the sublime experience, in Kant it is not the object but man's own imagination which is felt as 'robbing' itself of its freedom as reason registers a different order that is foreign to the structures that man's 'I' imposes on the world. Thus, there is in Kant a double, in some ways paradoxical, move whereby the paradigm 'I' seems to deprive itself of its imaginative powers but, at the same time, also experiences itself as strengthened through surrendering itself to reason and to a purposiveness that seems 'other' to its own empirical concerns.

The pleasure does not simply come from the 'I' surrendering itself to an absolute—the supersensible or the demands of reason—as Strauss suggests in his reading of Kant in *Subjects of Terror*; the pleasure comes through keeping in play the tension between the (paradigm) empirical imagination that responds with awe to the fearfulness of nature, on the one hand, and to the (consoling) Ideas provided by reason, on the other hand. Those empirical subjects who are simply taken over by fear in a passive or reactive way (the Alpine peasants) never get as far as experiencing the tension, and neither do the 'Oriental' voluptuaries who have been softened through a life of sensuous gratification and ease; those empirical subjects (women) who should not subject themselves to the universals of abstract reason might feel pleasure, but should not do so. Although at an empirical level Kant argues that the sublime response is neither inevitable nor universal, the use of the phrase 'everyone *ought* to so judge' allows him to analyse the *a priori* structures of the judgements of taste, and to distance his own approach from that of the 'empirical' psychologists or physiologists such as Burke (CPJ: 20/239, 5/277).

Terror and the universal

Kant's tension-ridden account of the sublime is worth comparing with that of Hegel who discusses the sublime in terms of *art*, not nature, as in the case of Kant, and who is particularly concerned with the match between form and content as it develops through the history of religious culture. For Hegel the sublime is revealed in terms of an absolute which can be represented only negatively, and in terms of that which escapes finitude.

> In the sublime ... the finite Appearance expresses the Absolute, which it is supposed to bring before our vision, but only in such a way that the Absolute withdraws from the appearance and the appearance falls short of the content.
>
> (Hegel 1835: vol. i, 339)

For Hegel the highest art is the beautiful, not the sublime. Thus, in the account of the unfolding and progression of art over history, the 'sublime' is represented primarily by the preclassical period in which form and content are not in harmony.

For Hegel it is the 'flight beyond the determinateness of appearances' which 'constitutes the general character of the sublime' so that 'the meaning, as the universal, towers above individual reality and its particularity' (i, 303, 378). He refuses the adjective 'sublime' for the pantheism of Indian art in any strict sense, because the kind of excessiveness that it reveals—although not beautiful—does not propel us towards the Absolute (i, 340). Hebrew poetry is allowed as an example of the sublime, but only in a negative sense, as an inadequate representation of the 'imageless Lord of heaven' and his 'power and dominion' (i, 321). Classical art is beautiful, not sublime, because in classical art the universal is adequately expressed through the particular. Even Romantic art which, in stretching towards the unrepresentable, has to forego the beauty and harmonious match of form and content which characterises classical and Greek art, is not subsumed under the banner of the 'sublime' in any positive sense. Instead it is described in terms of two realms that have become divorced: a 'spiritual realm, complete in itself' within which the self 'bends' the 'otherwise rectilineal repetition of birth, death and rebirth' into spirit via a 'return into self' and, on the other hand, the realm of the external which 'now becomes a purely empirical reality by the shape of which the soul is untroubled' (i, 527).

Hegel clearly has Kant in his sights in making these comments. In Hegel's account of Romanticism (and Kant), a gulf opens up between the space–time of the empirical self and the realm of the spirit that seems to reach out to the Absolute, but is only a distortion of the space and time of the material world— a false ('bent') infinity of spirit that is overly self-contained and independent of the empirical. This is not the kind of infinity that Hegel sees as genuine, because with separation comes limitation. If this self-enclosed circle of the absolute is separated off from the empirically real, its apparent infinity is limited and finite. What Hegel wants is an infinity expressed in the world: a God who is not distinct from the world and a universal that is adequately expressed through the symbolic form that it adopts. Neither sublime art nor Romantic art can express the ideal relation between the universal and its instantiation, although both can be stages on the way in the development of the Spirit.

In his discussion of the Terror of the French Revolution in *The Phenomenology of Spirit*, Hegel also represents death in the Terror in terms of a gap that has opened up between 'the *individual* and the *universal* consciousness', and in ways that make the Terror analogous to the sublime (1807: 357, §586). In the 'universals' of revolutionary France there is no advance to 'the reality of an organic articulation' which would maintain itself in 'an unbroken continuity'. Instead, freedom has become abstract. On the one hand there is 'simple, inflexible cold universality'; on the other hand there is 'discrete, absolute hard rigidity and self-willed atomism of actual self-consciousness' (359, §586). If the individual is to merge with the universal in such conditions, it can only do it via death— and a death that is 'the coldest and meanest of all deaths'. Cutting the head off the individual (with the guillotine) is dealing only with the particular, not with the universal: it is attributed with 'no more significance than cutting off a head of cabbage or swallowing a mouthful of water' (360, §586).

For Hegel, it is in Romanticism and in the operations of the guillotine that the modern subject is born, but this is a subject alienated from the universal. We can now see what has happened in Strauss who has read Kant's account of the sublime through Hegel's account of the failure of the Kantian sublime—its false infinity—and the Terror of the French Revolution. For Strauss, as for Hegel in his account of the Terror, Kant's sublime moment involves a subject who sacrifices the 'I' for the 'universal' or the 'absolute' in ways that are too abstract, too estranged, not sufficiently embodied or organic. The Kantian sublime is linked with bad infinity in ways that make it analogous to the (bad) sacrifice of the individual to absolute freedom in the Terror of the French Revolution.

Against such a reading of Kant, that of Lyotard serves as a useful corrective. To situate Lyotard's argument, for him the 'postmodern' sublime did not succeed the modern sublime in temporal terms. On the contrary, 'A work can become modern only if it is first postmodern. Postmodernism thus understood is not modernism at its end but in the nascent state, and this state is constant' (Lyotard 1982: 79). Identifying the sublime with that which falls outside the horizons of presentation, Lyotard suggests that there are two conflicting modes of response. The 'modern' response is that of the artist or philosopher who emphasises 'the powerlessness of the faculty of presentation' in a way that involves a 'nostalgia for presence' felt by the human subject; but in order for the powerlessness of the imagination to get a grip, there must first be an emphasis placed 'on the power of the faculty to conceive'—and this failure of representation does, for Lyotard, constitute the postmodern irruption within the modern sublime (79).

As we have seen, the Kantian sublime is not like beauty which can, at least in principle, be aligned with an unrealised (but ideal) universal consensus (of taste), and which Kant describes in terms of a particular that generates a new universal. The 'universal communicability' of the sublime cannot stem from the understanding (which is defeated) nor from sense in any immediate way (since what is registered is painful and disharmonious), but instead involves Ideas which are thrown up by reason and which relate to another 'higher' realm: that of the supersensible in which man is not determined at all, but is a free and moral agent whose actions are determined by the universal and by duty, rather than by sense. Lyotard is insistent—most explicitly in the detailed reading of the third *Critique* that he offers in his *Lessons on the Analytic of the Sublime*—that Kant's demand for universal communicability in the case of sublime feeling is a demand that undercuts itself, since the sublime 'escapes' all 'demands for universal communication':

> The sublime feeling is neither moral universality nor aesthetic universalization, but is, rather, the destruction of the one by the other in the violence of their differend. This differend cannot demand, even subjectively, to be communicated to all thought.
>
> (Lyotard 1991: 239)

For Lyotard, what is distinctive about the Kantian sublime is its link with 'the differend': a 'conflict between genres of discourse' that emerges out of the incommensurability of language games (Lyotard 1983: 136; and see Lyotard 1989, 324–59). In political terms, the differend involves a conflict or dispute that is irresolvable because it brings into play at least two language games which would describe what is at stake in incommensurable terms. Any resort to 'solving' the dispute by appeal to one of the language games simply covers up the difference and rests on something that is, from the perspective of the language game adopted, 'unpresentable'. The pleasure in the Kantian sublime involves 'the incommensurability of reality to concept' and 'two "absolutes" equally "present" to thought' (1982: 79; 1991: 123). To fail to register these incommensurable absolutes—through moving up to a higher level—is to cover up or cover over difference.

Lyotard allies his own celebration of irreconcilable 'language games' with Kant's account of the 'chasm' between competing faculties in the moment of the sublime (Lyotard 1982: 81). To unpack this move, it is useful to bear in mind that for Lyotard 'language games are the minimum relation for society to exist' and that in *The Postmodern Condition*—to which, in English translation, the 1982 essay is appended—there is an emphasis on the 'agonistic aspect of society' (and also of language games) (1979: 15). To be a 'language partner' in a society is not to be an atomistic unit, but is to occupy a position in a network of 'messages that traverse them, in perpetual motion'. Each linguistic 'move' provokes a 'countermove'; but the countermove that is no more than a reactive response is 'not a "good" move'. Novelty is not just a matter of new content, but of 'displacement': a disorientation (a new orientation) that comes from making 'an unexpected "move" (a new statement)' (1979: 16).

37

In the case of the individual who is responsive to the Kantian sublime, his response will remain wrought by tension that always pulls away from the universal: 'pleasure derives from pain' and there is also a mismatch between understanding and sense, since 'the imagination fails to present an object which might, if only in principle, come to match a concept' (Lyotard 1982: 77, 78). For Lyotard's Kant this mismatch is not something that is sublated, in that sensibility and empirical imagination do not simply give way to the higher powers of abstract reason in some kind of ultimate 'sacrifice'. Instead the tension between the 'higher' imagination and empirical imagination is both preserved and celebrated, as is the tension between 'sense' and 'reason'. There is an emphasis on the conflict of the faculties in Kant's account of the sublime—indeed it is this very tension that generates pleasure.

For Lyotard, postmodernism is an irruption in the aesthetics of modernism, and this irruption is present in Kant, specifically in his account of the sublime. For Lyotard, 'modern aesthetics is an aesthetics of the sublime, though a nostalgic one' (1982: 81). Taking Kant as key to the aesthetics of modernity, he calls that art modern which uses its 'technical expertise' 'to present the fact that the unpresentable exists' (78). For the 'modern' this 'unpresentable' figures in terms of absence or loss. By contrast, for the 'postmodern' sublime absence is not loss, nor unreachable excess. The postmodern aesthetic denies itself 'the nostalgia for the unattainable' and instead revels in 'the unpresentable in presentation itself' (81). Interestingly, Lyotard finds in Kant not just the origins of modernity, but the postmodern moment. In other words, in Kant's celebration of the tension inherent within the moment of the sublime—a tension presented in Kant in terms of the conflict of 'faculties'—Lyotard finds the 'postmodern' irruption within modernity itself. He concludes the 1982 essay by opposing Kant to Hegel and linking Hegel to systematicity, uniformity, totality and 'terror'; Kant is, by contrast, linked with a pleasure that is generated by irreconcilable conflict (82).

Towards an ethics of discord

Lyotard's essay was written as a response to Habermas' attack on 'neoconservatives' such as Foucault. Lyotard finds in Habermas' call for a withdrawal from radical, avant-garde thinking 'the mutterings of the desire for a return of terror, for the realization of the fantasy to seize reality' (Lyotard 1982: 71–72, 82). This fantasy is, according to Lyotard, Hegelian in its nostalgia for 'the whole and the one' and for a 'reconciliation between language games'. 'But Kant knew that the price to pay for such an illusion is terror.' Thus Lyotard's 'answer' to Habermas ends by countering the 'transcendental illusion' of Hegelian unity with a call to arms, and by recruiting Kant in the battle against the 'terror' of systematicity: together they will 'wage a war on totality' (81, 82).

Lyotard's 'answer' to Habermas is thus double-pronged. Habermas' critique of avant-garde thinkers might be interpreted as aiming for the kind of social unity in which all the elements of a society fit organically (as within the Hegelian absolute), but that, Lyotard says, would be to fail challenge the (Hegelian) notion of a 'dialectically totalizing *experience*'. Alternatively, Habermas might be recognising competing discourses and social groupings, but see the possibility of synthesising them at a higher level. That is also problematic for Lyotard, who is implicitly mocking Habermas for positioning himself on the side of Enlightenment thinkers and criticising Foucault and others as 'neoconservative'. After all, the Enlightenment gave rise to the Terror of the Guillotine, with Robespierre explicitly appealing to 'public virtue' as he argues that the good citizen will recognise Terror as the necessary instrument of equality and democracy. Indicating that the liberatory moment in modernity is not the 'modern' moment (of an appeal to consensus) but the postmodern moment (of allowing the singular and the universal to exist in tension, side by side), Lyotard indicates that what is needed is a critique of any such notion of a 'real synthesis' between heterogeneous language games (73).

In his *Reflections on the Revolution in France*, Burke—also, above all, an Enlightenment thinker—mounts an explicit attack on Rousseau and Voltaire as the philosophical sources for the 'tragedy' that emerges once 'consensus' or the abstraction of 'the people's choice' are used as the grounding for justice and virtue. Burke has a valid point, but his actual argument is weak, depending as it does on an evocation of 'natural' and 'manly' feelings, hallowed by tradition—feelings that seem to rule out the possibility of any social change—as the only defence against the impending tragedy of revolutionary Terror. Kant's answer to 'terror' is far more interesting, and this is what Lyotard's response to Habermas enables us to see. Thus for Lyotard—but not in the much more Hegelian reading of Kant on the sublime that we find in Strauss—at the heart of the sublime is a recognition of irresolvable conflict or difference.

I do not think Lyotard should be read as denying that Kant's account of the sublime is 'modern', as well as 'postmodern'. He is not refusing to acknowledge that there is in Kant's account of the sublime a nostalgia or longing for completion—or that reason plays a role in generating the pleasure via an appeal to a higher (supersensible) order and system. In this respect Paul Guyer is much too short with Lyotard in his edition of Kant's *Critique of the Power of Judgment* (*CPJ*: xxxi–xxxii, 355n.). Instead Lyotard's point seems to be that the enjoyment of the sublime is instigated by irresolvable discord, and that a tension between faculties—and between levels of discourse—is integral to Kant's account of the sublime. The pleasure that is generated is not simply that of reason gaining control, but due to the tensions that are created as reason and the empirical imagination confront the unpresentable and the unconceptualisable, from a double perspective that combines pleasure (sensual) with the *a priori* universality of reason. As such, Lyotard's postmodern sublime privileges an irruption within the space–time order that is imposed on phenomenal reality by Kant's transcendental self as Lyotard works to open a hiatus in modernity, as well as within Kant's account of the operations of judgement itself.

For Lyotard, it is Hegel who will seek to close down the possibilities of thinking discord productively, without a final synthesis, not Kant. And it is Lyotard's Hegel who abandons the sensible in favour of spirit, the universal or the absolute, and who offers a totalising 'metanarrative' which is analogous to the 'terror' that occurs under totalitarian regimes when subjects cannot make claims to be different. It is also Lyotard's Hegel who seeks to subsume the differend under the universal. Reading this back onto the philosophies of the sublime, we could either say (as Hegel himself said) that the sublime involves a failure to adequately express the properly organic and complete universals of spirit, or we could read the Kantian sublime (as Strauss does) in a Hegelian manner, as the sacrifice of the sensuous and the empirical imagination in favour of the abstract universals of reason and freedom, abstractly considered. Lyotard offers a strong—and philosophically interesting—defence against both these strategies.

For Lyotard, the Hegelian move involves covering over absolute difference through offering a philosophy that privileges a universal which will encompass difference. The 'other' has been silenced and rendered permanently unpresentable, but in the name of 'spirit', logic', the progress of history and of 'reason'. The terror is bound up with the act of silencing, or rather with the feeling of being silenced and with the recognition that it would be self-defeating to make one's claim in terms of the metanarrative (or institutional structures) that cannot recognise difference as absolute. He situates Habermas in terms of a Hegelian tradition that assumes that all speakers can (and should) agree on 'which rules or metaprescriptions are universally valid for language games' and which also assumes 'that the goal of dialogue is consensus'. For Lyotard, by contrast, agreement on rules and a metanarrative is both impossible and undesirable and, furthermore, 'consensus is only a particular state of discussion, not its end. Its end, on the contrary, is paralogy' or the opening up of dissension and difference (1979: 65–66). Arguing that not everything that is new opens up difference in the manner of the paralogism, Lyotard stresses the importance of irresolvable difference (the differend) in advancing knowledge. Privileging consensus as an ideal 'tends to stabilize'. Such an ideal has its uses, but 'what is striking'—and what generates 'new norms for understanding'—is when someone 'comes along to disturb the order of "reason"', and when the capacity for explanation is itself destabilised by a power that 'generates blind spots and defers consensus' (1979: 61).

Thus, the Lyotardian account of the sublime produces a triple move that is strategically productive in terms of opening up the differences within Western modernity that are covered over by notions of a universal good or the culture of consensus. First, Lyotard opposes any conception of merit that would entail sacrificing another individual for the sake of an abstract justice or public virtue. Second, Stockhausen's implicit romanticisation of a performative act that pushes its audience 'towards resurrection' via a kind of spiritual 'leap' is also opposed. It is not that there are no universals in the Lyotardian moment of the

Kantian sublime, but that the universal and the singular are kept together, in tension, and given equivalent weight. Third, however, Lyotard would also categorise as a variety of 'terror' the notion that there is one and only one description of any act that is valid: the language of categorising the act in terms of murderous terrorism and perhaps even 'absolute evil' (as viewed from the perspective of America and the West) does not overwrite the competing language of religious martyrdom and heroic self-sacrifice (as viewed from the perspective of the fundamentalist extremists).

The sublime and the real

One of the merits of Lyotard's postmodern sublime is that it can register that competing descriptions of an act do not block off all other moral (or value) judgements of that act. Nor does it leave the audience with nothing but subjective 'feelings', in Burkean fashion. Instead, moral and other value judgements need to start by looking at how the tension is preserved between individuals and universals. Any universal that seeks to silence difference—by murdering its opponents, for example, 'to make a point' or to educate its opponents—has not respected the logic of the Kantian sublime that Lyotard uses as a basis for a non-consensual ethics. This is a useful way to think about how one both registers multicultural differences and multiple narratives, whilst also refusing any move that suggests that we are stuck with moral relativism and are bereft of principles that could provide the basis of condemning mass murder or the inevitability of the sacrifice of the individual for the 'greater good'.

I want to hang on to this insight. Nevertheless it is also necessary to consider what other modes of 'difference' have been forgotten through Lyotard's celebration of a postmodern sublime that is an irruption in the modes of Western modernism, since his strategy also throws up a new cluster of differends. Lyotard's 'postmodern' move does not take us to a position outside the structures of Western modernity from which to determine what might—or might not—count as a candidate for the modern or postmodern sublime. To see the limitations of Lyotard's analysis it is useful to turn back to the World Trade Center Towers attack.

Would the events of September 11 2001 have counted as sublime for Kant? We have seen that Kant is no Burkean: he breaks the necessary connection that the young Burke established between terror and the sublime in his *Philosophical Enquiry*. But neither does Kant argue, as did the older Burke, that war can never be sublime. If actual terror was felt, then the sublime is ruled out. If there was both terror and the transcendence of terror, and an event that was so unimaginable that it challenges the bounds of conceptualisation, then the sublime is in play—except that Kant suggests that the rational man *should only* be able to master his terror in the case of a war that 'is conducted with order and reverence for the rights of civilians'. And 'September 11' certainly would not count for Kant in that respect.

41

Kant does allow that terrifying acts of war can be morally improving, but he does not advocate Stockhausian terrorism in which the individual is sacrificed to abstract freedom or the good which operate as 'supersensible' and universal Ideals. Where the 'universal' comes in is with reference to Kant's description of how the ideal rational man *ought to* respond to the infinite or indefinitely great power that seems to threaten his self. But to answer the question of how the paradigm rational man should respond to a potentially sublime event, Kant smuggles in embodied and material differences—sexual difference, ethnicity, cultural and historical specificity—into his account of the idealised 'sublime' response. Kant thinks of 'universal communicability' in terms of the pleasure of the paradigm rational man who is male, non-effeminate, non-Oriental and probably urban, in that he needs to inhabit an environment in which fear is no longer a necessary survival response. As we will see in more detail in the next chapter, such a man also needs to have received the right kind of education that trains him to be his own master and think and speak for himself (see also Kant 1784). The wars that such a man encounters must also be the right kind of civilising (European?) wars.

Lyotard emphasises that the pleasure of the Kantian sublime is generated by dissonance and discord. But what Lyotard does not register is the ways in which Kant's ideal of universal communicability is still encoded through cultural and sexual difference. Lyotard's silence about empirical differences within the imagined community that founds modernity is symptomatic. Kant's idealised modern subject who has a specific body—even as he transcends embodiment— has, in effect, been replaced by Lyotard's postmodern framework that privileges paralogy and dissonance, but which thinks incommensurable difference in terms that also write out material, cultural and embodied differences. Sex, 'race', ethnicity and cultural difference (dis)appear as differends in Lyotard's abstract analysis of agonistic 'language games'. They seem to be registered, but only in Lyotard's terms.

Would 'September 11' have counted as sublime for Lyotard? I remain unsure. For Lyotard it is 'Auschwitz' that represents the hiatus within the narratives and ideals of Western modernity which give birth to his account of the postmodern sublime. Lyotard warns us that in terms of listening to Holocaust testimonies we do not know how to ask the right questions or hear the answers that are given. The narratives of the survivors disappear into the silence of the differend for those who did not themselves witness the event. Thus Lyotard comments in *The Postmodern Explained*, 'All that is real is rational, all that is rational is real: "Auschwitz" refutes the speculative doctrine. At least this crime, which is real, is not rational' (1988c: 29).

Elsewhere in this text Lyotard remarks: 'As for a politics of the sublime, there is no such thing. It could only be terror. But there is an aesthetic of the sublime in politics' (1988c: 71). Lyotard is contrasting here the way that the imagery of the sublime enters into political events—either cynically (as employed by the Fascists for example) or innocently (in France 1968)—and

42

what might be involved in thinking through a politics that is based on the postmodern sublime. In contemplating the unspeakable horrors of Auschwitz, Lyotard pushes Kant back towards the Burkean sublime—since he represents the sublime as necessarily bound up with terror—and, like the elderly Burke, he seems to silently contradict his earlier position as he refuses to pursue the potential of his earlier writings for thinking the politics of the sublime in the face of real-life terror.

Lyotard describes modernity in ways that yoke the rights of the individual together with the 'universal' either via a direct appeal to reason or via a kind of imagined consensus amongst 'rational' men. The postmodern sublime becomes that discordant moment within modernity which forces us to register the incommensurable differences and tensions that are at its heart. In treating the Holocaust as typical of the sublime in politics, we can see how Lyotard's 'postmodern' Kantianism incorporates a framework of reality and narrative that is grounded in the history of the civilisation, culture and 'reason' of the West.

Why is Auschwitz so often evoked as the paradigm example of the sublime in the scholarly literature on this subject, and not, for example, The Middle Passage in which slaves were transported from Africa to Britain, Europe and the Americas or the genocide of the aboriginal peoples in Australia? As Marcus Wood has recently argued in *Blind Memory* (2000), the imaginative and conceptual tensions generated by the horrors of the slave trade produced a kind of blindness and a cluster of images and fictions that serve as a kind of screen that covers over the experience itself which has fallen outside the horizon of representation. What gets counted as sublime is that which 'we' (Western) subjects find hardest to cover over or 'screen' out through fantasy imagery or metaphors that contain the horror within manageable bounds. Not only historical distance but also the geography of Europe, the Americas and the West have helped shape the bounds of what is—and what is not—fundamentally disturbing to a civilisation that conceives of its own modernity in terms of consensual rationality and a communicative ideal.

Lyotard's use of the 'postmodern sublime' might provide a valuable first step towards finding the basis for an ethics of discord within the structures of Western modernity, but its limitations should also alert to the ways in which 'we'—Western democratic 'persons'—consign to the limbo of the 'non-modern' or the 'pre-modern' those societies in which the individual/universal relation was never configured in such terms. Even the question of what might or might not function as an example of the 'sublime' will be imaginatively skewed to express the values of a Western civilisation which has, in practice, placed a greater emphasis on the rights, welfare and lives of Western 'persons' than on non-Western subjects.

Thus, even if 'September 11' represents an irruption into a modernity and into modes of imagining within which we (Europeans) are all Americans now, it does not tell us which political horrors *should have* generated incommensurable narratives, but have failed to do so because the acts of witnessing have met only the silence of indifference in the Western press. Lyotard does discuss the questions of '*What ought we to do?*' and '*What ought we to be?*', but he approaches these questions via the analysis of the languages of legitimation. Empirical and cultural differences are registered, but he claims that his language-based approach is 'more radical than any other (politicological, sociological, or historical)' (Lyotard 1988c: 39 and ff.). Like Kant, he seems to want to rid philosophy of empirical difference, whilst drawing on it to distinguish between 'transcendental freedom (an Idea that is unpresentable, scarcely even conceivable)' and '"empirical freedom" (if there is such a thing)' (70). The question that Lyotard's analysis raises is not simply whether there are multiple narratives that might be provided for this event (the answer is 'yes'); nor whether these narratives are incommensurable in terms of the framework of meanings ('yes' again); but 'why remain complicit with Kant's occlusion of materiality and questions of power from the domain of aesthetics?' Why in the end turn back from making an ethics and aesthetics of discord also a political event?

3

KANT AND THE UNFAIR SEX

For the eighteenth-century Scots 'moral philosophy' encompassed both ethical and aesthetical enquiries, and the French *philosophes* also moved easily between the two realms. It was with Kant that the distinction between ethical and aesthetic attitudes to the world was sharpened. But this division would work to the disadvantage of women who frequently found themselves entirely excluded from the ethical sphere, or granted a different—inferior—form of moral consciousness. The question of women's relationship to the aesthetic has been the subject of much debate in the wake of Kant. It is, therefore, ironic that although the present-day opponents of feminism have been able to grasp that there might be a place for feminist ethics or feminist political theory within the discipline of philosophy, the notion of feminist aesthetics has been found much more baffling and has attracted opposition, even from within feminism itself.

Thus, one of the most important feminist art historians, Griselda Pollock, has argued that feminists should 'stop merely juggling the aesthetic criteria for appreciating art' and 'reject all of this evaluative criticism' (Pollock 1988: 26). In literary criticism also there was too quick a move to neutral ground 'beyond' feminist aesthetics (Felski 1989). Whereas feminists emerging from the Marxist and socialist traditions have wanted to legitimise value judgements in ethics and politics, feminist aesthetics was regarded as necessarily ahistorical and essentialist in approach; as conservative, or, at best, confused. It was only gradually that feminists emerging from these traditions found a place for feminist aesthetics as an important part of the processes of political change (Wolff 1993).

This hostility to a feminist aesthetics is produced, at least in part, by the acceptance of an idea that Kant developed in the *Critique of the Power of Judgment* (1790). There Kant argued—in a way that he did not in the 1764 essay *Observations on the Feeling of the Beautiful and Sublime*—that a truly aesthetic value judgement must be 'disinterested': must abstract from all use value and material value, and concentrate solely on the object or artwork considered as form. We saw in the last chapter that even a progressive philosopher like Jean-François Lyotard is in the end complicit with the Kantian demarcation of aesthetics, denying that there ever could be a 'politics of the sublime'. What the argument of this chapter will suggest is that feminist philosophers should refuse Kantian markers for the boundary between the aesthetic and non-aesthetic realms and register the links between the aesthetic, the ethical and the political. Indeed, we will see that despite Kant's attempt to treat moral and aesthetic philosophy in purely formal terms (in terms of the 'universal'), questions of the material and the empirical insistently intrude so that, in the end, his reiterated comments about women's moral and political incapacities produce profound fractures within his system and undermine its overall coherence—although not its continued influence.

In the last chapter I indicated that Kant places whole classes of humans outside the imagined community of rational beings who can—or should—take pleasure in the sublime via the transcendence of fear. Not only is Kant scathing about the 'voluptuaries of the Orient' who respond to pleasure in a passive fashion, he also treats the paradigm rational person as both manly and male. Kant's failure to include (more than) half of the human race within the bounds of his account of 'universal' moral duty and aesthetic response is of more than merely historical interest. As Corey Robin puts it in *Fear: The History of a Political Idea* (2004), an account of the liberal self is 'Kant's bleak gift to modern morals'—and one that is (still) subject to a variety of criticisms from contemporary political and legal theorists who both register its continuing influence as well as seeking to resist its power. Bizarrely substituting the pronoun 'she' for the (supposedly) gender neutral 'he', Robin sums up Michael Sandel's criticism of Kantian moral philosophers for treating the self as,

> an 'active, willing agent', who chooses her beliefs rather than embrace or discover those she has inherited from parents, teachers, and friends. She is not bound by her 'interests and ends.' She 'possesses' such ends but is not 'possessed' by them. She lurks, like a spider, behind all the strands connecting her to the objects of the world—content in her remove, autonomous at the center of her austere web.
>
> (Robin 2004: 63; Sandel 1982)

Robin suggests that Kant's treatment of terror is fundamental to his overly autonomous conception of the self, and contrasts Kant's approach with that of his predecessor Montesquieu who, in his *Persian Letters* (1721) and *The Spirit of the Laws* (1748), had treated the self as 'a fragile being severed from its basic goods and the world's objects'. Robin explains:

> Montesquieu made it possible for subsequent theorists to think of fear, redefined as terror, as an experience unhinged from the life of the mind. If a person were rational or moral, Montesquieu suggested, he was not likely to be found among the terrorized. Kant picked up on this contrast between terror, on the one hand, and selfhood, on the

other, only he turned it in an entirely different direction. Like the despot, Kant sought to strip the self of its contingent features—its particular ends, its attachment to immediate circumstances, its objects of desire. But where the despot uncovered a creature ripe for terror, Kant discovered an agent of moral freedom, a pure good will, attuned solely to the dictates of reason, who could act upon the requirements of duty without the 'admixture of sensuous things'.

(Robin 2004: 64)

Although Montesquieu matters to Kant much less than Robin suggests, Kant's treatment of fear and terror is certainly integral to the development of his critical philosophy. This chapter will provide a detailed exploration of Kant's comments on women and moral and political personhood, paying special attention to his changing attitudes to the sublime and to fear. I will argue that Kant's demand that each human being be treated as a free person as far as moral agency is concerned is at odds with his comments on 'the fair sex' whom Kant represents as morally and politically unfair. As we will see, it is utterly inappropriate for critics or supporters of Kant to substitute the pronoun 'she' for 'he' as a means of making Kant's argument more inclusive, since it is more than a merely contingent feature of Kant's system that the ideally autonomous and spider-like self is gendered as male. Women are allocated wifely (*weiblich*) virtues suitable to the job of securing the survival of the species or the race, with the language of moral 'duty' and 'character' restricted to the males. In fact it would seem that, in order to explain how human civilisation is able to develop or survive, Kant requires women to respond to their emotions in a different way to men.

Insofar as female ethics is concerned, Kant serves as a precursor to Freud who argues that, ethically speaking, women possess a different—inferior—form of moral consciousness:

I cannot evade the notion (though I hesitate to give it expression) that for women the level of what is ethically normal is different from what it is in men. Their super-ego is never so inexorable, so impersonal, so independent of its emotional origins as we require it to be in men.

(Freud 1925: 342)

Analogously, in *Observations on the Feeling of the Beautiful and Sublime*, Kant informs us that women do not distinguish between good and bad actions on the basis of a moral sense, but by means of aesthetic taste:

The virtue of a woman (*Frauenzimmer*) is a *beautiful virtue*. That of the male sex should be a *noble virtue*. She will avoid the wicked not because it is unright, but because it is ugly; and virtuous actions mean

47

to her such as are morally beautiful. Nothing of 'ought', nothing of 'must', nothing of duty. To her all orders and every gloomy compulsion is intolerable. She does something only because it pleases her, and the art is to make her find pleasing only that which is good. I hardly believe that the fair sex is capable of principles, and I hope by that not to offend, for these are also extremely rare in the male.

(*Obs*: 2/ 231–32, p. 81, *corr*.)

Here, in this early essay, Kant links women to the aesthetic realm of the 'beautiful' and excludes them from the moral and also from the sublime. As we saw also in Chapter 1, Kant contrasts women's ideally '*beautiful*' understanding with that of the male which 'should be a *deep understanding*, an expression which signifies identity with the sublime'. For Kant the beautiful action is the graceful action which appears 'to be accomplished without painful toil'. Study, deep thought and 'strivings and surmounted difficulties' might 'arouse admiration', but 'belong to the sublime'. As such, profound reflection is unsuitable for women 'in whom unconstrained charms should show nothing else than a beautiful nature' (*Obs*: 2/229, p. 78).

Although Kant indicates that some (few) women are capable of the sublime, he judges this to be unnatural and, insofar as it is contrary to beauty, even 'disgusting' (*ekelhaft*) (2/233, p. 83). 'Laborious learning or a painful pondering, even if a woman (*Frauenzimmer*) should greatly succeed in it, destroy the merits that are proper to her sex' (2/229, p. 78). Citing the names of two of the best known French women 'geniuses' of the time—the humanist scholar Anne Lefèvre-Dacier and the philosopher Émilie du Châtelet—we are told they might 'as well even have a beard' (2/229–30, p. 78). Such women are not sexually attractive and thus cannot fulfil nature's purpose which is to propagate the species. Given Marquise du Châtelet's four children and her celebrated affair with Voltaire—which survived her simultaneous liaison with another younger man—Kant's claim repeats an extremely odd, but nevertheless entirely conventional, cliché about the physiological attributes of a woman who not only translated Newton, Aristotle and Virgil, but also wrote original works of moral and metaphysical philosophy herself (Battersby 1989; Waithe 1991).

For Kant, writing in 1764, women remain—or *ought* to remain—at the level of the superficial; the 'unconstrained charms' of the ideal woman '*should* show nothing else than a beautiful nature' (italics added). Given Kant's famously narrow view of true moral judgement (as involving duty, obligation, principle and the overcoming of obstacles), this would seem to imply that the Kantian woman is completely excluded from moral agency. This inference might be dismissed in that these comments are found in an early essay which falls outside the bounds of Kant's critical system. However, as we will see in this chapter, Kant cannot be defended in such a way. The consistency and systematicity of Kant's edifice of pure and practical reason will be shaken as we press on the fractures that his account of sexual difference reveals.

In the 1760s Kant's critical system had yet to be formulated. Instead, Kant seems to have been tempted by David Hume's 'mitigated' scepticism—what Kant termed 'zetetic' scepticism—as a block to that type of unrestrained fear that leads humans into superstitious belief and religion (Zammito 2002: 183). In the critical writings—conventionally dated to the publication of the first edition of the *Critique of Pure Reason* in 1781—Kant would move away from Hume and develop the ideal of the autonomous (noumenal) self or person who transcends terror; but, as we will see, Kant's later solution applies only to certain classes of human beings and continues to exclude women. In this respect it is interesting to look at Kant's *Remarks in the Observations of the Feeling of the Beautiful and Sublime*: a series of often bad-tempered observations (many of which concern women) that Kant made around 1764–65, in the margins and on a series of loose-leaf inserts to his own text of *Observations* (Kant 1764–65, 1991). Unfortunately, despite their importance to non-anglophone feminist philosophers, most of these have been omitted from the recent English translation of Kant's *Notes and Fragments* (Kant 2005; Zammito 2002: 125–31, 402n.–404n.). However, something of their flavour can be gleaned from a rough on-line translation (Cooley and Frierson 2005).[1] Here we can see Montesquieu mentioned, but what we also find is a kind of poisonous combination of Jean-Jacques Rousseau and Hume with regard to the nature and education of women.

Hume had persistently associated women with fear-based 'superstition' and with a consequent subservience to priestly power (Battersby 1981). But Hume did not debar women from the study of history, the classics and philosophy as a way of blocking religious delusion (Battersby 2005). Insofar as women's education was concerned, Hume was happy for women to be treated as equals except in one specific respect, and this concerned the need to inculcate the entirely 'artificial' virtues of 'chastity' and 'modesty' which, he says, exclusively 'belong to the fair sex'. To secure this non-natural—but nevertheless politically useful—good, Hume emphasised that women need a more restrictive education than men. The Humean woman needs to care about her reputation, and she needs to be taught to feel 'shame' in the case of infidelity. The non-natural, female virtues of modesty and chastity are justified on utilitarian grounds, not as something 'natural' to women's mental or emotional constitution (Hume 1739–40: 570–71; Hume 1751: 166, 195).

For Hume, women are naturally fearful (and libidinous), but moral education and philosophy act as useful social controls. By contrast, in his *Remarks in the Observations* Kant complains that Hume is too willing to admit women in to the philosophical domain:

Mr. Hume believes that a woman (*Frauenzimmer*) who has no knowledge of the history of her fatherland or of Greece and Rome cannot ever maintain company with people of understanding. But he does not consider that women are not put there to support the men in their ponderings, but as recovery from these. History is of no use without some degree of philosophy, even if it were only that which concerns what is moral (*moralisch*). But a woman (*Frauenzimmer*) only needs that part of history, concerning customary behavior (*Sittlichkeit*), that relates to her sex.

(Kant 1764–65: 20/183)

Here Kant seems to be making the type of distinction between the full duty-based morality of the ideal male and the well-mannered behaviour of the ideal female that we will see him making more than 30 years later in his published lectures on *Anthropology* (*Anth*: 7/306). And in the *Remarks* Kant makes this point via an argument with Hume concerning female education and feminine virtues.

For Kant, Hume's solution to the question of female virtue is no longer enough. Instead, Kant takes his cue from Rousseau's *Émile* and advocates women's exclusion from all deep scholarship and from the sublime (Rousseau 1762; Mahowald 1978: 103–15). Indeed, Kant argues that the ideal woman is—like Emile's partner Sophie—no more than the partner and helpmate for the male. Insofar as the understanding is concerned, her role is fundamentally recreational. But since Kant also accepts—like Hume, and unlike Rousseau—that woman is initially fearful, the Kantian woman is doubly disadvantaged: debarred from ameliorative education, the Kantian woman is left marooned in her initial state of 'natural' terror. Disappointingly, Kant seems not to register this as a blind spot of his system, noting in the *Remarks*:

Before one inquires into the virtue of a lady (*Frau*), one must first ask whether she needs it. In the state of simplicity there is no virtue. In men, a strong inclination to protect and honesty, in women (*Weibe*) sincere surrender and cajolery. In conditions of luxury the man must have virtue (*Tugend*), the woman honour (*Ehre*).

(Kant 1764–65: 20/64)

Although this (depressing) note may be no more than Kant's response to Rousseau's *Emile*—which Kant first read in 1763—and an elaboration on the French philosopher's distinction between the virtues required in simple socie-ties and those required in more degenerate conditions of luxury, it does not (alas) contradict what Kant says elsewhere about women's lack of a moral sense. They are aligned with 'simplicity' and 'nature'; in developed societies they do not need moral (as opposed to social) virtues at all.

In an apparent attempt to get round the Humean objection that would allow some specifically female virtues such as chastity and modesty that need to be inculcated via education, in the *Remarks* Kant explicitly denies that chastity is a moral virtue. Like Hume, Kant registers that women are not naturally chaste, but (unlike Hume) he treats shame as either linked to sexual embarrassment or to a 'general concept of honour' which cannot be described as morally virtuous (1764–65: 20/96, 89). Even more worryingly, unlike Rousseau (who does, at least, describe the education of the ideal woman, Sophie, in great detail), Kant's own lectures on education—based on courses delivered over many years, but published by a student in 1803—seem to entirely overlook the problem of women (Rousseau 1762; Kant 1803: 9/439–99). It's as if women were not only absent from his audience, but also from the human race. This is particularly curious in the light of the fact that the history of the city of Königsberg is intertwined with that of the Russian Empire, being occupied by the Russian Army between 1758 and 1762. Kant had strong links with several Russians during the years of occupation, and presumably retained an interest in Russian affairs (Kuehn 2001). Given the formidable education of the Russian Empress, Catherine the Great (1762–96), her reputation as a supporter of the French *philosophes* and her role as a reformer of the Russian legal system and Empire, Kant's reticence seems quite remarkable. As we will see later, his silence on the subject of the education of women links to the fact that the Kantian woman lacks both 'character' and 'personhood' in the technical senses in which Kant uses these terms.

In the published version of his lectures on *Anthropology* (1798/1800), Kant comments that the womanly (*weiblich*) principle that equates truth with 'what the world says' can hardly be reconciled with the notion of character 'in the narrow sense of the word' (7/308). We can find similar sentiments, even more bluntly expressed, in some of Kant's notes (written during the 1770s) on anthropology: 'young people and women (*Frauenzimmer*) don't yet have character. Do not accord with themselves', and again even more emphatically: 'women (*Weibern*) ... have little character at all. When one knows one, one knows them all' (KGS: 15/759 no. 1495; 520 no. 1176). However cruel these observations might seem, they are nevertheless consistent with his later elucidation on the notion of 'character' where it becomes apparent that character is not something that one is born with, but that one attains through overcoming bodily drives and feelings: 'The man of principles has character. Of him we know exactly what to expect. He does not act on the basis of his instincts, but on the basis of his will' (*Anth:* 7/285). Described in such a way, it is hardly surprising that the Kantian woman does not have 'character'. Neither, it seems, should she seek to attain it via the educative process. But, without 'character', women will also be a puzzling exception to the account of moral duty and will that Kant developed in his critical philosophy after 1781.

Persons, humans and women

The concept of personhood is integral to Kant's moral system and also to his political ideals relating to autonomy and independence; but Kant was (at best) ambivalent about whether women count as moral beings or persons in the same sense as the males. In his critical philosophy Kant distinguished between the *transcendental* self and the *transcendent* or noumenal self which he also, at times, refers to as the 'person'. The transcendental self is a necessary condition of knowledge of the phenomenal world; it cannot be intuited in any direct fashion, but it is nevertheless that 'I' which must be supposed to persist through a linear sequence of temporal moments as a condition of our being able to order our experience into a unified whole. In the *Critique of Pure Reason* Kant also argues that a particular kind of space—Euclidean, Newtonian, with persistent and unchanging substances—is also necessary for this temporal ordering to take place (CPR: B274–79, Bxxxix fn.). The space–time framework is imposed by the I, but the transcendental I can only be known in relation to the spatio-temporal (and causal) framework that it provides (CPR: A103–10, B136–42). Thus, the transcendental self grounds the phenomenal world in which there is no freedom and within which the synthetic *a priori* principle that 'Every event has a cause' applies (A189–212, B232–56; A444ff. = B473 ff.).

Although I have argued elsewhere that Kant's transcendental self is by no means ungendered (Battersby 1998: 61–80), and although breakdowns in the structures of this persistent or transcendental 'I' are also relevant to Kant's concept of the sublime, the focus of this chapter will be on the noumenal self or person. This aspect of the self is linked to freedom, not to the deterministic space–time structures supplied to the phenomenal world by the I. Although the *transcendent* or noumenal I is also not directly intuitable, it falls outside the horizons of the space–time world which, Kant argues, is the only type of world that we are capable of *knowing*. That the noumenal self exists is a matter of faith (rather than knowledge), but it is also a necessary presupposition of moral discourse and *practical* reason. Thus Kant argues that as far as moral judgement is concerned, each person has to be treated *as if* he were free, and *as if* he had an immortal soul that could be held responsible for its actions. The noumenal self or person—free, responsible, autonomous, a choosing *agent*—grounds the ascription of blame or praise as far as morality is concerned. Thus, although we cannot *know* either our own selves or others as persons, Kant's official doctrine is that moral judgement entails personhood as a kind of necessary fiction. Moral discourse would break down if we treated our own selves (or other humans) as no more than empirically determined, or as no more than passive animals or desiring machines. This is why it is extremely damaging to Kant's system that he seems ambivalent as far as female personhood is concerned.

In a late work, *Religion Within the Boundaries of Mere Reason* (1793/94), Kant divides the determining forces of human behaviour into three main types: animality/*'Tierheit'* (instinctual drives, passions etc.); humanity/*'Menschheit'* (the ability to judge, reason and posit ends for action based on a comparison between the self and others); and personality/*'Persönlichkeit'* (the capacity to act in accordance with the dictates of reason and the will and to be morally accountable) (RWB: 6/26–28). Reading Kant's remarks about women in the *Anthropology From a Pragmatic Point of View* (1798/1800) and elsewhere in the light of this division, it becomes clear that for Kant women are fully animal and full (but subordinate) humans, but he sees no need for them to develop their full potential for personality—and his comments on fear, transcendence and the sublime even suggest that women have a duty to remain non-persons.

Thus, in his lectures on *Anthropology*—lectures which continued to be delivered late into his life—Kant claimed that in primitive societies woman is no more than a 'domestic animal' or '*Hausthier*' who follows her male who leads the way 'with weapon in his hand' (*Anth*: 7/304). Although Nature is said to have created woman for the purpose of improving society, it is clear that Kant thinks that woman's 'charm' is a sham. Woman might appear a tender, delicate, domestic, nurturing—'beautiful'—companion for the male, but there are strong and dominating passions underlying this façade. Even in that type of 'barbaric civic society' that tolerates polygamy, the most favoured woman imprisoned in the Harem knows how to gain control over her man. Monogamous marriage functions to the advantage of the female and increases her control (7/304). Woman—who is created by Nature to civilise and refine the male through her power to charm him into obedience—is not herself 'so delicate in her choice (in matters of taste) as the man, whom Nature has built more coarsely'. All woman wants, according to Kant, is a man whose physique indicates he has the 'strength' and the 'ability' to protect her. This is fortunate, since should the woman be repelled by the crude 'beauty' of the male, and should she be 'refined in her choice', the woman would need to do the courting—and this would be 'degrading to the worth of her sex even in the eyes of the man' (7/306 *corr.*). What Kant is, in effect, noticing in these lectures on *Anthropology* is that Burke's account of the 'beautiful' and 'the sublime' produces puzzles if women are included into the account not simply as (ideally beautiful) objects, but as fully human subjects. Women are an anomaly and fall outside the rules of 'natural' taste.

As others have also noted, Kant's position on women and personhood is not stable (Mendus 1987; Pateman 1988). Thus, in discussing marriage in *The Metaphysics of Morals* (1797/98), Kant seems to suggest that women (like men) are indeed persons. Kant argues that a wife (*Weib*) surrenders her status as a person on getting married through a kind of—inalienable—contract that is performatively produced in two stages: by the marriage ceremony and by the subsequent sexual act (6/277–78). This surrender is performed only with respect to the husband, who also surrenders his personhood to his wife. Thus, marriage is described as 'a reciprocal giving of one's very person into the possession of the other' (6/359). To that extent, the husband and the wife have an 'equality of possession of each other as persons … and also equality in their possession of material goods' (6/278). This reciprocity and equality mean that it is inappropriate for either partner to treat the other as a sexual object or as a means to an end and 'neither is dehumanized through the bodily use that one makes of the other' (6/359).

This account would seem to entail that women are (at least prior to marriage) persons in their own right. But the picture darkens when Kant moves on to discuss personhood in the section on 'civil personality' later within the same text. Kant defines civil personality as the 'attribute of not needing to be represented by another where rights are concerned' (1797/98: 6/314). The problem is that Kant also insists that civil personality belongs only to those citizens who are economically independent, and that independence 'requires a distinction between *active* and *passive* citizens, though the concept of a passive citizen seems to contradict the concept of a citizen as such' (6/314). Kant's examples of passive citizens include: apprentices; domestic servants; all minors (*Unmündige*); private tutors (as opposed to school teachers); tenant farmers (as opposed to leasehold farmers); the woodcutter Kant hires to work on land that Kant himself owns; 'the blacksmith in India' who brings his own hammer, anvil and bellows into other people's houses when he goes to work (as opposed to 'the European carpenter or blacksmith who can put the products of his work up as goods for sale to the public'); and 'all women (*Frauenzimmer*)'. Kant sums up the logic behind this curious list with the claim that the passive citizen is 'anyone whose preservation in existence (his being fed and protected) depends not on his management of his own business but arrangements made by another (except the state)' (6/314).

Trying to make sense of these claims, it is tempting to argue that Kant must be suggesting that all women start out as moral persons, but the wife (*Weib*) surrenders her civil personality along with her moral personality when she enters the married state. The phrasing that Kant adopts in a short essay of 1793—*On the Common Saying: That May Be Correct in Theory But It is of No Use in Practice*—might be thought to strengthen this reading since there it is the wife '*Weib*' and the child who are linked as 'natural' dependants (1793: 8/295). However, this solution founders as it is noted that in the passage on 'civil personality' in the *Metaphysics*, Kant uses the term *Frauenzimmer*: a now fairly derogatory for women, but one that was in the eighteenth century used in a more generalised sense—and one that Kant comments on in his *Remarks* on his 1764 essay *Observations on the Feeling of the Beautiful and Sublime*. There Kant associates *Frauenzimmer* with women's positioning within the private, as opposed to the public sphere, via the links with a room (*Zimmer*) and the spatial confinement of women (Kant 1991: 55; Kant 1764–65: 20/69).

It should also be pointed out that the German word '*Weib*' is also commonly used in German for 'woman' as well as for 'wife': an ambiguity that makes Kant's views on women particularly difficult to untangle. Where there is ambiguity, I have corrected the standard English translations of Kant to render *Weib* as 'wife', since this would be the more generous interpretation of Kant's meaning. However, the use of the term *Frauenzimmer*—and, on occasion, *Frau* (lady)—would seem to indicate that the lack of civil personality is not simply a consequence of the wife's economic dependence on a propertied male, since this lack apparently characterises all women, whether married or not. In his Notebooks Kant seems to use the three words interchangeably, and it seems fairly implausible to seek to defend Kant in this way, especially since Kant also asserts that the only valid marriage contract is one based 'on the natural superiority of the husband to the wife in his capacity to promote the common interest of the household' (Kant 1797/98: 6/279). A morganatic marriage which made the male the economic dependant is declared as invalid as a prostitution contract or as a contract for sex outside marriage. Although we are told that women and others whose existence depends on the will of another retain their 'freedom and equality *as human beings*' (6/315), it would seem that this does not extend to women's status as persons. For Kant, there would seem to be an underlying moral inequality that makes it appropriate for wives to be economically dependent on their husbands.

As in *Religion Within the Boundaries of Mere Reason* (1793/94), in *The Meta-physics of Morals* Kant makes a distinction between 'a human being (*homo phaenomenon, animal rationale*)'—'a being of slight importance' who 'shares with the rest of the animals, as offspring of the earth, an ordinary value'—and 'a human being regarded as a *person*, that is the subject of a morally practical reason' who as '*homo noumenon*' is 'exalted above any price' (1797/98: 5/434–35). Officially Kant's doctrine in *The Metaphysics of Morals* is that women are not civil personalities, but are moral persons who surrender personhood as they enter the marital state. Unofficially, however, this position is ridden with tensions in that moral personhood is said to be incompatible with servility: the person 'is not to be valued merely as a means to the ends of others or even to his own ends'. The person 'possesses a dignity (an absolute inner worth) by which he exacts respect (*Achtung*) for himself from all other beings in the world'. As a consequence, the human being regarded as a person will compare himself with every other person 'and value himself on a footing of equality with them' (6/435). Thus Kant's official doctrine of personhood is undermined by his insistence that women are 'natural' dependants.

As we have seen in the last chapter, respect (*Achtung*) is the term for that mental attitude which is bound up with the moral law and with the sublime. But it seems that in *The Metaphysics of Morals* it is male human beings who command respect, women who are the object of love (and protection). The division that Kant made in his early essay of 1764 between male and female virtue has not gone away, but remains in disguised form (*Obs*: 2/231–32, p. 81). It is the males who are linked with duty and obligation and a moral law which is 'noble' and which engenders respect; the virtue of women is linked to their status as humans, not persons. Although women can have, at best, a 'beautiful virtue', Kant's comments in *Anthropology From a Pragmatic Point of View* (1798/1800) make it clear that he thinks women frequently fall short of this ideal when they seek to step outside the private sphere. Here he represents married women as either insufficiently vocal for civic independence or as too mouthy to speak well about property rights before a Court of Law.

This (unpleasant) passage plays on the connotations of the German term '*Mund*' which means a human (not an animal) 'mouth' and is thus linked with the voice. Kant moves between what it is to attain majority in civic matters

(*Mündigkeit*), being a minor (*unmündig*), and having a guardian (*Vormünder*) or male custodian (*Curator*) who represents the minor or wife. Women are compared to children who 'are naturally unable to speak for themselves (*unmündig*)', so that 'their parents are their natural guardians (*Vormünder*)':

> The wife (*Weib*), whatever her age, is declared incapable of speaking (*unmündig*) for her self in civic matters; the husband is her natural custodian, but it is another man who acts in this capacity if she shares property with her husband.—Although it is of the nature of her sex that the wife (*das Weib*) can work her mouth enough (*Mundwerks genug hat*) to speak for herself and for her husband, even in a court of law (where it is a question of what is Mine and what is Thine), so one could describe her as over-wordy (*übermündig*) according to the letter of the law. However, just it is not in the nature of women (*Frauen*) to be drafted to go to war, so a woman cannot personally defend her rights or take up civic duties, but only through her representative. This inability to speak for herself (*Unmündigkeit*) in public affairs makes her only the more powerful as far as domestic welfare is concerned, since it is the male's nature to feel himself called to respect (*achten*) and defend the rights of the weaker.
>
> (*Anth: 7/209 corr.*)

Although this passage ends with a reference to respect, it is not wives that bring forth this response, but only their status as weaker beings requiring the protection of the males. Once again Kant justifies the political and legal subordination of wives in terms of the natural weakness of women.

Published in 1798, with modifications introduced in the 2nd (1800) edition, Kant's *Anthropology* was based on the popular lecture course that Kant delivered on a regular basis from 1772 onwards. As such, this text—with its misogynist comments on women—cannot simply be dismissed as belonging to Kant's precritical phase, especially since in the lectures Kant takes up themes that can be found elsewhere in the critical system. Thus, in the *Anthropology* Kant asserts both that it is 'comfortable' to make oneself a civil minor (*unmündig*) and that minority is 'degrading' (*Anth: 7/209*). Analogously, in the opening paragraphs of Kant's most famous essay, 'An Answer to the Question: What is Enlightenment?' (1784), we can also find the claim that it is 'comfortable' to be a minor who is deemed incapable of speaking for himself (*unmündig*). And here Kant also suggests that it is an act of kindness on the part of the males to act as guardians and speak for the women. But the 1784 essay accuses the whole of the 'fair sex' of cowardice and of being too lazy to 'take the step into *Mündigkeit*' which translates as 'majority' but also connotes 'speaking for themselves' (1784: 8/35). Kant puts forward 'Enlightenment'—defined as freedom from tutelage—as a goal for all humans in their struggle to emerge from 'self-incurred minority' (*Unmündigkeit*). Here Kant seems to suggest that women, as well as men, should treat themselves as having the capacity for freedom and full civic responsibility (8/41). Elsewhere, however, Kant fails to address the question of the education and cultural formation of women that would make this outcome a possibility—and, in his Notebooks and *Observations on the Feeling of the Beautiful and Sublime*, Kant even suggests that the education of women is positively undesirable.

It would seem that Kant cannot make up his mind about women; he is sure that they do not yet have civic personhood, but he seems unsure about whether this is due to 'the nature of her sex' or to the historical condition which has made them choose the 'comfortable' option of remaining political minors. What is clear is that in his justification of this inequality he time and time again reverts to the language of the 'natural'. Thus, in *On the Common Saying*, we once again see Kant refusing wives—*Weibe*, so perhaps even all women— the same legal privileges as men. Here Kant asserts that the right to freedom belongs to 'every member of the communal being (*Wesen*) as a human being (*Mensch*) insofar as the human is a being (*Wesen*) capable of having rights at all' (1793: 8/291 *corr.*). On the other hand, Kant once again places gender restrictions on the membership of the commonwealth in ways that exclude the wife or woman (*Weib*):

> Every one who has a right to vote on this legislation is termed a citizen (*citoyen*, that is a citizen of the *state*, not a *bourgeois* or burger of a town). The only necessary qualification, aside from the *natural* one of not being a child or a wife (*Weib*), is that he be *his own master* (*sui juris*): that he own some sort of *property* ... from which he can live, so that in other words whenever he needs to acquire things from others this is through a process of alienating what is his.
>
> (1793: 8/295 *corr.*)

Kant is not talking here about treating all humans as autonomous and noumenally free 'persons', but is analysing human rights at the level of subordinate, but equal, membership of the state. But even at this level, Kant makes an exception for married women—and perhaps also for all women. Kant envisages the validity of constitutional law as dependent on each property owner having one vote, so that possessing more property does not give more voting rights. But although he maintains that '*all* of those who have this right to vote must agree that the public law is just', he refuses propertied wives (or propertied women?) the right to vote, whilst insisting that they must also obey the law (8/296 *corr.*). Moreover, the condition of being without property brings with it a law of subservience that makes the male who is not his own master equivalent to a child or a wife: 'one must obey as a child its elders or a wife her husband' (292).

On the Common Saying is directed against Thomas Hobbes' account of the social contract as having its origins in self-interest. In a way that is reminiscent of Jean-Jacques Rousseau, Kant offers an account of the origins of the social contract that is not intended as a historical account, but as a kind of fiction—'an *idea of reason*'—that can provide a justification of the legal and civil code as long as the following conditions are met (287). For a State to formulate just laws, it needs to respect:

1. The *freedom* of each member of the society as a human being (*Mensch*);
2. The equality of each member of society with every other member as a *subordinate* (*Unterthan*);
3. The *independence* of every member of a communal whole, as a *citizen*.
   (8/290 *corr.*)

For Kant such a society is just because each man has the capacity to gain property, and thus to become a voting member in the state: he is arguing against hereditary prerogatives that would bar mobility from the propertyless to the propertied class (292–93). Unfortunately, however, married women with property are positioned as 'natural' subordinates within the state. And in the *Anthropology* Kant makes the matter worse when he remarks: 'The wife (*Weib*) becomes free by marriage; whereas the man (*Mann*) loses his freedom thereby' (*Anth*: 7/309 *corr.*). Kant seems not to recognise that wifehood involves legal and civic sacrifices on behalf of the woman—and he also does not notice the conflict between his theory ('all should be equal or be treated as if they have the potential to become equal') and his practice ('but not women').

In *Groundwork of the Metaphysics of Morals* (1785) Kant famously declares that his account of moral duty and moral law has been purged of all elements of the empirical and the anthropological, so as not to distract from the validity of his *a priori* arguments which bind the noumenal self to an ideal of a free and autonomous will as the supreme legislator for moral values (1785: 4/389). But there are enough elements of the empirical and the anthropological remaining in Kant's later writings for us to be able to see that his account of freedom is gendered. It is not that women start out as needing to be treated *as if* they were autonomous and free agents in the same way as the men, but then surrender this autonomy as they enter into the married state; it is rather that women are natural inferiors and have a sexually determined incapacity to act in accordance with the dictates of reason and their own will. In terms of the vocabulary that Kant develops in *Religion Within the Boundaries of Mere Reason* and expands on in *The Metaphysics of Morals*, moral personhood is not an ideal for women, whether married or not.

In her classic account of the failure of social contract theory to deal with marriage and other sexual contracts, Carole Pateman provides an accurate and forceful account of Kant's shifty and shifting account of marriage (Pateman 1988: 168–73).What she does not sufficiently emphasise, however, is the consequences of this in political and metaphysical terms. Politically speaking, Kant's treatment of marriage is symptomatic of his refusal to allow women a voice within the original social contract—an *'idea of reason'*—which grounds the idea of the ideally just state and civil society. Kant's *'idea of reason'* leaves women permanently disenfranchised, muzzled in the courts of law and without any public voice. Metaphysically speaking, Kant's inability to think whether woman is a person (*homo noumenon*) or even the equivalent to a male on the relational and societal level of the merely human (*homo phaenomenon, animal rationale*) produces profound fractures within his critical system. There is no simple way of healing these fractures, since Kant remains ambivalent about whether women have or have not a duty to struggle for a voice of their own (*Mündigkeit*) and for moral or civic personhood. And this has implications for the philosophy of the sublime that Kant develops in his later writings.

Duty and the sex that fears

In Kant's precritical *Observations* it was the difficult, the challenging and the overcoming of obstacles that Kant most valued; these are the characteristics identified with the 'sublime', and restricted to male human beings. Women are devalued insofar as they seek to render themselves sublime. There is thus a difference in this early work between Kant's claim about women's moral capacities—that women just do not happen to be able to follow moral principles—and his aesthetic claim that women should never attempt the sublime. In this early work, Kant makes superficiality and ease aesthetic duties for women. The question that raises itself for the aesthetic/ethical boundary is not, therefore, simply to do with Kant's 'factual' errors about female nature, but about the duty that Kant imposes on women to remain in the immediate, and to leave their powers of reason undeveloped. These tensions remain in Kant's late texts, even though his analysis of the beautiful and the sublime change in some quite fundamental ways, and specifically in ways that made the question of the 'beauty' of women much more marginal to Kant's thinking.

In the precritical *Observations* woman was amongst the paradigm examples of the 'beautiful'. In the *Critique of the Power of Judgment*, by contrast, it is objects in nature that have become the paradigm, and a special analysis is required to explain how the term 'beautiful' can be applied to human beings at all. Kant's examples of the sublime in the third *Critique* have also changed so as to place less emphasis on (male) humans (of certain racial types) and more on natural objects. However, great military commanders and geniuses still count as sublime—along with bold, overhanging and threatening rocks; clouds piled up in the sky; great waterfalls; storm-ridden seas; earthquakes and volcanoes (*CPJ*: 260–63). All of these would also have qualified as 'sublime' in *Observations*, but Kant no longer describes the sublime as a passive response to the overwhelming, the powerful, the massive and the colossal. In the *Critique of the Power of Judgment* it is not objects in nature that are *in themselves* sublime or beautiful; rather these are qualities read on to nature by human beings (203, 256).

In *Observations* Kant could see no transcendent element in the human response to beauty. It was all just a matter of *Reiz* (normally translated as 'charm' in English, but also suggesting 'attraction')—and Kant quite specifically made sexual attraction the underlying *Reiz* (*Obs*: 2/235 ff., pp. 86ff.). In the *Critique of the Power of Judgment*, on the other hand, beauty has a transcendent element: it is consistent with attraction (including sexual attraction), but a response is aesthetic insofar as the experiencing subject abstracts from all *Reiz*—and hence from all use-value and material-value—and concentrates solely on the form of the object. The pure aesthetic reaction is 'disinterested'. And, since such a pure response will not generate the peculiar feeling of the sublime, the latter can never be as purely aesthetic as the appreciation of beauty (*CPJ*: 223, 226).

The pleasure in the beautiful comes from the mind's creation of a (phenomenal) reality that seems purposively designed to accord with human capacities (*CPJ*: 219ff.). Beauty—and this will include an appreciation of the female form—involves pleasure in constructing and forming nature in such a way that it seems non-threatening. The sublime, by contrast, involves registering nature as a noumenal, super-human, non-constructed infinity: it involves *Rührung* (usually translated as 'emotion', but with connotations of 'psychic disturbance' or 'turbulence') (245). In the sublime, the mind 'is not merely attracted by the object, it is also repelled by it', and by its formlessness and '*limitlessness*', in particular (245, 244). As we saw in the last chapter, in Kant's developed critical philosophy the sublime requires both an appreciation of the terribleness of the object surveyed and a (simultaneous) transcendence of terror (260–61). The state of mind characteristic of pleasure in the sublime is *Achtung* (respect)—a word that Kant uses in his moral philosophy to express the moral man's subservience to duty and to the moral law (1788: 5/73). And it is Ideas of reason that prevent the potential for terror degenerating into actual fear as nature is registered as a potential infinity, with the power to nihilate the self (*CPJ*: 257ff.).

For Kant the pleasure of the sublime is closed off to all except the man who has been 'prepared by culture' for a receptivity to 'moral ideas', and who has been educated into confidence in the power of his own ego to confront nature at its most fearsome (*CPJ*: 264, 269). According to Kant, this will exclude those who have been taken over by the spirit of trade, by base self-interest, softness (*Weichlichkeit*) and cowardice (263). A 'tenderhearted (*weich*) but at the same time weak (*schwach*) soul, which reveals a beautiful side' (i.e. an ideal woman) could never have the right attitude of mind; but the non-ideal woman would also be unlikely to qualify. Kant is scathing about all timorous, 'whimpering' and oversensitive humans whose emotions do 'in fact enervate the heart' (273). Comparing these emotions with 'the motion we are glad to have for the sake of health', he dismisses these feelings as 'passive' and as analogous to the 'agreeable exhaustion' felt by 'the voluptuaries of the Orient' after their bodies have been 'kneaded, and all their muscles and joints softly pressed and flexed' (273–74). When the pleasure comes from outside, and is not generated from within the self, such pleasures are not even compatible, Kant says, with the category of the beautiful which belongs to aesthetics in a pure sense. It is clear that Kant's morally educated subject who appreciates the sublime is not only not female, he is also not like the effeminate 'Oriental' male who receives pleasure from a source outside his own self.

Kant's analysis of the sublime is thus intimately connected with his gendered (and Orientalist) notion of personality. A man proves his superior moral excellence by his ability to experience the sublime. And it is significant to note in this context that *Achtung*—the attitude of respect that is an integral part of the experience of the sublime—is described as a 'feeling' (*Gefühl*), but one which might seem obscure or 'dark' (*dunkel*) in that it is not like any other feeling: 'it is not one *received* by means of influence', but is 'instead a feeling *self-wrought* by means of a rational concept' and also one that 'infringes on my self-love'. Respect is 'the *effect* of the law on the subject' in a direct way. As such, it is 'specifically different' from other sensuously generated feelings which produce either 'inclination or fear'. Respect can be reduced to neither of these affects, although 'it has something analogous to both' (1785: 4/401n.).

Writing here in the *Groundwork of the Metaphysics of Morals* (1785), Kant brings together his deontological morality and his account of human personality through the claim that 'The *object* of respect is therefore simply the *law*' and 'Any respect for a person is properly only respect for the law (of righteousness etc.) of which he gives us an example' (4/401n. *corr.*). For Kant the morally good act is not the one performed out of sympathy or love, but through a kind of thought experiment whereby I seek to universalise my action. This is the law, and the morally good rule is the one that would be valid for all. Through his analysis of the sublime in the *Critique of the Power of Judgment* Kant emphasises the appropriate education and character that is necessary for respect for the law. In so doing, he broadens his previously deontological system of ethics into an account of the virtuous or good man (aretaics). But in drawing the divide between 'respect' and 'fear', Kant re-draws the gender divide and returns to Greek notions of warrior virtues. War, we are told, is both sublime and more likely than long periods of peace to produce those elite males capable of experiencing the sublime (*CPJ*: 263). Kant's paradigm rational man is neither fearful nor passive with respect to sensual experience. He is not female; and neither is he like the effeminate 'Oriental' male who is submissive in relation to his own pleasures and to other humans.

As in the *Observations*, Kant does not make it a logical impossibility for a woman to thrill to the sublime; but in these late works there is no inference that women should be educated into the kinds of courage and self-confidence that would enable them to rise above fear. On the contrary, Kant claims in the *Anthropology* that it is appropriate for the female sex (*das weibliche Geschlecht*) to be timorous in the face of physical danger. Since the future of the human race is in the hands—or rather the womb—of women, to ensure the continuance of the species women should be concerned with their own physical safety (*Anth:* 7/306). But this is an important rider to the Kantian system, because such feelings will debar women from developing *Achtung*: that reverential attitude necessary for experiencing the sublime; for acting in accordance with universal duty; for imaginative access to the noumenal realm, and hence for visionary insights of a religious nature. Kant's women are thus not incapable of becoming 'persons' in the full sense that Kant outlines in his *Religion*, but have no duty to do so. On the contrary, although Kant's women count as 'humans', their duty is to remain also akin to his instinct-driven 'animals'.

Kant concludes this point in the *Anthropology* not by demanding that female weakness should be corrected by women themselves, but instead by requiring males to act as the protectors of women. Since Kant then goes on immediately to make reference to a kind of 'cultivated propriety' (*gesitteten Anstande*) that substitutes for true (duty-based) virtue in the case of women, we can be sure that Kant had recognised the implications of this gendering of human excellence (7/306 *corr.*). Here, in the context of thinking about women and children, Kant condones actions motivated by feeling as integral to human culture and refinement, but only to one half of the human race. Here he seems to be recognising that there can be duties that are not based on universalisability or abstract freedoms, but on membership of a community in which there are nested dependencies. At this level our duties towards an other are not simply duties towards a 'person' (abstractly considered)—free, autonomous, and equal to all other persons. Instead there are other duties that stem from our status as humans; as Kantian humans we might lack autonomy, but we are nevertheless able to judge, reason and posit ends for action based on a comparison between the self and others in the community.

Kant regards females as natural subordinates to the males. Judging from his remarks in the *Anthropology*, this is because he regards emotion as necessary to women's constitution, and an important part of their make-up given their procreative duties:

> As Nature entrusted to woman's (*weiblichen*) womb her most precious pledge, namely the species (*Species*), and the embryo through which the breed (*Gattung*) should propagate and perpetuate itself, so nature was fearful for the preservation of the same and planted this *fear* into woman's nature, as fear of *bodily* injury and a timidity towards similar dangers; through which weakness of this sex comes the call for legitimate masculine protection.
>
> (7/306 *corr.*)

It is also because of this natural difference in the emotional constitution of women and men that Kant also insists that female (*weiblich*) virtues and vices are different 'not only in kind but in motive' from those of the (*männlich*) male (7/307). It is not that there is no space for emotion in Kant's account of human nature, but that his account of virtue—and political justice—privileges those who are able to transcend emotion and fear in particular, as we see clearly in Kant's analysis of the sublime. Whether 'Oriental' males may ever be educated into the transcendence of emotion is left somewhat unclear; it depends on the racial and cultural type (and will be considered further in the next chapter). By contrast, it is clear that Kant's ideal woman is a wife who either cannot or *should not* be trained to transcend her emotions in such a fashion.

In an extended section leading up to an analysis of cowardice in the *Anthropology*, Kant takes up the distinction between 'sthenic' affects (which are exciting and exhausting) and 'asthenic' affects (which are sedative and relaxing) from John Brown's *Elementa Medicinae* of 1780 as a way of gendering the response to fear (*Anth*: 7/256, 255). The emotions of fearfulness (*Bangigkeit*), anxiety (*Angst*), dread (*Grausen*) and horror (*Entsetzen*) are only masculine insofar as they 'muster the strength for opposition'. 'Patience is, accordingly, not courage. Patience is a feminine virtue'—and one, Kant notes, shown by males of certain culturally inferior types (such as the North American Indians) (257). Sthenic resistance to emotion might involve the transcendence of the sublime; but it might also involve laughter: 'Laughter is masculine (*männlich*), while weeping is feminine (*weiblich*) (effeminate [*weibisch*] in the case of men)' (255–56). Even in experiencing helplessness in the face of an evil such as death, Kant insists that the male must not 'be moved to weep'—although he does allow that the man might be allowed to 'have tears in his eyes'. Open weeping 'would be transgressing against his own sex, and so, with his femininity (*Weiblichkeit*), he would not be able to serve as protector of the weaker sex' or be able to provide a model for women who make 'masculinity a duty' and wish the man to behave like the courageous hero in a 'book of Knights' (263 *corr.*).

Kant seems happy to leave woman at the level of the 'asthenic', responding to emotion in a merely passive manner. In so doing, he traps women in the phenomenal, leaving them incapable of the full moral personhood or civil personality that raise the ideal males above the merely animal and the merely human. Both the self and the transcendence of the body and its instincts are thought by Kant in ways that take the male subject (of European origins) as norm. Women either *do* or *should* respond to threatening events with fear, but this means that they are disqualified from making adequate moral judgements and also from appreciating the sublime. Although Kant claims in his precritical work (*Obs*: 2/ 231–32, p. 81) that women are motivated to 'avoid the wicked' because they have developed a taste that enables them to discriminate between the 'morally beautiful' and the 'ugly', in Kant's mature works, the ideal woman's lack of personhood means that she cannot even be said to respond to the beautiful with the disinterestedness that is necessary to a full aesthetic response. Ironically enough, it would thus seem that the status of Kant's women as non-persons debars them not only from the moral realm, but also from the aesthetic.

Kant and feminism

Some feminist philosophers have sought to defend Kant against the charge of misogyny, and Ursula Pia Jauch has even read him as 'a feminist "*avant la lettre*"' (Jauch 1988). But given Kant's framework for theorising freedom, personhood and education, this claim is implausible. It is, however, worth noting that, since there is space within the Kantian system for emotion (albeit for an emotion that is ultimately transcended), there is also a possibility of radicalising the Kantian system by emphasising the empirical impossibility of ever completely transcending emotion and becoming entirely 'disinterested'. However, for Kant the desirability of obeying duty (in ethics) or being disinterested (in the matter of aesthetic judgement) is not based on empirical fact, but on a logical ideal, so he would not necessarily dissent from the claim that he is privileging a state of mind that is impossible in practice. But there is something politically (and philosophically) undesirable in separating theory from practice in the Kantian fashion.

To claim that there is a space for emotion within the Kantian system (and to see the possibility of radicalising Kant) is, however, to dissent from the more standard feminist response to Kant's ethics which is altogether more hostile. Robin May Schott, for example, has criticised Kant for portraying, 'the ideal man as a highly disciplined, apathetic creature who values pain above pleasure, whose greatest enjoyment consists in the relaxation following work, and who finds no place for love in his life' (Schott 1988: 109). But this criticism rests on a misunderstanding of Kant's praise of 'apathy': a state of mind that Kant is careful to explain did not for the Stoics involve indifference to emotion, but which instead involved the transcendence of emotion (Kant 1797/98: 6/408–9). Although Kant's ideal male does not succumb to drunkenness or drugs—'certain mushrooms, wild rosemary, acanthus, Peruvian chicha, South Sea Islanders' ava, and opium'—which 'weaken, as poisons, one's vitality', the ideal Kantian male can share in the 'masculine' pleasure of laughter, as we have seen (*Anth*: 7/170, 255). And far from advocating relaxation, Kant advocates an active control of pleasures and pain, excusing the man 'whose eyes are shining with tears, as long as he does not allow them to fall in drops, still less accompany these with the disagreeable music of sobs' (7/256).

Similarly when Schott criticises Kant for delineating emotion as 'an intoxicant which one has to sleep off' and passion as putting the self 'in chains', she registers Kant's distinction between an affect (*Affekt*) and a passion (*Leidenschaft*), but without apparently grasping that Kant graded emotions (such as anger) above passions (such as hatred) (Schott 1988: 105–6). Emotions are affects, says Kant, that come before reflection and can therefore be transcended once reason comes into play. Much worse is a passion: 'a sensible *desire* that has become a permanent inclination' through the force of habit. A passion can be indulged with a 'calmness' that 'permits reflection and allows the mind to form principles upon it'. Since it can exist alongside reason, passion is condemned as a 'vice' and as '*properly* evil'; emotion, by contrast, is 'childish and weak' but, since it is natural, it is not in itself morally evil (Kant 1797/98: 6/407–8). What is wrong with Kant's account of emotion and of sexuality from a feminist point of view is not simply that he downgrades so-called 'feminine' character stics of mind, as Schott's analysis would suggest, but rather that he tries to re-establish the old (Aristotelian) sexual polarities that bind rationality, creativity and the highest moral duties to the bodies of an elite of *males*. Kant implicitly lines up all *women* on the side of 'weakness'. Women either cannot—or should not—transcend fear. Males should ideally transcend fear, and only the (male) human being who has reached these lofty heights can be said to represent the universal—and make valid judgements of taste or to be fully moral.

Similar remarks apply to Kant's comments on sexual desire. Schott suggests that Kant has a hostility towards sex analogous to that of the Christian mystics. She claims that Kant is so reluctant to mention the sexual act that he uses 19 different Latin phrases on one page, rather than discuss it in his own tongue (Schott 1988: 113). But in the *Lectures on Ethics*, Kant's Latin phrases serve to make more explicit his detailed catalogue and grading—in German—of the variety of sexual perversions (Kant 1930: 27/390–93, pp. 169–71). Kant's text continues the German 'Natural Law' tradition of finding justifications for social order that do not rest simply on divine law. Thus, Kant's assertion that masturbation, male homosexuality, lesbianism and intercourse with animals are vices more heinous than incest is established on the basis of an appeal to reason, not to God or simply to instinctive repulsion.

In the same series of *Lectures* Kant argues against those who promote the 'mortification of the flesh'. Bodies require discipline; but 'discipline can be of one of two kinds: we may have to strengthen the body, or we may have to weaken it'. The 'fanatical and monkish' virtues of starving and wasting the flesh are compared unfavourably with those of Diogenes. 'We must harden our body as Diogenes did' (27/379, p. 158). It is probable that Kant did not know that Diogenes was famous for his acts of public masturbation (Kant's most terrible vice), as well as for living simply in his barrel. Nevertheless, Diogenes is a most interesting choice of hero. Kant suggests here—as he will also argue in his *Religion*—that it is not man's animal nature as such that is evil, but rather the failure of a man to harden himself (and it is surely a '*him*-self') into a person (*RWB*: 6/34–36).

Can male sexuality be controlled? And how about female sexuality? These are the questions that require urgent answers once the traditional Aristotelian and Christian answers have been rejected. Kant speculates that the origin of evil in society comes from the fact that males mature sexually in their mid-teens, but cannot (on average) afford to get married until their mid-twenties (Kant 1786: 8/116n.). It is not that Kant's ideal male lacks desire, as Schott suggests, but that he transcends and controls desire. He also controls and governs female sexuality—even though charm ('*Reiz*', and hence sexual attractiveness) is still registered in the *Anthropology* as integral to female nature (*Anth*: 7/305.).

Despite the lively debate engendered within the community of feminist philosophers concerning the ways in which Kant's anthropological comments on sexual and racial difference impact on his moral philosophy, within the world of more orthodox Kantian scholarship these topics still too often continue to be treated as unimportant and merely contingent features of Kant's system. This is, presumably, why it was not thought worthwhile to translate Kant's comments on women in *Remarks in the Observations of the Feeling of the Beautiful and Sublime* (1764–65) and in the Notes of his various lecture courses on *Anthropology* in the important recent English edition of Kant's *Notes and Fragments* (Kant 2005). Those who, like John H. Zammito (2002) or Susan Meld Shell (2003), recognise the importance of this topic to Kant's thinking are, too often, dismissed as mere 'historians of ideas' who are not engaging with the 'philosophical' structures of Kant's systematic philosophy.

But Kant's comments on sexual difference are more than empirical asides, and are *philosophically* significant. In them we see how he registers the importance of emotion to bodily and species survival—but only to one half of the human race. Since it is clearly unsatisfactory for him to have devised a 'universal duty' that excludes women, Kant's system of morality requires major revision. In this context, however, it is worth noting that Kant makes some useful points about the different attitudes that are open to those educated into bodily transcendence and those encouraged to respect their bodily desires and emotions. We could allow that, in our society, models of virtue and personhood are indeed gendered—or that the experience of the 'sublime' might indeed be different for women—without, in any way, endorsing Kant's conservative conclusions about female nature or his failure to address the question of the education of women.

Despite this limited defence of the Kantian project, it does nonetheless remain true that Kant scholars have been altogether too eager to find excuses for Kant. Thus, for example, in *Freedom and Anthropology in Kant's Moral Philosophy*, Patrick Frierson does register that Kant's reflections on women and various races are both 'well-known and embarrassing', but the philosophical implications of Kant's views on women are handled in a brief footnote which treats them as irrelevant to the critical system as a whole (Frierson 2003: 34, 173n.). Frierson explains that at the time these remarks would have been 'entertaining' asides, and that they are not fatal to Kant's account of anthropology as a branch of 'universal knowledge' since they 'are meant only to refer to the gender or race under discussion'. Indeed, the discussions of race and gender 'do not have the systematic place that the accounts of the character of the individual and the species do'.

That Kant's accounts of moral character and of personhood are gendered at a conceptual level and that his account of the human species is racially skewed is put to one side. Instead, Frierson argues that Kant's moral philosophy is consistent with his anthropological theory and that it is precisely the non-empirical and universal account of freedom and moral character that 'makes Kant both distinctive and attractive' (163). According to Frierson, what remains a 'Kantian legacy for today' is the limits of the empirical and the fact that the (universal) freedom that Kant advocates as a moral ideal cannot be contaminated by the empirical (164). If this remains the message for today, then it is one that needs to be strongly rejected. We need to resist the Kantian tendency to theorise a mode of observation and response that is cut off emotion and mood, and that also fails to register the social, historical and political contexts. Ethics, politics and aesthetics need to be linked back to anthropology and to material differences. This will also need to be borne in mind in the next chapter which starts by considering the way that, at a merely metaphorical level, Kant links the sublime with Judaism and Islam and also with the 'feminine'.

4

KANT'S ORIENTALISM: ISLAM, 'RACE' AND ETHNICITY

In this chapter I will consider Kant's 'Orientalism': a term which I will use in the sense in which Edward Said defines it: as 'a style of thought' which does not simply deal with 'facts' about the Orient, but which builds on texts, images, myths and hearsay to fabricate an identity for the 'Orient' as that which is exotic and peculiar—not like 'us', whether 'us' is defined as European, the West or simply as 'the Occident'. The geographical limits of the Orient are diffuse, but typically it 'designated Asia or the East, geographically, morally, culturally', including Egypt, Arabo-Islamic peoples, Turkey, North Africa, the Middle and Far East and sometimes also India (Said 1979: 31).

The Oriental subject was represented as an *object* of knowledge for the superior Westerner, with the identity of Europe itself emerging via the representational strategies for delineating the alterity of the East. In earlier chapters we have noticed how Kant refuses the overly passive 'Oriental' subject the capacity for appreciating the sublime. We have also registered Gil Anidjar's claim that the nineteenth-century discourse on the 'religions of the sublime' has contributed to the emergence of 'the Semite' and 'the Muslim' as 'enemies' of western modernity, and his claim that this development is 'a direct consequence of Hegel's learning from Kant' with respect to the sublime (Anidjar 2004). It is now time to look in more detail at Kant's own comments on race and the Orient, and to see how his treatment of non-European 'otherness' differs from his treatment of woman as other. This will also involve some further consideration of Kant's own deployment of the imagery of the feminine 'other'.

Scattered across the *Critique of the Power of Judgment* (1790) and *Religion Within the Boundaries of Mere Reason* (1793/94) and other late writings, can be found a handful of passages in which Kant links the sublime to the monotheistic religions of Judaism and Islam. Thus, in a footnote to *Religion Within the Boundaries of Mere Reason*, Kant depicts the man who is taken over and moved by the feeling of the sublime as enraptured not by the sublime object, but by a vision of his own destiny and his relation to the 'law', backing up his claim by reference to the example of Judaic Law handed down to Moses on Mount Sinai:

> The majesty of the law (like the law on Sinai) instils awe (not dread, which repels; and also not charm [*Reiz*], which invites familiarity); and this awe arouses the respect of the subject toward his master, except that in this case, since the master lies in us, it rouses a *feeling of the sublimity* of our own vocation that transports us more than any beauty.
>
> (RWB: 6/23n. *corr.*)

Kant makes these comments on the sublimity of the Mosaic Law in response to an objection to his moral philosophy put forward by Friedrich Schiller (1759–1805) who had accused Kant of representing the relationship between morality and '*gracefulness*' (*Anmuth*) in overly oppositional terms. Against Schiller, Kant argues that moral duty and grace cannot be reconciled, and then deploys a series of elaborate allegorical images that link the sublime to the masculine and 'grace' to the feminine. Although it might be appropriate to represent the glories of humanity by means of 'the figure of virtue' with the '*graces*' (*Grazien*) in attendance, Kant says, it is 'only after subduing monsters' that Hercules becomes the leader of the muses:

> a labor at which those good sisters shrink back in fear and trembling. These same attendants of Venus Urania become unchaste sisters (*Buhlschwestern*) in the train of Venus Dione as soon as they meddle in the business of determining duties and try to provide incentives for them. — Now, if we ask, 'What is the *aesthetic* constitution, the *temperament* so to speak *of virtue*: is it courageous and hence *joyous*, or weighed down by fear and dejected?' an answer is hardly necessary. The latter slavish frame of mind can never be found without a hidden *hatred* of the law . . . .
>
> (RWB: 6/23n.)

Kant's metaphorical allusion here is to the two different Venuses (or Aphrodites) in Roman and Greek mythology. Venus Urania was born from Uranus, god of the heavens, and came to represent one of the nine Muses: the celestial Venus of philosophy and religion. Her attendants were 'The Three Graces' or 'Charities': feminine personifications of charm and loveliness. But there was a second Venus or Aphrodite, the daughter of Zeus and Dione, who came to represent profane, as opposed to sacred, love. This 'Common Aphrodite' or 'Venus of the People' oversaw sex and the procreation of children. As such, her concerns were those of the body, and alien to those of the mind or soul, and her attendants were a type of temple prostitute. Kant wilfully conflates the two different goddesses, alluding to the inability of the female Graces to subdue confront sublime 'monsters' without experiencing fear. The sublime 'majesty' of the moral law cannot be reconciled with the merely graceful, because the 'slavish frame of mind' which is linked to the feminine is not just indifferent to virtue, but involves a concealed 'hatred' of the law. Here, in this late work,

Kant's metaphors suggest that feminine fear is not simply amoral, but also *immoral*—beauty remains gendered as feminine, with the sublime as masculine, even at the level of artistic symbolisation.

Whether Kant's Oriental subject is as 'slavish' as his female subject is the question that this chapter will address. As we will see, Kant manages to combine a relatively positive attitude to Islam and to the Arab with extremely hostile and prejudicial comments about 'Oriental' nations, cultures and races. This chapter will focus on Islam, the Arab, Turkey and Kant's specific comments on 'the Oriental'. Kant's complex engagement with the 'Egyptomania' of the German Romantics will be considered more fully in Chapter 5 where we will see how Kant deployed the imagery of the 'most sublime' Isis, despite distancing himself from those of his contemporaries who portrayed the Old Testament 'religions of the sublime' as masking a more ancient and more fundamental mode of sublime response.

Kant and Old Testament religions

To understand Kant's use of the example of Moses receiving the Ten Commandments from Jehovah on Mount Sinai to illustrate sublimity in *Religion within the Boundaries of Mere Reason*, it is useful to look back at a passage in the *Critique of the Power of Judgment* (1790) where the necessary failure of the imagination with respect to the sublime is also portrayed in terms of the Laws handed down to Moses:

> Perhaps there is no more sublime passage in the Jewish Book of the Law than the commandment: Thou shalt not make unto thyself any graven image, nor any likeness either of that which is in heaven, or on the earth, or yet under the earth, etc. This commandment alone can explain the enthusiasm (*Enthusiasm*) that the Jewish people felt in its civilized period for its religion when it compares itself with other peoples, or the pride that Mohammedanism inspired.
>
> (CPJ: 274)

This passage has often been misinterpreted and read as if Kant were claiming that art should not seek to represent the sublime, and it clearly is the case that Kant regarded nature (not art) as the more effective means of rousing sublime feelings. However, as the next chapter will show, Kant himself sees no difficulty in describing an art object—a vignette depicting the veiled Isis—as exemplifying the sublime. Kant is far less puritanical about graven images than many of his critics suppose. Instead, Kant uses the examples of Judaism and Islam to make a double point. First, he argues that the imagination becomes more powerful 'precisely because' it enters a realm in which sense experience is lacking, so that the pleasure of the sublime becomes linked to 'a presentation of the infinite, which for that very reason can never be anything other than a merely negative presentation'. Second, he argues that our own 'representation of the moral law' is of an analogous type. Thus, the fact that the moral law is abstract (and not capable of being portrayed via concrete presentations) does not detract from its power. On the contrary, Kant says,

> It is exactly the reverse: for where the senses no longer see anything before them, yet the unmistakable and inextinguishable idea of morality remains, there it would be more necessary to moderate the momentum of an unbounded imagination so as not to let it reach the point of enthusiasm (*Enthusiasm*), rather than, from fear of the powerlessness of these ideas, to look for assistance for them in images and childish devices.
>
> (274)

Although the point is obscured in many of the English translations, Kant is using the term '*Enthusiasm*' in the almost technical sense employed by anglophone writers on religion. Examples include Lord Shaftesbury in *A Letter Concerning Enthusiasm* (1708) and David Hume, who repeatedly ascribed 'enthusiasm' to a disorder of the imagination. For Hume—most obviously in his essay 'Of Superstition and Enthusiasm' (1741)—'enthusiasm' was linked to hope, pride, and an over-confidence in one's own mental capacities, leading to false and over-optimistic beliefs relating to the nature and power of the god who was worshipped. For Hume, it was 'enthusiasm' that produced the delusions of the Quakers, the Shakers and other religious mystics. As such, 'enthusiasm' was opposed to 'superstition' which was linked to a disease of the passions (especially fear and timidity) and to a different kind of false belief, induced by an over-reliance on priests and authorities. In his *History of England* (1754–62) and his *Natural History of Religion* (1757), Hume often used 'superstition' as a synonym for Roman Catholicism (Battersby 1981). Kant makes frequent reference to all these works by Hume.

Kant suggests that both the 'enthusiasm' of Judaism and the 'pride' of the Mohammedans are allied to the sublime. However both the Islamic and Judaic modes of the religious sublime are also represented as inferior to that of the (entirely abstract) moral law which 'carries with it no risk of *fanaticism*' (*Schwärmerei*) (CPJ: 274–75 corr.). Kant defines the latter as '*a delusion of being able to see something beyond all bounds of sensibility*' and 'to rave with reason'. As such, 'fanaticism' is contrasted not only with the proper relation to the moral law, but also with '*Enthusiasm*'. The latter is a 'delusion of sense' (*Wahnsinn*) whereas 'fanaticism' is a more deep-seated 'delusion of mind' (*Wahnwitz*). In effect an equivalent to Hume's 'superstition', it is 'brooding' fanaticism that Kant regards as the most serious failing: the confusion of mind that it engenders 'is least of all compatible with the sublime'. In 'enthusiasm' the imagination is simply 'unreined' and produces the type of religious delusion that is 'a passing accident'. By contrast, 'fanaticism' (*Schwärmerei*) is a 'disease' that 'destroys' the understanding and is a 'deep-rooted, oppressive passion'.

Kant associates 'fanaticism' not with Islam or Judaism, but with those governments who 'have gladly allowed' religions to be represented by 'such supplements' as images and 'other childish devices',

> and thus sought to relieve the subject of the bother but also at the same time also of the capacity to extend the powers of his soul beyond the limits that are arbitrarily set for him and by means of which, as merely passive, he can more easily be dealt with.
>
> (275)

As we saw in the last chapter, Kant treats female subjects in precisely the way that he complains about here—sparing them the 'bother', but at the same time in effect denying them the 'capacity', for transcendence in respect of the sublime. Kant is, in other words, accusing a State religion that emphasises the role of ritual worship and of 'images and childish devices' of feminising the subject and rendering him *slavish*. As in *Religion Within the Boundaries of Mere Reason*—published three years later—Kant is presenting the ideal religion as universal, as in conformity with the moral law, and as shorn of all elements of ritual, mystical revelation, of ornamentation or what he calls '*parerga*'—a term I will come back to in Chapter 5. Kant is promoting the pared-down religion of the Enlightenment, which emphasises moral reason, and he positions both Judaism and Islam on the side of the Enlightenment in this respect. Associated with the lesser delusions of 'enthusiasm', these two types of monotheism count as preferable—historically passing—phases on the way to an even more abstract and universal form of religion: one that aligns religious belief with moral duty and brings it 'within the boundaries of mere reason'.

As Gil Anidjar has registered in *The Jew, the Arab: A History of the Enemy*, Kant's reference to the sublime in Judaic and Islamic traditions is intriguing, especially since it is to be found immediately after one of the paragraphs in the *Critique of the Power of Judgment* where Kant refers to the 'voluptuaries of the Orient'. As we have seen, Kant suggests that these Oriental degenerates are prevented from experiencing the sublime through an overly passive relation to their own bodies—in particular, through having 'their muscles and joints softly pressed and flexed' (*CPJ*: 273–74; Anidjar 2003, 120ff.). In Chapter 1 of this book we also saw Anidjar making the claim that the invention of the racial and ethnic category of the 'Semite' (including both the Jew and the Arab) in the nineteenth century can be traced back to Hegel's reading of Kant on the sublime. For Hegel, Anidjar claims, 'both Jews and Muslims are thoroughly submitted, they are *slaves*. They are slaves to their god', and there is a kind of 'horrifying beauty' about their enslavement (Anidjar 2004).

However, in *The Jew, the Arab*, Anidjar seems implicitly to recognise that what Hegel says about Semites stands in complete contrast with what Kant himself says, despite the comments on 'Oriental' lethargy and passivity that precede those on the Jewish and 'Mohammedan' religions. Anidjar poses a long series of questions relating to the slipperiness of Kant's vocabulary, and the way it shifts between talking about a 'people' as opposed to a 'religion', as well as to the puzzling nature of the 'feelings' of 'enthusiasm' and 'pride' which Kant here associates with Judaism and Islam: 'How do religion, enthusiasm, Judaism, pride, politics, apathy, and Islam relate to each other? Do they, in fact, relate? And if so, under what logic of distinction, by means of what conflict?' (Anidjar 2003: 124). Anidjar (quite rightly) notes how Kant's reference to Jewish Law in the 'famous and frequently discussed passage of Kant on the *Bildverbot* [the ban on images]' has received extensive commentary, but that the reference to Islam seems to have been neglected by the commentators, as a way of explaining why his own 'lack of competence' has prevented him from providing a satisfactory answer to the multiplicity of questions posed by Kant's comments on Judaism and Islam.

Whilst not able to do full justice to this topic within the framework of a book on the question of the sublime, it is certainly possible to add to Anidjar's analysis, so that we can see how, for Kant, questions of 'race' and of true (and false) religions need to be kept apart. Kant debars racially and culturally inferior peoples from access to the sublime; but this prohibition does not extend to either the Jews or the Mohammedans whose failings with respect to religion are described in *Religion Within the Boundaries of Mere Reason* in quite other terms. Indeed, in contrast with Anidjar's interpretation of Hegel on Islam and the sublime, for Kant the problem with Mohammedanism is not that the believers in Islam are 'slavish' and 'submitted' to their God, it is rather that they suffer from an excessive over-confidence—a disorder of the imagination allied to 'enthusiasm'—that has (temporarily) led them astray.

Thus, in another important footnote to *Religion Within the Boundaries of Mere Reason* Kant also links Islam to 'pride' as he contrasts it with Judaism, Hinduism and Christianity. Once again we are told that, 'Mohammedanism is distinguished by its *pride*, because it finds confirmation of its faith in victories and in the subjugation of many peoples rather than in miracles, and because its devotional practices are all of a fierce kind' (*RWB*: 6/184n.). Furthermore, Kant then goes on to link the '*slavish* cast of mind' not to Islam, but to certain ways of inculcating the Christian faith, specifically in reference to 'priestcraft' and an emphasis on 'pietism or false piety' which he defines as 'conducting oneself passively in view of the divine blessedness expected through a power from above'. It is thus a false relation to Christianity—not Christianity *per se*, but also not Islam or Judaism—that Kant associates with loss of self 'reliance', 'constant anxiety' and 'self-contempt' (6/184n.). By contrast, Kant adopts a much more positive tone as he registers here that Islamic pride is a 'remarkable phenomenon' of 'an ignorant though intelligent people', and suggests that this excessive pride was caused by Mohammed's 'fancy' that he alone had freed man from polytheism and 'restored to the world' a monotheistic concept of God. Here again we see Kant suggesting not that the Islamic subject is 'slavish' or in thrall to State religion, but has the inflated—but nevertheless excusable—

over-confidence of 'enthusiasm'. Far from possessing the 'contempt for oneself' that is associated with the *'False devotion (bigotterie, devotia spuria)'* of the Christian who misunderstands 'humility' and 'virtue' and hence submits himself to his God, Kant's Muslim possesses an utterly non-slavish arrogance insofar as religious belief and practice is concerned (184n.–185n.).

There are, admittedly, a few passages in Kant's writings that suggest a different assessment of Islam. Thus, for example, in his *Essay on Illnesses of the Head* of 1764, Kant distinguishes the morally good 'enthusiast' from the 'fanatic' (including the visionary and the *Schwärmer*), but then says it is fanaticism that has driven Mohammed towards a princely throne (*KGS:* 2/267). Clearly, the use of this vocabulary here contrasts with his remarks in both the *Critique of the Power of Judgment* (1790) and also *Religion Within the Boundaries of Mere Reason* (1793/94). Furthermore, in the *Critique of Practical Reason*, Mohammed's paradise is described as one of a variety of mystical 'monstrosities' that obtrude on reason (1788: 5/120–21). Kant's more developed position is, however, that neither Judaism nor Islam is flawed in a way that is irredeemable. Apart from the problems of excessive pride, Kant's principal objection to Islam in *Religion Within the Boundaries of Mere Reason* is that it overemphasised religious practices as a way of securing salvation (*RWB:* 6/194). As Kant argues at some length, religious rituals and customs should be regarded as mere '*parerga* to pure reason': they ornament it but fall outside the boundaries of a true (enlightened) religion (6/53).

Kant certainly does not seem to associate Islam with the 'slavish' fanaticism of State religion—something that seems surprising in terms of later developments and current stereotypes, but which nevertheless reflects the Enlightenment ideals and values that Kant sought to promote. Thus, for example, Frederick the Great of Prussia (1740–86)—the monarch with whose enlightened religious views Kant profoundly sympathised—welcomed Turks into Prussia, proclaiming:

> 'All religions are equal and good, if only the people who follow them are honourable people. And if the Turks and heathen came and wanted to live here in our land, then we would build mosques and churches for them.'
>
> (Şen 2002)

A large number of Muslims—including Bosnians, Albanians and Tatars—changed to the Prussian side in the wars with Russia that took place in Frederick the Great's reign. Frederick demonstrated their welcome by allowing the appointment of an Imam for the 'Prussian Mohammedans' in the troops (Abdullah 1981: 15–16).

The difficulties of the Muslims in Prussia increased only after the death of Frederick the Great in 1786, and this was when Kant's own difficulties with Prussian State religion also intensified. The new ruler, Frederick William II, was a religious fanatic and mystic of the Rosicrucian variety, and the 1793 edition of Kant's *Religion Within the Boundaries of Mere Reason* was quite badly mangled by the censor. Like many other Enlightenment philosophers, Kant confines his most important criticisms of state religion to his footnotes (in an evident attempt to escape the attentions of the censor). In his footnotes— many of which were added only in the 1794 edition—we can see Kant defending his (and Frederick the Great's) 'enlightened' form of Christianity against the new Prussian orthodoxies. In these late texts Kant has a rhetorical purpose as he deployed the examples of Islam and Judaism for Enlightenment ends: to counter the new Christian 'piety' and rituals of the Prussian State.

Kant's primary complaint against Judaism as a religion is that it withdraws from the 'universal' and excludes other peoples and cultures from participating in its values and blessings. Kant's strong claim is that, in its original form, Judaism cannot count as a religion at all, since it was 'only a collection of merely statutory laws supporting a political state'. Maintaining that the original patriarchal religion of the Jews involves no belief in a future life, Kant even asserts that 'Judaism as such, taken in its purity, entails absolutely no religious faith'. Thus whilst, on the one hand, Kant is happy to credit 'no longer patri- archal and uncontaminated Judaism' with making both Christianity and Islam possible, he also insists that insofar as the history of religion is concerned Christianity emerges out of the 'total abandonment of the Judaism in which it originated' (*RWB*: 6/125–28).

Anidjar argues that it was Hegel's reading of Kant on the sublime that con- tributed to the invention of the category of the Semite and the positioning of the Jew and the Muslim as the 'enemies' of the West, but Kant himself might best be described as a (fair-weather) friend of Islam who suggests the followers of Mohammed come close to the 'sublime' religion of pure reason. The 'pride' of the Mohammedans and their overemphasis on ritual are relatively minor mistakes compared to the ingrained madness that comes from the subjection of a people to Catholic or other religious authorities. Kant prefers 'Mohamme- danism' to Roman Catholicism, to extreme modes of Christian mysticism, to Judaism and also to Egyptian polytheism or deism. Thus, Kant also argues against those who regarded Egypt as the origin of subsequent forms of mono- theism, asserting that the ancient Egyptians were mere 'heathens', 'blinded by superstition': their concept of God was no more than 'that of deism, or rather that of the most wretched polytheism' (Kant 1817: 28/1124–25).

Kant's (predominantly positive) analysis of Islam as a religion does, however, need to be kept separate from his (primarily negative) comments on impure, ill-adapted or degenerate races, nationalities and 'peoples' (*Volk*). As I will demonstrate, Kant is (relatively) generous in his comments on the Arabs (whom he counts as members of the 'white' race), whilst nevertheless con- tinuing to be extremely insulting about other 'Oriental' peoples (both 'white' and 'non-white') who continue to be denied the capacity to experience or appreciate the sublime. Analogously, despite his relatively positive assessment of the Hebrew religion, especially in relation to the sublime, Kant also makes abusive remarks about the 'Jews', 'Palestinians' and 'Hebrews'—terms used by Kant as synonyms—who are described as a nation of 'merchants' and 'deceivers' who live amongst us (*Anth*: 7/205–6n.). Through reading Kant via Hegel, Anidjar has simplified the picture and missed the particular—and peculiar— mode of late eighteenth-century racism that Kant deploys. For Kant neither the Arab nor the Muslim is 'the enemy'; neither is 'submitted' to his God in a slave-like way. But neither is the 'Semite' the enemy; the category of the 'Semite' was still in the process of emerging, and does not correspond to Kant's way of drawing racial or ethnic boundaries, as we will see. But Kant's comments on the 'Oriental' are nonetheless racist—or, more precisely, 'ethnicist'. Indeed, Kant adopts a most pernicious form of racism which pre-dates—but nevertheless acts as a disturbing precursor to and influence on—modern notions of 'race' and ethnicity.

Kant on race and ethnicity

Before considering in detail Kant's comments on the Arabs, the Turks and other 'Oriental' peoples, it is necessary to look in some detail at Kant's theory of 'race' and its relation to modern notions of ethnicity. Kant's most extensive contribution to eighteenth-century debates on these topics is to be found in a precritical work, 'Of the Different Human Races' (Kant 1775/77). Kant does modify his position later to some extent, especially with regard to his account of teleology; but the fundamental principles remain unchanged, as we can see from his 1788 essay 'On the Use of Teleological Principles in Philosophy' in which Kant defends himself against some fundamental criticisms of his view of race voiced by Georg Forster in 1786 (*KGS*: 8/159–84). In the 1775 essay Kant argued against those monogenists, including Linnaeus, Buffon and Cuvier, who had maintained that all human beings belong to one single race, but also against the polygenists, such as Voltaire and Lord Kames (Henry Home), who had asserted that there were several distinct species of mankind (Greene 1954). Firming up the division between 'species' and 'race', Kant's own claim is that in origins there was one human species that divided into four distinct races of mankind. Difference is explained in terms of a variation of these basic, *a priori*, types.

Kant's four original races were '(1) the white race; (2) the Negro race; (3) the Hun race (Mongol or Kalmuck); and (4) the Hindu or Hindustani race'. Kant includes the Arabs as one of the varieties of the white race, along with the Moors, the Turkish-Tatars and the Persians and those inhabitants of Asia who are not specifically mentioned elsewhere. The Negroes include the inhabitants of the rest of Africa and New Guinea. The Kalmuck race is said to include the Huns, the Mongols, the Lapps and Amerindians, and to exclude the Chinese who are viewed as being of 'mixed race' (consequent upon an ancient mixing of types (3) and (4) in and around Tibet). In one half of the

Indian continent the Hindustani race is described as being 'very pure and ancient'; but, by implication, it is 'mixed' elsewhere (1775/77: 2/432–33, pp. 11–12).

What makes Kant different from the polygenists is his insistence that the four original races can and do interbreed. Kant ties the 'wisdom' of nature to its tendency to vary itself and to perfect itself, driving human beings to 'develop all of their talents and approach the perfection of their calling'. Although the interbreeding of the four races might result in a weakening of the original 'hereditary stock', such 'half-breed resemblances' soon vanish as members of the individuals belonging to the 'stock' change their diet or settle in a new geographical location (2/431, p. 10). Without any notion of genetic inheritance— or even a clear idea of how the processes of sexual reproduction work—Kant indicates that most of the apparent differences between different nations and cultures can be explained in terms of a variation on the four underlying 'pure' races. Climate and diet produce such profound changes in the basic varieties of humans that—if reinforced by intermarriage amongst similar cultural types— they can even produce changes in 'the family stock' and produce changes in 'the reproductive power'. Furthermore, Kant also argues that some differences between cultural types are to be explained by the fact that the underlying 'pure' race has yet to adapt to the new climate, despite having inhabited the country for a long time. The characteristics of the American Indians ('a Hunnish race not fully acclimatised') and the Lapps (another Hunnish race 'only recently driven into this [arctic] region from a milder climate') are both explained in this way (Kant 1775/77: 2/533–34, pp. 11–12).

In order to maintain a distinction between four—and only four—'races' of mankind, Kant has disregarded an enormous amount of counter evidence, especially since each of the four races includes such a range of varieties and geographical locations. Kant seems to have based his distinction of the four races largely on skin colour—white; black; red-brown; olive-yellow—but hair colour and type, the shape of the eyes and some questions of temperament and character also play a role. What plays no role at all in Kant's account is groupings of languages, but it was this that would contribute so much to the emergence of the (artificial) category of the 'Semite' in the subsequent century.

As Bernard Lewis explains, the term 'Semite' comes from 'Sem', the Greco-Latin version of the Biblical 'Shem': the oldest of Noah's three sons, and thus one of the three lines of descent for all mankind after the Biblical Flood had drowned all human beings, except for Noah and his offspring (Lewis 1999). Christians—and to a lesser extent Muslims and Jews—came to accept that the three sons of Noah represented three original racial groups. From 'Ham' were descended the dark-skinned peoples of Africa; from Sem the group that included the Hebrews; from Japheth the Persians, the Greeks and those people who later became categorised as Aryans. This (implausible) view combined in the late eighteenth century with the philological analysis of languages to produce the new category of the 'Semite'—which included the Arab as well as the

Jew—as opposed to the Aryan, which included members of those cultures whose languages were Indo-European or Indo-Iranian ('Aryan'). Although 'Semite' was a term that was devised to categorise cultural and linguistic groupings, by the end of the nineteenth century it was being misused and acting as a marker of 'race'.

Kant was orthodox enough in a Christian sense to argue—on 'rational' grounds—that all races were descended from one common ancestor, and made a point of insisting that his account was consistent with that of the story of Adam and Eve in *Genesis* (Kant 1786: 8/110). But his account of the subsequent four races is quite distinct from the philologists' groupings of cognate languages and cultures that was emerging around that time (Bernal 1987: 224–38). This does not mean, however, that Kant was even-handed in his description of the four races. Kant asserts that the original humans must have originated 'between 31 and 52 degrees latitude in the old world': an area stretching from Alexandria to London, so including Turkey, Tehran, Baghdad, Jerusalem, Athens, London, Paris, Rome and Southern Germany, but excluding Cairo, Amsterdam, Berlin, Russia, most of Poland and also Königsberg. The 'old world' is the area of the 'greatest riches of earth's creation' and also 'where human beings must diverge least from their original form' (1775/77: 2/440–41, p. 19). The 'noble blond' (*Hochblond*) is the first northern deviation from this most basic and perfect type, and is listed as the 'first race', emerging as a result of humid cold; this would include the Prussians and many of the other 'deviations' in Northern Europe. The 'copper red' Americans are listed as the second race, being produced by 'dry cold'; the Senegambian black figures as the 'third race' and the effect of 'humid heat'; and the 'olive-yellow Asian Indians' the fourth race, produced by 'dry heat' (2/441, pp. 20–21).

Since Kant describes the Asian Indians as being of a 'true gipsy color', and as suffering from such excess of bile that their very skin colour is 'virtually jaundiced', it is clear that his is by no means a neutral description (2/439, p. 18). This is even more apparent when Kant ascribes the universal 'stink' of the Negroes as being due to the 'harmful absorption of the foul, humid air' which produces an excessive evaporation of phosphoric acid through the skin. Analogously, the 'half-extinguished life power' of the American Indians is attributed to an excess of acidity which also causes the skin to be of a 'reddish iron rust colour' when they live in the North and a 'darker copper colour' when in the South. The unsuitability of native-Americans as slaves—in contrast with Negroes—is used as evidence of their 'lack of ability and durability' (2/437–38, pp. 16–17). Although a weak life power is also said to be 'entirely natural' to the inhabitants of cold regions, this is not mentioned as a fault of the 'first race'—the 'noble blond'—which does, by contrast, escape all criticism, except for 'a tendency to scurvy'.

The *hochblond* race is characterised by 'tender white skin, reddish hair, and pale blue eyes', and said to inhabit 'the northern regions of Germany'. We are told that, as a stock, this *hochblond* type was good enough to have persisted 'as a race, if the further development of this deviation had not so frequently been interrupted by interbreeding with alien stocks'. At this point Kant indicates that he has provided an approximation of 'the real (*wirkliche*) races', and provides a table that runs from the first 'noble blonds' to the fourth 'olive-yellow' Indian variations (2/441, p. 20). Clearly, although Kant has not the vocabulary of the 'Aryan' and 'Semite'—and although he argues (on grounds of practicality) against the controlled breeding of non-degenerate human types—we can find in Kant's account of the origins of the human 'race' a distinctively Northern and European bias that would later be commandeered by the German anti-Semites (2/431, p. 10).

Coming back then to the question of the 'Oriental' and effeminate males and men of other inferior cultural groups who are said by Kant to be unable to appreciate the sublime, it would seem as if this incapacity does, for Kant, involve a mix of racial and cultural disadvantages. Kant has nothing against Islam as such, and Arabs and most Turks are also allowed into the 'white race'—even, for the most part, falling within the latitudes of perfection in which human civilisation was said to have originated. On the other hand, in *The Metaphysics of Morals*, Kant criticises Mohammedanism for having allowed opium, whilst prohibiting alcoholic spirits, with opium specifically linked to an inability to measure—and hence to a lack of judgement (1797/98: 6/428). In the *Anthropology* opium is linked to long-lasting 'mental debility' and also to the kind of false bravery exhibited by the Turks. Thus, Kant indicates that the Turkish 'madmen' who seem courageous cannot really be said to transcend fear because they have no accurate estimate of the dangers they are facing (*Anth*: 7/ 217, 256). Both of these 'facts' would suggest the inability of the Turks to experience the sublime, since in the *Critique of the Power of Judgment* both judgement and the transcendence of fear are made necessary prerequisites for the awe and respect that the sublime demands.

This makes it sound as if Kant made the Turks' incapacity to transcend fear and access the sublime no more than a historical accident, and consequent on their use of opium. In the *Anthropology* Kant is, however, much more harsh, declaring firmly that whereas Russia cannot yet be said to have a definite character that belongs to its people and Poland has lost the character that it once had, 'the nationals of European Turkey never have and never will have what is requisite for a definite character of a people [*Volkscharakter*]' (*Anth*: 7/ 319 *corr.*). Kant is talking here about the character of a people (*Volkscharakter*), rather than about the kind of individual character that we saw, in the last chapter, Kant linking to moral personhood, to rational agency, and to the 'man of principle' who overcomes his bodily drives and feelings on the basis of his will (7/285). Nevertheless, it seems clear from the continuation of the passage in the *Anthropology* that the denial of a *Volkscharakter* to the inhabitants of European Turkey is linked to the question of moral character, since Kant claims that he is not discussing 'the artificially acquired (or artfully lost) characteristics of nations', but 'the innate, natural character which, so to speak, lies in the blood mixture of the human beings' (7/319 *corr.*). Kant is as dismissive of the character of people from European Turkey as he is of that of women, again suggesting that when Kant denies the effeminate 'Oriental' males the capacity to appreciate the sublime, it is the Turks whom he has in mind. And the problem, it seems, is not just due to the fact that the Turks befuddle their minds with opium and soften their bodies by recourse to massage and the delights of the Harem, the problem lies in the very composition of their blood.

Kant adopts a more generous assessment of the Arabs, but they are associated with two modes of mental disorder: 'unbridled' and 'unruly' imagination. The first merely produces fables and fictions; the second leads to a complete loss of control and to believe in things that could never possibly exist (*Anth*: 7/181). Here, in the *Anthropology*, Kant associates the latter form of fantasy with the same 'delusion of the senses' (*Wahnsinn*) which he had, in the *Critique of the Power of Judgment*, ascribed to the disorder of '*Enthusiasm*' and that we have also seen him link with 'Mohammedanism' (*CPJ*: 274 *corr.*). The Arabs—described as a 'nomadic' people—are also ascribed the type of 'passion' that acts as a drive to freedom. Here again Arabs are credited with 'pride', even to the extent that 'they look with contempt on settled peoples'; and once again this leads on to a discussion of 'the affect which is called Enthusiasm'. Hunting peoples might be ennobled by such a feeling of freedom, but because this feeling is generated by the senses, and not by moral laws, it threatens to become a 'passion' (*Leidenschaft*) as opposed to a mere 'affect'. Here Kant insists that only humans have passions, and that passions are reason-driven and so are not a part of our animal nature. However, by identifying the passions as '*ambition, lust for power* and *avarice*', the tendency to passion is clearly not condoned (*Anth*: 7/268–70). This passage thus fits with Kant's criticism of strong passion that we have noted elsewhere (Kant 1797/98: 6/407–8).

Although Kant does not discuss the *Volkscharakter* of the Arabs in the *Anthropology*, in his early *Observations on the Feeling of the Beautiful and Sublime* (1764) Kant does discuss their 'national characteristics', describing them as 'the most noble people of the Orient, yet of a feeling which easily degenerates into the adventurous'. The Arab, Kant says, is 'hospitable, generous and genuine, although at the same time his stories, histories and above all his sentiments are shot through with something of the wonderful'. Here, once again, the Arabs— 'the Spaniards of the Orient'—are allowed a proximity to the sublime that is denied to the Turk who falls into the grouping of Oriental peoples who are not considered worthy of discussion since 'they display few signs of a finer feeling'. Apart from the Arabs, only the Persians are allowed good taste—they are 'the French of Asia'—with the Japanese ('the Englishmen of this part of the world') also allowed some merit (*Obs*: 2/252, pp. 109–10).

Kant's prejudice against Turkey and against the peoples of the Orient is expressed again in the (so far untranslated) notebooks of those of his students who attended his *Lectures* on anthropology during the years 1772–89 (*KGS*: 25/

1ff.). Although in the winter of 1784–85 Kant can be found admitting that his account of the national characteristics of the various peoples might involve something of a caricature, it is notable that in almost every session his lecture course concludes with an extended discussion of 'the character of nations', 'the character of the sexes' and 'the character of the human species'. And in each of these sections we see Kant repeating—slightly altering, extending and also elaborating on—his views about nations, peoples and races. Kant, famously, never travelled himself. His biased opinions are, however, not simply the result of unthinking prejudice, but are an outcome of extended (and evidently often uncritical) reading, together with attention to hearsay and gossip which Kant then shared with his students. No doubt some of his views came from his close friend, Joseph Green, an English merchant, who not only travelled but also devoured travel literature; Kant discussed his philosophy with Green in the greatest detail from the time they met, around 1765, until Green's death in 1786 (Kuehn 2001: 154). The fact that the section on national character is missing from the very final set of lecture notes that we have available cannot lead us to conclude that Kant had outgrown these views, since we see remnants of these opinions incorporated in the published version of the *Anthropology* (1798/1800), in the *Critique of the Power of Judgment* (1790) and in *Religion Within the Boundaries of Mere Reason* (1793/94).

In 1772–73 Kant tells his students that amongst the Asian nations only the Persians have taste: where 'Tataric blood has been passed down, that has made a nation coarse and without taste'. Kant immediately cites the Turks as an example of this. They 'are distant from all fine sentiments': they do not dance; their music is 'so ponderous as to be melancholy'; they have a 'quite unbelievable seriousness'; and also (in an apparent contradiction with the last assertion) that they 'do nothing but smoke tobacco and drink coffee'. Kant does seem to allow that the Chinese have taste, but this is dismissed as 'private' (as opposed to public) taste, in other words as being unable to fulfil the requirement of universal communicability that Kant will later make a necessary condition of the beautiful (*KGS*: 25/400–401).

Likewise, in the lectures of 1775–76 Kant asserts that the differences between the 'Oriental' and the 'European' do not vary across different regimes or ages. In comparison with the European, 'All oriental peoples are totally incapable of judging according to concepts' and are 'unable to discriminate a single instance of morality or justice on the basis of concepts'. Being incapable of conceptual thought, and basing their judgements on 'appearance'—and 'shape (*Gestalt*) and intuition (*Anschauung*)', in particular—Kant also declares Oriental peoples incapable of philosophy, mathematics and the appreciation of beautiful music. The Oriental mind cannot grasp 'harmony' which instead appears simply as 'confusion'. Kant registers the 'sensuous beauty' and apparent 'excellence' of Chinese painting, but dismisses this as mere 'handiwork' rather than involving any understanding, declaring that 'in them we find neither an idea of the whole nor taste'. Of Orientals generally he asserts,

In their buildings we find no sublimity, order, proportion, delicacy, fineness nor taste which all rests on concepts. True beauty consists of an accord between sensuousness and understanding, and this they lack. Because they are incapable of concepts, so are they also incapable of true honour, and know nothing about this, since to have a love of honour and a desire for honour is something quite other than the glitter of haughtiness.

(25/655–56)

As I will argue in the final chapter of this book, this exclusion of the Chinese from 'public taste' is a serious handicap for later philosophers, like Hannah Arendt, who sought to base a broadly liberal political philosophy on Kant's account of aesthetic taste. It is true that these lectures on anthropology belong to Kant's precritical period, and he had yet to develop his mature theory of the relationship between the sublime and the beautiful. In particular he seems to assert in this section something that he will later deny, namely that beauty involves conceptual understanding. Nevertheless, it follows from his depiction of 'Oriental' peoples in this section that they will be incapable of the sublime as described in the *Critique of the Power of Judgment* and, as we have seen, elements of this caricature of the Oriental creep into Kant's comments on the sublime in the third *Critique*.

For Kant the difference between conceptual thought and the data (intuitions) presented by the senses is that concepts group particulars together and deal in generalities, whilst intuition presents us only with singularities. In the lectures we see that the problem with Kant's 'Oriental' man is that he is trapped in sensuousness and mere detail. He is incapable of generality, let alone universality or the longing for absolute totality that is integral to the Kantian sublime. Not only do Oriental buildings lack sublimity, but Oriental writings are a mere 'work of flowers', and of a style that is 'sprawling, pictorial and full of flowers'. Warning Europeans against importing these stylistic excesses, Kant compares the Orientals unfavourably with the Greeks who were the first to develop conceptual thought— and hence 'philosophy, rhetoric, painting, sculpture' and the like (25/656).

Quite who gets counted into the category of the 'Oriental' apart from the Tatars, the Turks and the Chinese is left unclear—and also deeply puzzling given Kant's claim that Oriental man is incapable of loving his 'Father Land' and also has 'no capacity for the concept of god' (25/656). It's certainly hard to tie these comments on Oriental characteristics to Kant's much more favourable assessment of Islam as a religion. As we have seen, Kant has a particular prejudice against 'European Turks', and in the 1775–76 lectures on anthropology he also claims that 'The Poles and the Russians have more of the mix of Oriental characteristics than other nations in Europe' (25/661). Since we have already seen Kant claiming in the published version of the *Anthropology* that Russians and Poles lack character, this once again fits with the conclusion that 'Oriental' man is incapable of the sublime (*Anth*: 7/319 *corr*.).

Without general concepts, without universals, and hence without any 'real' moral principles, Kant's Oriental man is as incapable of transcending appearance as Kant's European woman. There are, however, two important differences. First, the Kantian woman is bound to immediacy via her emotions, especially via her propensity to fear; by contrast, the Kantian Oriental is constrained not by his emotions, but by the fact that he responds to the world in a too-particular fashion, privileging sense images and shapes. Second, whilst Kant makes the avoidance of the sublime a moral duty for women, in the case of Oriental peoples Kant seems to suggest that they simply lack the ability to either produce or to appreciate the sublime.

Which of these two modes of exclusion is the more disabling is a question that could be debated at length. Kant's views on 'race' and ethnicity are so obviously outdated and so coloured by prejudice that it is, perhaps, hard to give them any credit at all. By contrast, the notion that women are more emotional, more fearful, and less autonomous still finds support in cultural practices which often continue to socialise women to fulfil Kantian norms. However, norms are at least open to question, whereas presenting differences of race and ethnicity as simple 'facts' closes down the imaginative options of those who wish to contest Kant's overly abstract views of the self and of personhood. It becomes too easy to pretend that these, merely empirical, 'mistakes' do not bear on Kant's overall system. However, Kant's very way of marking out the 'truly universal' and distinguishing it from the 'merely particular' and the 'detailed' relies on racial and cultural norms that privilege the non-sensuous, the conceptual, the abstract and the logical as viewed from the perspective of 'old Europe'. Even Kant's distinction between beautiful art and that type of 'handiwork' that can be dismissed as mere 'craft' turns out to incorporate ethnic and racial determinants, along with his norms for the sublime.

Paul Gilroy has remarked that 'it is regrettable that questions of "race" and representation have been so regularly banished from orthodox histories of western aesthetic judgement, taste and cultural value' (Gilroy 1993: 9). He then pleads that 'further enquiries should be made into precisely how discussions of "race", beauty, ethnicity and culture have contributed to the critical thinking that eventually gave rise to cultural studies'. It is, however, not merely with reference to cultural studies that such basic research is needed; the question of the effect of 'racial' and ethnic stereotypes and paradigms in mainstream philosophy and aesthetics is also seriously under-researched. Furthermore, most recent scholarly work in this area has addressed these issues from a perspective that privileges the shared cultural traditions of Black American slaves or, alternatively, the European Jews.

Thus, whilst an account of the 'Slave Sublime'—as provided, for example, by Gilroy in the final chapter of *The Black Atlantic* (Gilroy: 187–223)—addresses the important theme of collective, unexpressed and ineffable pain, an 'Oriental sublime' would need to address some quite other blind spots in the history of philosophy. Kant's own comments on the 'Oriental' suggest that this would need to include how the 'public sphere' is distinguished from the merely 'private' or 'local'; how the 'universal' is distinguished from mere 'ornament' or 'parerga', as well as a reconceptualisation of stylistic unity, beauty and the work of art. How the question of parerga bears on the question of the sublime—and whether deconstructive strategies can ever be enough—is the topic of the next chapter which situates Kant's comments on the sublime Isis and Egypt in relation to the forever elusive 'feminine'.

5

EGYPT, *PARERGA* AND A QUESTION
OF VEILS

The argument of the last chapter has shown that, in Kantian terms, 'Oriental' cultures are capable only of producing an art full of unnecessary '*parerga*' or 'ornaments'. As Kant explains in the *Critique of the Power of Judgment*, where the *parerga* to a work of art are themselves beautiful they can intensify the pleasure, 'like the borders of paintings, draperies on statues, or colonnades around magnificent buildings'. Even though such ornamentation is 'not internal' to the artwork, it nevertheless adds to the pleasure 'through its form'. But Kant indicates that there is also a different kind of *parergon* which is not formally beautiful: in this case, 'it is, like a gilt frame, attached merely in order to recommend approval of the painting through its charm'. Here the ornament is merely 'decoration, and detracts from genuine beauty'. Kant then goes on to insist that sublimity 'requires another standard of judging' than that of the beautiful, since the latter excludes all 'charm', 'emotion' and sensibility' (*CPJ*: 226 *corr.*). However, in the *Anthropology* Kant also stresses that the *parergon* is also important when considering the 'artistic presentation of the sublime'. The 'description, embellishment (in secondary work, *parerga*) may be and ought to be beautiful'. These beautiful extras render the sublime 'an object of taste'; without them 'it would be wild, crude and repulsive' (*Anth*: 7/243).

Jacques Derrida has, famously, explored the means whereby Kant evokes our ability to take pleasure in the sublime and represent the unrepresentable, only by pushing to the borders—as *parerga*—that which enables Kant's system to close in on itself as a unity:

> Philosophical discourse will always have been *against* the *parergon*? But what about this *against*?
>
> A *parergon* comes against, beside, and in addition to the *ergon*, the work done [*fait*], the fact [*le fait*], the work, but it does not fall to one side, it touches and cooperates within the operation, from a certain outside. Neither simply outside nor simply inside. Like an accessory that one is obliged to welcome on the border, on board.
>
> (Derrida 1978a: 419)

Derrida's strategy is to use this supplementary—but nevertheless entirely necessary boundary of the Kantian *parergon*—to disturb our vision, and allow us to see an 'other' that Kant himself refuses and represses. Insisting that 'Framing always supports and contains that which, by itself, collapses forthwith', Derrida tries to 'welcome on board' a different kind of unrepresentable, which does not function as that which is 'beyond' representation, but which is unseen and undervalued because of the way in which it inhabits the margins (427). In particular, in the body of his writings Derrida pays attention to the displaced 'feminine' and the 'Jew' that philosophy treats as its 'enemy'—as what 'it will always have been *against*'—but which help define what can be (and what cannot be) represented in philosophy itself.

In the wake of Derrida, a school of literary and cultural criticism has developed which looks to deconstruction to develop a positive account of a 'feminine' sublime. As Joanna Zylinska explains, the notion of the 'feminine sublime' that she is putting forward,

> is born from the excess that the earlier theorists of the sublime attempted to tame or annul. I am not interested, however, in determining whether or not there *is* a sublime which is specific to women. Instead, I use this term to explore instances in which absolute and incalculable alterity can no longer be housed by the discursive restraints of traditional aesthetics, leading, as a consequence, to the eruption of affect and the weakening of the idea of the universal subject.
> (Zylinska 2001: 8)

Zylinska then goes on to equate 'death' with 'the ultimate source of fear in the experience of the sublime', and to interpret 'the feminine sublime' as a 'recognition' of 'mortality and finitude to which the self is exposed in its encounter with absolute difference' (8). Equating the 'feminine' with textual and artistic excess—with that which is pushed beyond the margins of representation—and that functions as "'a point of semiotic turbulence'" (35), Zylinska proposes a 'feminine sublime' that does not ward off that which is feared or seek to strengthen the 'I' in the manner of the Kantian sublime, but welcomes the feared 'other':

> The feminine sublime does not domesticate the object that might be a source of threat but rather accepts the amorous relationship of pleasure and pain, life and death, and the potential dispersal of the self.
> (31)

For Zylinska, this new 'feminine sublime' will involve an abandonment of aesthetics with its concern with the subject–object relation, and instead entail a move to Levinasian ethics which involves "'respect for the alterity of the other'". As such her feminine sublime will function as "'a site of resistance to aestheticism'" (31).

Zylinska's approach is indebted to that of Barbara Freeman, *The Feminine Sublime: Gender an Excess in Women's Fiction* (1995), and this last phrase is taken from her. However, Zylinska is much less interested in women's artworks than Freeman, and in her analysis we see one of the tensions that was implicitly there in Freeman's work: the lack of coincidence between the 'feminine' and 'women'. I will come back to Zylinska's argument later on in this chapter, but here it might be noted that Kant's philosophy of the sublime is also situated in the domain between ethics and aesthetics, and cannot be assumed under the heading of 'aestheticism'. As we have seen, for Kant the 'sublime' is fundamentally different from the 'beautiful' and is not simply an 'object of taste'. Only the *parerga* and embellishments of the beautiful can render it tasteful. For Kant, the sublime is always to be understood in terms of the 'moral law', personhood and duty. Furthermore, Kant secures the universality of the experience of the sublime only by overlooking or downgrading material and cultural differences between subjects, so that the attainment of the experience of the sublime is ruled out either at an 'empirical' level (in the case of the Oriental subject, for example) or on moral as well as empirical grounds (in the case of women).

Zylinska and other advocates of a 'feminine sublime' advocate a strategy that is almost the reverse of mine. Zylinska professes no interest in a sublime that might be 'specific to women', but nevertheless claims to be adopting a strategy that involves a 'weakening of the idea of the universal subject'. But what is puzzling about this methodology is the apparent universalising of 'the self' and 'affect', as if it were *always* the case that *all* human selves respond to sublime in always identical ways—so that what one 'really' is terrified of in the case of the sublime is a mask for 'death'. But this is to treat the female, the raced or the ethnically specific subject as no more than the 'other' of the (European) philosopher who locates the 'feminine', the 'Jew', the 'Muslim', the 'Arab' or the 'Oriental' as the longed-for and/or excluded 'other' that props up his own 'universal' or 'neutral'—and never properly historical or culturally specific—account of 'our' truths, fears, pains and pleasures.

In order to explore further the differences between the different kinds of 'other' in the Kantian texts, this chapter will explore the background to a passage in the *Critique of the Power of Judgment* (1790) in which Kant describes the sublime in terms of a veiled feminine goddess who forever eludes the human subject, but whom all men must respect. This passage seems to fit with Zylinska's demand for an aesthetics of 'absolute and incalculable alterity'. However, I will be concerned to show that the elusive and excessive 'other' inhabits Kant's texts on the sublime, on religion and on morality in a variety of conflicting ways. There is the ever-elusive 'feminine' figure of Isis hidden seductively behind her veil, together with the entirely abstract evocation of 'the Jewish people' and 'Mohammedanism' who get near to an appreciation of the sublime via the ban on graven images. Derrida's—often brilliant—strategy with respect to the analysis of the Kantian *parergon* brings certain of these exclusions into focus, whilst at the same time preventing us from seeing how historical specific—and how important—is Kant's *simultaneous* attack on flesh-and-blood women, on 'Orientals' and others of an 'inferior' cultural or racial type. The continued emphasis on the 'absolute and incalculable alterity' in the aesthetics of the 'feminine sublime' continues to erase the historical, material and political dimensions of the sublime of embodied *female* and *'raced'* and ethnically distinct subjects.

Kant amongst the Egyptians

In the last chapter we saw that Kant was dismissive of Egyptian religion which is described as heathen 'superstition' and as mere 'deism, or rather that of the most wretched polytheism' (Kant 1817: 28/1124–25). Kant's dismissive comments on Egyptian religion are perhaps surprising in the light of a footnote to the *Critique of the Power of Judgment* (1790) where, famously, Kant asserts:

> Perhaps nothing more sublime has ever been said, or thought more sublimely expressed, than in the inscription over the Temple of *Isis* (Mother *Nature*): 'I am all that is and that was and that shall be, and no mortal has lifted my veil.' *Segner* made use of this idea by means of a vignette, rich in sense, placed at the beginning of his theory of nature, in order to prepare the mind of his apprentice [*Lehrling*], whom he was ready to lead into this temple, through a sacred shudder [*heiligen Schauer*] and ritual attentiveness.
>
> (*CPJ*: 316n. *corr.*)

For deconstructive and psychoanalytic readers of Kant this passage is a gift, apparently showing that Kant's privilege of the masculine subject rests on a hidden 'feminine' sublime that acts as Kant's 'Other' and that inspires him with horrified fear. Thus, for example, Sarah Kofman has read the veiled Mother Nature who is encountered by the young male apprentice in Kant's text, in terms of the Freudian castration complex (Kofman 1982).

In Kofman's explication, the sublime and necessary veiling of Mother Nature conceals the monstrous Other of Freudian psychoanalysis: the woman whose mutilated body lacks a penis. For Kofman, Kant's 'respect' for the veiled and sublime Isis is an instance of fetishistic fear, and reveals both an aspect of Kant's warped sexuality and also the underlying misogyny of Enlightenment man's 'respect' for women. Kofman's analysis is powerful, but her psychoanalytic account loses the specificity of Kant's conservatism about sexual, racial and ethnic difference. As we will see, Kant entered into a debate with his male contemporaries with respect to the sublime and veiled Isis, with Kant accusing other male philosophers of representing the sublime in an overly feminised fashion.

To fill in the historical background: it seems likely that Kant's reference to the figure of Isis in the footnote to the 1790 text can be traced to an acquaintance with Karl Leonhard Reinhold's pseudonymous publication on *Die Hebräische Mysterien oder die älteste religiöse Freymaurerey* (*Hebrew Mysteries or the Oldest Religious Freemasonry*) which was published in a journal for freemasons in 1786 and then as a book in 1788 (Assmann 1997, 1999). In 1787 Reinhold was appointed as the inaugural occupant of the first Professorial Chair devoted to the new Kantian philosophy. His own, enormously influential, *Letters on the Kantian Philosophy* had begun to appear in the journal *Der Teutsche Merkur* in 1786, and the young Professor corresponded regularly with Kant from 1787 onwards. He was, indeed, the person to whom Kant first announced his project for a critique of aesthetic taste (*KGS*: 10/513–16).

Reinhold is an intriguing and important 'Enlightenment' philosopher who had started out as a Jesuit before becoming a Barnabite monk and parish priest, concerned with Catholic reformation and religious toleration. He converted from Catholicism to Protestantism and then embarked on a philosophical trajectory that took him through materialism, atheism, Leibnizianism and Humean scepticism to Kantianism and his subsequent attempts to reform and complete the Kantian system. This led him in 1798 to adopt the standpoint of Fichte and then, even later, to develop a philosophy of language. Reinhold is best known for the writings of his Kantian phase (1787–98), but he had been initiated as a freemason in Vienna in 1783 and his influential account of the 'Hebrew Mysteries' was published in 1786 shortly before his conversion to Kantianism. In it, Reinhold explored the philosophical underpinnings of masonic rituals, equating the concept of 'nature' as the theological deity of natural religion with Isis, the goddess of the Egyptian mysteries. Eighteenth-century freemasonry presented itself as deistic, and Reinhold describes its 'mysteries' in terms of the origins of an ancient and underlying religion out of which the various forms of monotheism evolved.

In Reinhold's text we find not only reference to the veiled image of a goddess at Egypt's ancient capital, Sais, and also to the veiled Isis (Assmann 1997: 118). Reinhold quotes (in translation) the passage on 'Egyptian Rites' from Voltaire's *Essai sur les moeurs et l'esprit des nations* (*Essay on the Customs and Spirit of Nations*) of 1753. Voltaire had made reference to Isis and to two inscriptions—'I am all that is' and 'I am all that is, was, and shall be, and no mortal has ever lifted my veil'—and had also asserted that the Egyptians, the Jews, the Arabs and the Turks all called the most supreme being by a similar sounding name: 'I-ha-ho' or 'I-ha-hou' or simply 'Hou' in the case of the Arabs and the Turks (Voltaire 1753: ch. 22). Reinhold, however, links the meaning of the Hebrew word Jehovah or Yahveh—which he translates quite conventionally as the 'I am that I am' of *Exodus* 3, 14—with the inscription on the statue of Isis. Addressing his fellow freemasons, Reinhold remarks:

> Who amongst us, my brothers, does not know the ancient Egyptian inscriptions: the one on one of the pyramids at Sais: *I am all that is, was, and shall be, no mortal has ever lifted my veil*, and that other

beneath the statue of Isis: *I am what there is* (Ich bin, was da ist)? Who amongst us, my brothers, does not understand the meaning of these words so well—as in earlier times the *Egyptian initiate* must have understood them—and does not know that through them the essential *Being* (Daseyn), the meaning of the name *Jehovah*, is in words expressed?
(Reinhold 1788: 54; Assmann 1997: 118 *corr.*)

According to Reinhold, the veiled goddess at Sais was the deity into whose mysteries Moses was initiated when he was rescued from the Nile by the daughter of the Pharaoh, and brought up as her son in the Egyptian court. In making this claim Reinhold was concerned to show that there is a universal concept of God, but that the rituals that different nations follow are culturally variable and introduce distortions. Thus, Reinhold presents Moses as wanting to initiate his people into the mysteries of nature, but—through despair at the impossibility of instructing a whole people quickly enough to lead them from Egypt back to the promised land—as betraying the underlying universalism of the religion that lay at its heart (Assmann 1997: 122–24). Isis, the supreme deity of the mysteries, becomes Jehovah: the god of the 'chosen people' who was deployed by Moses for nationalistic ends. For Reinhold, what has been lost in the transmission from Egypt to the Hebrews is the underlying deism and the mystery of the 'I am what there is' which demands respect. Reinhold is writing as 'Brother Decius', a freemason, and is purporting to explain various mysteries and rites of the freemasons in which ceremonies of initiation into the temple of Isis played a part. In 1791 similar themes would surface in the libretto of score of Mozart's *The Magic Flute* which also deploys masonic symbolism in relation to Isis and the 'Queen of the Night' (Chailley 1971; Lorraine 1995).

Assmann has argued that Reinhold's narrative that links Moses to Isis is not original and is indebted to a series of textual precursors, including Plutarch, Maimonides, Ralph Cudworth, John Spencer and William Warburton. However, Assmann also demonstrates Reinhold's influence on his German contemporaries, especially Schiller who was one of Reinhold's colleagues at the University of Jena. Indeed, Reinhold is even credited by some scholars with inspiring Schiller's interest in Kant's moral and aesthetic philosophy, especially his theory of the beautiful and the sublime. In '*Die Sendung Moses*' ('The Mission of Moses'), Schiller also deployed the image of a veiled Isis, suggesting (like Reinhold) that the Egyptians once had direct access to 'sublime' truths about 'the unity of God and the refutation of paganism'. The text was published in the journal *Thalia* late in 1790, but re-uses material delivered in a lecture in 1789 (so predating Kant's *Critique of the Power of Judgment* which was sent to press in Spring 1790). In it Schiller credits Reinhold's pseudonymous text. Although Schiller tells us that the key to the Egyptian mysteries is lost, he also indicates that particular symbols and rituals were passed down to Moses by Egyptian priests who had access to the inner sanctum of the temples at Sais and Serapis in Alexandria. Like Reinhold, he elaborates on the passage on the statue of Isis and the pyramid at Sais that could be found in Voltaire:

> Beneath an old statue of Isis one read the words: '*I am what there is*', and on a pyramid at Sais one found the ancient, remarkable inscription: 'I am all, what is, what was, what shall be; no mortal has lifted my veil.' No one was permitted to enter the temple of Serapis who did not bear on his chest or forehead the name Jao—or J-ha-ho—a name resembling in sound the Hebraic Jehova and probably also having the same meaning; and in Egypt no name was spoken with such veneration as this name Jao.
>
> <div align="right">(Schiller 1790; Pfefferkorn 1988: 120 <i>corr.</i>)</div>

Those who were initiated into these mysteries were named 'beholders' or 'ones who intuit' (*Anschauer* or Epoptes) since the discovery 'of a previously hidden truth can be compared to a passage from darkness to light, and perhaps also because they really and truly looked at the newly discovered truths in sensuous images'. In their hymns these beholders praise Jao with the words: '"He is one; self-existent; and to that one all things owe their existence"'.

Schiller's essay starts by emphasising that Christianity and Islam—'the two religions that govern the greatest part of the inhabited earth'—are both utterly dependent on the 'religion of the Hebrews'; but then Schiller seeks to demonstrate that the religion of the 'veiled goddess' underlies all three monotheistic religions. According to Schiller, Moses has betrayed the 'pure deism' of the original worship of the veiled goddess. For Schiller nature and its creator seem to collapse into each other, and are alternatively female (Isis) then male (Jao/Jehovah). But the beholders of the sublime are part of a closed and privileged 'brotherhood' and are male. He thus, in principle, allows access to a 'hidden truth' that might be unveiled via a process of intellectual intuition, and returns to a kind of neoplatonism that privileges the male 'beholder' of the truth that is hidden behind Isis' veil.

This scenario re-appears four years later in Schiller's poem 'The Veiled Image at Sais' ('*Das verschleierte Bild zu Sais*') where it becomes evident that it is no more than a contingent (historical) fact that no man (no male) now alive is sublime enough to negotiate the way out of the darkness, to see the truth in sensuous images—and remain sane (Schiller 1795). The poem opens with a young man whose 'hot thirst' to know 'all' has driven him to Egypt and to Sais. Encountering the veiled image of 'truth', he hears the voice of a goddess who tells him both that 'no mortal shall raise the veil until I myself raise it' and also that 'whoever will, with profane and guilty hand/ lift the holy, forbidden veil beforehand/ ... will *see* the truth'. Schiller's young, daring novice answers defiantly:

'Whatever might be beneath, I'll raise it!'
He shouts in a loud voice: 'It I will see.' See!
Shrieks back a long, mocking echo.

Speaking, he raised the veil.
'What', you ask, 'and what was shown him there?'
I do not know. Unconscious and pale,
The priests found him there the next day
Stretched out at the feet of Isis.
All that he saw and experienced
His tongue never made known. For ever
Was the gladness of his life gone,
And a deep grief took him to an early grave.

Schiller's texts on the veiled Isis were enormously influential. It was from Schiller that Beethoven copied out the two sentences relating to Isis: '*I am what there is*', and '*I am all, what is, what was, what shall be; no mortal has lifted my veil*'. These sat framed on his desk, as a kind of deist manifesto, during the final years of his life, together with a third formula also taken from Schiller that seems to have been added later: '*He is one; self-existent; and to that one all things owe their existence*' (Assmann 1997: 122, 246n.). And half a century later George Eliot would remark dryly in her essay 'A Word for the Germans' that the Germans 'cannot write about drama without going back to the Egyptian mysteries' (Eliot 1963: 389).

Like 'The Mission of Moses', Schiller's poem contributed to a philosophical debate about access to the noumenal, and hence about intellectual intuition and a kind of (male) passivity. In his critical writings, Kant had reserved the capacity of intellectual intuition for unknowable—but not unthinkable—super-human beings (including God). Schiller, by contrast, does not deny man (males) the capacity to see what is hidden behind the veil of appearances; he only denies that there are now males strong enough—sublime enough—to actively seek the truth in the manner of the male hierophant. Unless the male is passive, and is simply granted a vision of the truth behind the veil—by a kind of neoplatonic inspiration—Nature will punish him. For Schiller, access to the sublime involves passivity and activity—along with a *male* viewing position that takes truth and the feminine as the desired object.

Now you (don't) see her

Kant himself returned to the figure of a veiled Isis in a short late essay of 1796, 'On a Recently Prominent Tone of Superiority in Philosophy'. Kant has an unnamed but nevertheless quite specific opponent in sight, Johann Georg Schlosser, in this essay which starts with a dig at masonic '*lodges*', and the notion that superior knowledge is to be equated with 'a sort of unveiling of a mystery', whether it be of an Egyptian, 'monkish' or alchemical type (Kant 1796: 8/389; 2002: 427). Kant mocks such mystagogues who treat themselves as superior because they claim 'a power of *intuition*' that gives them a knowledge of the supersensible that is altogether better than 'a power of knowledge *through concepts*'. This is, Kant sarcastically suggests, as unreasonable as 'the *Arab* or Mongolian' whose nomadic lifestyle leads him to regard the herding of horses and sheep as more admirable than working in a town (1796: 8/389–90). Kant then moves on to contrast worthwhile Aristotelian philosophical 'labour' (*Arbeit*) with recent writers who adopt 'the latest mystico-Platonic idiom', and whose philosophy prioritises ease, passivity, inspiration and intellectual intuition (393, 399). Kant mocks those philosophers who adopt 'the art of the *pseudo-Plato*' and claim '"to approach the goddess of wisdom so closely that one may hear the *rustle* of her robes"' and who '"though unable to lift the veil of Isis, can yet make it so thin that one can *divine* the goddess beneath it"'. Perhaps thinking not only of Schlosser but also of Schiller's 'The Veiled Image at Sais', in which the man who peers behind the veil is punished by madness, Kant sarcastically remarks that 'the platonizing philosopher of feeling' is careful not to make the robe of Isis completely transparent—'otherwise it would be a seeing, which is certainly to be avoided' (399).

Kant then proceeds to satirise the 'pure *metaphysics*' of the 'new Platonist' who relies on analogical reasoning even as he alerts us to '"the danger of the emasculation (*Entmannung*) of a reason become so highly strung through metaphysical sublimation (*Sublimation*) ... "'. By contrast, what has 'emasculated' (*entmannt*) and 'lamed' reason, says Kant in his own voice, is a false relation to the empirical that comes from supposing that we can see beneath Isis' robes. The veiled Isis must remain as inexhaustible labour, and the 'empirical elements' that are supposedly discerned underneath the veil should not be mistaken for universal laws (8/400 *corr.*). Those 'men of might' who have recently claimed 'to have caught this goddess by the hem of her garment and seized hold of her' are simply giving themselves airs (401n.). But there is, Kant says, something on which both sides can agree:

> The veiled goddess, before whom we both bow the knee, is the moral law in us in its inviolable majesty. We hearken to her voice, indeed, and also understand her command well enough; but on listening are in doubt whether it comes from man himself, out of the absolute authority of his own reason, or whether it proceeds from another being, whose nature is unknown to him, and which speaks to man through his own reason.
>
> (8/405).

Thus, in terms of Kant's own earlier use of the Isis imagery and the debates around Reinhold and Schiller, Kant himself seems to suggest that, in contemplating the 'sublime' veil of Isis, what is demanded is a reason of the type that belongs to a manly (unemasculated) male. The apparently penetrative act of intellectual intuition promoted by the neoplatonic mystagogues feminises reason in that it signifies a passive and dependent relationship to the empirical. In terms of the vocabulary of Kant's own critical system, he is suggesting that Nature, the moral law, and the noumenal truth concealed behind the 'veil of Isis' should be treated as 'regulative principles' which cannot be exhausted by any particular experience—not even by the sum of experiences—but which direct us 'to regard all combination in the world *as if* originated from an all-sufficient necessary cause' (*CPR*: A619/B647).

For Kant, it is the faculty of reason that drives man onwards in his quest for certainty and absolute knowledge (A293ff./B249ff.). The regulative principles of reason are 'rules' which direct us in a never-ending and restless search for a basis for reason which needs no further support, and which consequently dictate 'a regress in the conditions for given appearances, in which regress is never allowed to stop with an absolutely unconditioned' (A509/B537). Through the restless probing of reason, these regulative principles extend our understanding of the space–time world and help us fill in the gaps in the phenomenal reality that is created by the 'I'. But it is also this endless searching of reason that brings us face to face with the inexplicable as it reaches out towards the infinite and that which eludes the understanding. The 'manifoldness, order, purposiveness, and beauty' of the world puzzle 'our weak understanding' whilst acting as a kind of lure to reason, and generate the experience of the sublime in which:

> all speech concerning so many and such unfathomable wonders must lose its power to express, all numbers their power to measure, our thoughts themselves all definiteness, and even our thoughts lack boundaries, so that our judgment upon the whole must resolve itself into a speechless, but nonetheless eloquent, astonishment.
>
> (A622/B650)

Although Kant is careful to say that we cannot prove that the unity of nature exists or that there is a god which created it, the 'I', and the drives of reason, create infinite nature (and even the idea of God himself) through its continuous striving.

For Kant, phenomenal nature remains no more than a construct of the transcendental self as it reaches out and seeks to extend its horizons in a restless attempt to attain completion. Phenomenal (empirical) nature must be constructed in such a way that is consistent with its invention by man, the law-giver, but it also needs to be created in such a way as to render it consistent with the laws of a supersensible (and unknowable) God who brought it into existence. The experience of the sublime reminds us of the infinity of nature and of its inexhaustible might. Nature/matter/the law/*what* is created are personified as female. The divine—or semi-divine—formative force that creates nature is not 'emasculated' by this act of creation, but only by a failure to regulate a proper distance between man, the empirical and the moral law. The 'other' that is created as the counterpole to the Kantian transcendental self is not truly alien or strange, but is simply the 'other' of the I. This 'other' is what the transcendental self reaches out towards: it is an elusive fiction that is required to stabilise the 'empirically real', phenomenal—but nevertheless never completely knowable—world that the I fashions on the basis of its sense experience and conceptual apparatus.

Kant's scornful attack on the neoplatonic 'mystagogues' in the 1796 essay did not prevent subsequent German Romantic philosophers from deploying the Isis imagery in ways that depict man as able to access the absolute either via a lifting of the veil or by rendering it transparent (Padilla 1988, 190–201). Thus, similar themes can be detected in '*Die Lehrlinge zu Sais*' ('The Apprentices at Sais'), a story which Novalis started in 1798. Via his hero 'Hyacinth', Novalis identifies with the feminine: lifting the veil of the goddess at Sais and finding truth in the form of 'Roseblossom', the girl he loves. Novalis—who attended lectures on history and philosophy at the University of Jena by both Schiller and Reinhold—seems to echo Schiller, but reverses the implications, since Hyacinth is permitted to 'raise the veil' without punishment or madness.

Novalis allies 'truth' with 'woman', but we should not be misled into thinking that Novalis' celebration of the feminine involves a fundamental abandonment of the links between maleness and sublimity. A fragment from 1798 relating to the story, but eventually excluded, emphasises this point: 'One succeeded—he raised the veil of the goddess at Sais—But what did he see? he saw—miracle of miracles—himself' (Novalis 1978: 234). Hyacinth's discovery of his own self and his union with his female counterpart, Roseblossom, can act as parallels in the different versions of the story, since Novalis' hero retains his identity as a male who simply appropriates the feminine as the object of his own (male) quest. Novalis might seek to transcend normal (masculine, reason-based) access to the truth which is hidden behind the veil of appearances, but femininity and passivity are not his starting point. Rather, Novalis presents us with a hero, male enough (sublime enough) to take nature by force, to seek out the noumenal, and be rewarded with the double blessing of finding his true self and attaining a mystical union with his beloved. It is the supra-rational (but sane) male who achieves sublimity, not the female. Like Kant, Novalis makes the 'other' no more than the counterpart to the masculinised 'I'. But Novalis supposes that it is possible to encounter this sublime 'other' who is hidden behind the veil; for Kant it is the endless attempt to unveil the absolute that generates the empirically real and also the experience of the sublime.

Kant's comments on Isis reveal an interesting tension between his metaphoric deployment of the 'feminine' in relation to the sublime *object* of man's reason and the feminine *subject* who, as we saw at the start of the last chapter, is represented as incapable of 'subduing' sublime 'monsters' on account of her 'slavish' and fearful nature (Kant *RWB*: 6/23n.). Representing the sublime 'other' as a female goddess does not detract from the maleness of the viewing position that Kant's account of the sublime presupposes. The philosopher who searches after the (sublime) truth and the moral law remains paradigmatically male, even as the object of his quest is feminised. Kant's comments link the sublime to the inexhaustible task of forever seeking to uncover nature and the absolute. Like Goethe's *Faust Part Two*—which famously ends with the words 'The Eternal Feminine / Leads us onwards' ('*Das Ewig-Weibliche / Zieht uns hinan*'), Kant's (male) philosopher is drawn onwards and upwards in his pursuit of the ever-elusive feminine Isis, and it is through the pursuit—not through the uncovering—of the absolute that Kant's phenomenal reality is shaped (see Goethe 1833).

'In so far as is Allowed'

In *Moses the Egyptian* Jan Assmann comments on Kant's use of the Isis imagery in the *Critique of the Power of Judgment*, but he does not seem to know Kant's late (and extremely acerbic) essay of 1796. Even his analysis of Kant's remarks on the veiled Isis in the third *Critique* misrepresents Kant on the sublime, since Assmann's interpretation suggests that Kant is to be allied with those who think it possible to see through Isis' veil (Assmann 1997: 129–31). According to Assmann, Kant is indebted to Schiller in his adoption of the 'language of initiation' into the Temple of Isis—a puzzling claim given the date of the publication of Schiller's text—and he also asserts that,

> Kant's main point is to emphasize the initiatory function of the sublime. The holy awe and terror which the sublime inspires in a man serves to prepare his soul and mind for the apprehension of a truth that can only be grasped in a state of emotional arousal.
>
> (131)

Although it might be true of Schiller that the sublime prepares us to see a 'truth', Assmann is mistaken when he suggests that the sublime is similarly configured by Kant. Instead, as we have seen, in Kant's philosophy the sublime teaches us primarily about the power of man's reason and our vocation for freedom. Assmann does, however, make an extremely important point, since he shows how Kant's description of the sublime 'vignette' in Johann Andreas von Segner's *Einleitung in die Naturlehre* (*Introduction to the Natural Sciences*) is seriously misleading, especially if the reader does not have access to the image.

We have seen how Kant claimed that the image in Segner's text can be linked to that most sublime thought, '"I am all that is and that was and that shall be, and no mortal has lifted my veil"' and to the 'inscription over the Temple of *Isis* (Mother *Nature*)' (CPJ: 316n. *corr.*). Adding to, and also correcting the information about the vignette that Assmann most usefully provides, it is evident that Kant was referring to an engraving by the celebrated

German artist Georg Daniel Heumann in the second (1754) edition of Segner's text. Heumann's frontispiece shows a crowned female figure, shrouded in a cloak that is pulled across her face in such a way as to reveal only part of her profile. She is clutching a musical instrument—most probably a zither—as she strides across an ill-defined landscape. There are mountains in the distance, and she is followed by three winged putti who cannot see her face. Behind her is a large, broken, creeper-covered, vase which rests on a large plinth that is inscribed on one side with barely legible Greek lettering and on the other with geometrical shapes. One of the cherubs leans against the pedestal, a finger to his lips in a gesture of silence; one measures the goddess' footsteps with a compass; one lifts the hem of her cloak, pointing with his finger in the direction that the goddess is travelling. In dominant letters across the bottom of the copperplate print we find the Latin inscription '*Qua Licet*': which translates as 'In so far as is Allowed'.

Assmann comments that it is hard to read the image in terms of the veiled image of Sais, and indicates that the artist wanted to show the difficulty of looking Nature/Isis directly in the face and the need to study nature *a posteriori*. But this might not even be a picture of Isis. Although Kant describes the vignette as 'rich in sense', it is unclear which goddess is represented here— probably the divine Aphrodite or Venus who was associated with the zither. Although Isis was often conflated with a number of other goddesses by the Romans, including Aphrodite, it is hard to read the image as Isis whose attributes usually include a horned crown, a round mirror-like disc and sometimes vipers, a bronze rattle or a lotus flower. Heumann is perhaps making reference to Ovid—much quoted (and illustrated) in the eighteenth century—who uses the phrase '*Qua Licet*' in Book 3, Elegy 8 of *Amores* in relation to the inventions of science, the despoiling of the earth after 'the Age of Saturn' (a desecration which is compared to the seducing and unveiling of a previously chaste maiden), and man's greedy aspirations to conquer the skies.

Illustrations of the veiled Isis seem common in scientific and Romantic texts written after Kant, and Assmann provides some illustrations. But Kant's chosen image does not fit the Romantic mould, and his comments on the Egyptians seem in many ways closer to Voltaire than to Reinhold or Schiller. Kant—who was clearly not expert in reading images—was obviously most impressed by the inscription 'Qua Licet' that bans touching more than the hem of the goddess' cloak. Assmann does not comment on the motto, but instead allies Kant with those who believed that a 'secret wisdom' inherited from Egypt is transmitted via the experience of the sublime (Assmann 1997: 134). Through thinking about the image of Isis, Assmann has, in effect, re-invented a misreading of Kant common amongst his contemporaries. It is this type of misreading that Kant is responding to in the abrasively scornful remarks on Isis in the 1796 essay. Kant wants us to understand that his own use of the Isis imagery differs sharply from those who thought it possible to penetrate 'the veil of Isis' via a type of intellectual intuition that Kant regarded as effeminate in its passivity.

Goethe, Schiller and the philosopher Friedrich Schlegel eventually all came to side with Kant in his arguments against the 'mystagogue' Schlosser. Indeed, as we have seen, Goethe expressed his gratitude to Kant for having 'brought us all back from that effeminacy in which we were wallowing' (Cassirer 1918: 270). Nevertheless Schlosser's deployment of the 'unveiling' imagery was by no means atypical of the German Romantic writers who stressed the power of 'intellectual intuition'.

Assmann aligns Kant with the 'European Egyptomania' that reached its climax in the late eighteenth century (Assmann 1997: 143). However, looking across Kant's writings on religion, we can see that, on the whole, Kant's comments on the Egyptian religions are both slight and slighting. Thus in the posthumously published *Lectures on the Philosophical Doctrine of Religion* (delivered between 1783 and 1786) Kant indicates that the religion of the Persians, Indians and other 'heathen peoples' was 'far more bearable' than that of the Egyptians (Kant 1817: 28/1125). Clearly, Kant does not follow Reinhold in believing that the invention of monotheism can be explained in terms of the way in which the historical Moses translated the underlying universals of the Egyptian mysteries into a Hebrew context. For Kant, true monotheism only emerges as Judaic Law becomes mixed with 'foreign (Greek) wisdom' to become something entirely unprecedented in the history of cultures (*RWB*: 6/128, 137).

Despite these drawbacks to the narrative about the cultural construction and transmission of 'Moses' as an 'Egyptian', Assmann does, however, give us enough information for us to see that Reinhold is key to the identification of the sublime with Isis, the goddess of nature, which then sparked a kind of dialogue between Kant and his contemporaries. The issues were the proper relation (or distance) between ideal (sublime) maleness and nature; the question of the relationship between the masculinised sublime (which Kant allies to the moral) and the feminised beautiful (which we have seen Kant representing as either amoral or even as immoral); and the question of how to access the supersensible 'mystery' that lays hidden behind the veil. What matters to Kant insofar as the sublime is not the unveiling of matter, but the incentive to its continued investigation. As Kant's (confusing) comments on the Segner vignette demonstrate, he maintains a bar on accessing the noumenal, and uses the search for the forever unobtainable and sublime absolute as a device for sending man back to measure and reflect on empirical reality.

There are, however, tensions in Kant that meant that he was read—by his contemporaries, as well as by Assmann—as deploying the sublime in a way that allowed the observer of nature and of art to penetrate behind Nature's veil. This meant that Schiller was not alone in turning to Kant, and then trying to 'correct' him. Schelling, Coleridge and Schopenhauer all made similar moves, so that the question of whether a man was male enough/sublime enough/genius enough to lift Isis' veil became a trope of Romantic and post-Romantic writing. Even Hitler would claim in *Mein Kampf* that it is 'Jewish' nonsense to suggest that Nature can be controlled: it is an Aryan task to lift 'one or another corner of her immense and gigantic veil of eternal secrets and riddles' (Hitler 1925–27: 261). Amongst the Aryan peoples is found 'the Prometheus of mankind from whose forehead the bright spark of genius has sprung at all times' and 'illumined the night of silent mysteries'; and the 'concepts of beauty and sublimity' are amongst those picked out by Hitler as important to the Aryan culture which the Jew 'contaminates' as he 'drags men down into the sphere of his own base nature' (263, 296). The history of the concept of the sublime—like the history of the term 'genius'—has become thoroughly intertwined with that of race and ethnicity.

Not just a 'feminine' sublime

Towards the start of this chapter I made reference to Zylinska's '*feminist* discourse of the *feminine* sublime' that is nevertheless entirely uninterested in the question of *female* artists and writers. Indeed, Zylinska indicates that to concentrate on the question of whether women write in the sublime mode would turn her 'project into a "women's thing" (a mere trifle)' and also 'leave the power structure unchanged' (Zylinska 2001: 32). Instead, with a specific appeal to Derrida (on 'woman' as the 'untruth of truth' hidden behind the veil) and also to Hélène Cixous, Zylinska employs the techniques of deconstruction to link what she terms the 'feminine sublime' to 'an ethical moment in which an absolute and indescribable otherness is welcomed' (Zylinska 2001: 14ff., 4). Equating the sublime with that unrepresentable excess which exceeds the grasp of the self as represented in the history of Western thought, Zylinska sets out to mobilise this excess and develop an aesthetics and ethics of the 'feminine sublime' that has the power to disrupt our models of rationality and selfhood.

What the above analysis of Kant and the Romantics on the sublime has shown, however, is that there are several different kinds of excess that relate to the sublime. There is, first, the 'feminine' (Kant's Isis) that draws the masculinised I onwards whilst forever eluding his grasp. There is, second, the 'feminine' of the German Romantics which can be uncovered, but not expressed, by the I; here again the self who searches after truth or his beloved is conceptualised as male and the feminine object is no more than the counterpole to masculinised self. Both these modes of 'feminine' excess are different from that non-sublime otherness that relates to the materiality of the 'female' (the bodies of women); and this *fleshy* mode of embodiment (with its duties of 'fear', of 'care' and of reproducing the species) is also different from those other modes of non-sublime 'otherness' that have been ascribed to 'Oriental' and other 'raced' subjects. The problem is that Zylinska's strategy concerns itself only with the 'feminine'—in its Kantian and post-Kantian modes—and plays down the dilemmas of flesh-and-blood women and other 'raced' humans with respect to the dilemmas they face with regard to their exclusion from the traditions of the aesthetics of the sublime. This is particularly clear in terms of the way Zylinska links the feminine sublime with death and man's fear of death, whilst overlooking the problem that faces the female human whose ontological positioning differs from the male's positioning insofar as her body links her to the Other not only through death, but also in relation to birth.

For her notion of a feminine sublime Zylinska looks to the 'subversive literary practice' of *'écriture féminine'* and, in particular, to the way in which it disturbs our notions of identity and rationality through exploring 'the liminalities, thicknesses and crevices of the linguistic texture' (2001: 33, 34). Drawing also on Lyotard's account of the sublime and his concept of *'décriture'*—"the writing [*écriture*] of the impossible description"'—Zylinska develops a notion of *'décriture féminine'*: 'Contradictory, insubordinate and a-rational, *décriture féminine* is also a discourse of transgression, crossing over the boundaries drawn for the maintenance of the self's identity' (37, 39). Zylinska then turns to Emmanuel Levinas' philosophy which is read as also undermining the self's identity in ways that draw on and also contribute to the discourse of the sublime (72). In Levinas' 'Ethics as First Philosophy', we are told, the primacy of the self is undermined through "*the irruption of the face* into the phenomenal order of appearances"' and through encountering the strangeness of another, fellow human:

> 'in its expression, in its mortality, the face before me summons me, calls for me, begs for me, as if the invisible death that must be faced by the Other, pure otherness, separated, in some way, from any whole, were my business. It is as if that invisible death, ignored by the Other, whom already it concerns by the nakedness of its face, were already "regarding" me prior to confronting me, and becoming the death that stares me in the face.'
>
> (Levinas 1989: 82, 83, quoted Zylinska 71)

As elsewhere in *On Spiders, Cyborgs and Being Scared*, it is clear that for Zylinska the experience of the sublime involves an encounter with something so irredeemably strange and overwhelming that it brings the self face to face with its own death. For Levinas, the encounter with the face of the Other occurs as such a primordial level that it precedes ontology, and Levinas describes his ethics of responsibility for the other as 'first philosophy'. He argues that "'a horror of the other that remains other"' is integral to philosophy, and that the sudden irruption of the other's face into my world is a powerful antidote to the metaphysics and ethics of the West that seeks to reduce the absolute other to a pole of the self. For Levinas it is the stranger (*l'étranger*) who disturbs the 'egology' that is the ontology of classical metaphysics, and thus it is the face of the other (the stranger) that reminds me of my responsibility whilst also providing an ethical disruption to 'the being at home with oneself' (Zylinska: 71).

Zylinska suggests that we follow Derrida's suggestion and read Levinas as offering "'a sort of feminist manifesto'" (Derrida 1997: 44; Zylinska 73). But what Levinas' ethics offers is a manifesto of the *feminine*, not one that is concerned with the bodies or the historical situation of the *female*. Although the Levinasian Other is a human other which cannot be identified with the Isis of Kant or the male Romantics, it nevertheless suffers from many of the same drawbacks. Thus, Levinas links the alterity of the Other to the 'feminine' which he links to 'virginity, voluptuousness, eroticism and pretence', as well as to the 'modest' and 'the passivity of the "Beloved"' (Zylinska: 72–73). In Levinas' philosophy 'absolute' otherness remains an abstract affair insofar as all humans are similarly positioned in relation to death and to the fear of death that irrupts by means of the face. What Levinas' philosophy cannot deal with is a subject-position that can incorporate otherness within it in a more physical way, and so does not find the 'naked' face of the stranger the starting point for the relationship between the 'other' and the I. What Levinas' philosophy leaves out of account is those modes of excessiveness that are bound up with the specificities of the 'otherness' of the body that is deemed capable of pregnancy and birth.

Since otherness is already incorporated within the flesh-and-blood physicality that is the normative subject-position for *females* in the history of European culture, Levinas' ethics of respect for the face of the other overlooks the self–other relationship seen from the position of the female subject. In a sense Zylinska has recognised the difficulties Levinas has in dealing with sexed bodies (74ff.), and she tries to add in Luce Irigaray's objections to the way that Levinas represents the other in non-corporeal—and non-sexual—terms. Thus, in her 'Questions to Emmanuel Levinas' Irigaray objects:

> Who is the other, if the other of sexual difference is not recognised or known? Does it not mean in that case a kind of mask or lure? Or an effect of the consumption of an other [*Autre*]? But how is this transcendence defined?
>
> Furthermore, this non-definition of the other, when the other is not considered to have anything to do with sexual difference, gives rise to an infinite series of substitutions, an operation which seems to me to be non-ethical. No one can be radically substituted for the other, without depriving the other of identity.
>
> (Irigaray 1990b: 181–82, quoted Zylinska: 74)

I take Irigaray to be indicating that the 'other' that Levinas claims to respect is a *feminine* 'lure' (analogous to Kant's sublime Isis) and, as such, serves as a 'mask' for a different kind of 'other': the flesh-and-blood *female* who falls outside the Levinasian frame. Levinas cannot see women in their sexed specificity, and substitutes another kind of otherness (the neutered face) for women's flesh that is deemed so material as to be incapable of transcendence.

Zylinska quotes Irigaray and seems to register her objection, but then quickly moves back to Derrida and the ethics of the 'feminine' in a way that shows she has missed Irigaray's point (Zylinska: 79ff.). Zylinska's concern is to use excess to destabilise the ego. But the 'I' that she seeks to disrupt is already sexed as normatively male, and there is thus no emphasis on the puzzles that arise with regard to transcendence from the perspective of the female human who does not have to 'welcome' an 'absolute and indescribable otherness' in the manner of Levinas. For the pregnant mother 'the other' or 'the stranger' is already within, as Iris Marion Young's phenomenological account of her relationship with her own pregnant body and the birth of her child makes clear:

> Pregnancy challenges the integration of my bodily experience by rendering fluid between what is within, myself, and what is outside, separate. I experience my insides as the space of another, yet my own body. . . .

> The birthing process entails the most extreme suspension of the bodily distinction between inner and outer. . . . Through pain and blood and water this inside thing emerges between my legs, for a short time both inside and outside me. Later I look in wonder at my mushy middle and at my child, amazed that this yowling, flailing thing, so completely different from me, was there inside, part of me.
>
> (Young 1990: 163)

As I have argued in *The Phenomenal Woman*, an ontology of the *female*—not *feminine*—subject entails thinking the normality of the body that can give birth. Without ever implying that every woman either could or should give birth, what is necessary is to theorise natality and the relationship between I and its 'other' who is—or might be—found embodied within. The 'welcome' that is (or is not) extended to the foetus is by no means equivalent to the one demanded by the face of the absolute stranger in Levinas' ethics, and neither does death and the fear of death seem to be the link between the birth-giving mother and her potential offspring. I doubt that the fear of death is as 'universal' as Zylinska claims, but even if this were universal it would also be necessary to think the strangeness—and sublimity—of birth from the point of view of the embodied female subject.

What has disappeared from Zylinska's account is the birth-giving body as a different kind of excess: one that is linked to materiality and the *female*, as opposed to the 'feminine' otherness of the irruptive face. It is not that it is illegitimate to explore the notion of a 'feminine' sublime, but a concern with that feminine lure—Kant's veiled Isis—which acts as the 'other' of the male self is not identical with my own concern with the 'female' sublime, and this is because 'femaleness' is linked to embodiment in a way that 'femininity' is not. The unreachable 'otherness' of Isis is a necessary adjunct to Kant's system, and mobilising it only gives us access to the feminine lure—not to the materiality of the bodies of women for whom transcendence is not duty and immanence the ideal.

As we have seen, in Kant femaleness is bound up with that which is merely material and hence *beneath* personhood, not the kind of excessive 'otherness' that is bound up with the infinity of the cosmos or nature that acts as a horizon for—and a threat to—the (male) self. Zylinska's emphasis on the 'feminine' sublime does—like the traditional aesthetics of the sublime that it seeks to subvert—leave materiality behind as it privileges that which is 'other' to and 'beyond' the masculinised self. Fleshy difference and other material and culturally specific forms of exclusion also disappear through the adoption of a Levinasian frame which operates at too abstract and universal a level to capture the *philosophical* problems which are posed by thinking of the self as not detached from his or her familial, social and historical relationships, and also as not just contingently embodied.

I am not arguing that there is a 'real' essential biological difference that divides all males from females or one 'race' or ethnic group from all other groups or races. Our way of thinking sexual difference is—and has always been—subject to historical development and variation; and, as the last chapter on Kant's views of 'race' made clear, our 'modern' concepts of race and ethnicity are of very recent origin, and are also (fortunately) capable of being disturbed and displaced. However, it seems to me that the adoption of a model of a 'feminine' sublime is by no means the best way to rethink the 'excess' that has fallen outside the current imaginative and conceptual framework for imagining and theorising selfhood.

My own strategy is, therefore, *not* to argue that all female subjects or all Arab or black or 'raced' subjects must respond to the sublime in ways that would define them as a group in an entirely homogeneous way. My approach does, however, involve looking at the *specificity* of the exclusions relating to human differences, and considering, for example, how *women* artists and writers have responded to their positioning as 'other' and as barred from the sublime by virtue of their all-too-material bodies, as well as at the new modes of the sublime that have emerged out of these tensions. An analogous approach could also be adopted for artists and writers who have been assigned by our culture to one of the other 'race' or 'ethnic' groups. This would not involve treating the new 'raced' sublime in terms of unrepresentable excess, but in terms of the ways that those in the marginalised groups had sought to extend the boundaries of the effable and, in so doing, extended both the horizons of art and also our ways of conceptualising the self–other boundary.

It seems to me that this is what Paul Gilroy does in *The Black Atlantic*, since the account of 'the slave sublime' that he offers there does not simply stop with registering the way blackness has been excluded or allied with 'sites of ineffable terror in the imagination' (Gilroy 1993: 218). Instead Gilroy argues that we should investigate 'patterns of social remembrance' and 'the effects of protracted familiarity with ineffable, sublime terror on the development of a political (anti)aestheticism' (215). Identity itself is presented as fluid and as capable of being transformed as the emergent traditions and responses resonate together and generate historical change. Thus, Gilroy is concerned to develop a model of diasporic identity which pays attention to 'race' without seeking to reify it, and which also 'doesn't try to fix ethnicity absolutely but sees it instead as an infinite process of identity construction' (223).

Gilroy's own focus in *The Black Atlantic* is on the analogies between the experiences of blacks and of Jews in respect to the shared experience of collective pain. In the last chapter, I suggested that a rather different analysis would be required for Muslims, Arabs, 'Orientals' and other groups traditionally excluded from canonical accounts of sublime experience. But Gilroy's approach does, nevertheless, point to what is required. For Gilroy, the raced 'other' is neither simply one of the *parerga* to the systems of philosophy, nor is she a forever elusive 'excess' that haunts an 'I' which is forever fixed and stable in its identity. Instead race and ethnicity are made integral to the 'I', and difference is registered at the material, historical and cultural levels.

We need to return to history and detail the racial and cultural baggage employed to exclude whole races and peoples from the transcendence of the sublime; and, alongside this, we also need to investigate the range of responses by those who have been excluded. It is by these means that we can detect not merely the 'other' that haunts the margins of philosophical discourse as an ineffable excess, but also learn to recognise the 'other' who is present—but, in effect, invisible and silenced—*within* the history and discourses of Western modernity. In the last chapter of this book, I will indicate how, in *Philosophy in a Time of Terror*—in a dialogue on 'September 11' which was published not long before his own death in 2004—Derrida also seems to recognise the need for a more historical and political approach to these questions of the 'other' (Borradori 2003). But, as Anidjar's efforts to document 'A history of the enemy' in *The Jew, The Arab* makes clear, insofar as Islamic, Arab and 'Oriental' subjects are concerned, we are lacking much of the basic historical scholarship that would permit to see these 'others within'. In the next chapter I will, therefore, be focusing on the question of the 'female sublime' and seeking to distinguish this further from the 'feminine sublime'.

6

OURSELF BEHIND OURSELF, CONCEALED

To understand the severity of the problem facing women writers and artists who attempt the sublime it is necessary to fill in one other aspect of the history that links the female to base matter and refuses them access to the sublime. The anti-material bias in the aesthetics of the sublime as it developed in the eighteenth century can be seen in James Beattie's fanciful genealogy of the word 'sublime' in his *Dissertations Moral and Critical* of 1783: 'Grammarians are not agreed about the etymology of the word *sublime*. The most probable opinion is, that it may be derived from *supra* and *limus;* and so denotes literally the circumstance of being raised *above* the *slime*, the *mud*, or the *mould*, of this world' (Ashfield and de Bolla 1996: 180). This distaste for materiality continued in the nineteenth century, especially amongst those Romantic poets and philosophers who drew on alchemical symbolism. Despite the fact that many of these writers privileged the 'feminine', the alchemical metaphors indicate not only an aversion to matter but also a bias against the female, since in alchemy the female was aligned with 'the *slime*, the *mud*, or the *mould*, of this world' that was left behind as the vapours and spirits rose upwards during the process of alchemical transmutation.

The alchemical input into the language of the sublime is clearly registered in seventeenth-century dictionaries of the English language. Thus in Edward Phillips' *The New World of English Words* (1658), we find: 'Sulimation [sic.] (Lat.) a raising or carrying up on high: also a Chemical Operation, wherein dry exhalations ascending upward, stick to the sides of the Alembick' followed immediately by 'Sublimity, (Lat.) Height' (Wood 1972: 189–90). An alembic was the gourd-shaped glass vessel used in distilling during chemical and alchemical procedures; within it, base matter was 'sublimed', 'sublimated' or underwent 'sublimation' as it was heated in a metal crucible to produce a vapour that rose upwards, resolidifying on cooling into the purified sublimate. The alchemical significance of the language of sublimation never went away, although it is not much stressed in English Dictionaries from the eighteenth century onwards and is also curiously underplayed in recent scholarly attempts to trace the origin of the word 'sublime', even where the alchemical resonances are clearly present in the quotations that are examined (see, for example, Wood 1972).

The alchemical process involved an attempt to turn material that is 'cold', 'wet', 'sterile' and 'female' into a perfection of form (gold and androgynous) by first rendering it hot and dry (male). In alchemy the female is explicitly linked to matter; and to the imperfect: to blackness, coldness, wetness, inertness and the unformed (the changeable). According to the alchemists, all metals are composed of two immediate components: sulphur and mercury (quicksilver), although Paracelsus (1493–1541) adds a third element, salt. As Nicolas Salomon put it in the *Dictionaire hermetique*, published anonymously in 1695: 'the masculine or male sperm is sulphur'; 'the feminine or female sperm is mercury' (Salomon 1695: 190). For Salomon, mercury has mystical properties, but is by itself sterile: 'it resembles, say the philosophers, that of women who are too cold and wet, who would be relieved of their sterility if they were purged and heated, as Mercury is when it is purged in accordance with the rules' (191).

'Sublimation' involved a process of transformation of the imperfect and moveable into 'very subtle particles that attach themselves to the vessel' by the application of heat and the production of 'dry' (male) atoms (Salomon: 191). The transformation into the 'androgyne of the philosophers' occurs,

> when the male and female are united in the philosopher's mercury, i.e. when the two sexes are joined in the colour black very-black, which comprises perfect putrefaction. Here water is converted into earth, and the ancient enemies are made friends. And when earth turns into air, it becomes white, and when fire, red. And peace is made among the four qualities, that is cold, warm, dry and humid.
>
> (9)

In other texts—such as the anonymous German text *Hermaphroditic Child of the Sun and Moon* (L.C.S.: 1752)—the word 'hermaphrodite' is used instead of 'androgyne' for the perfection of form that combines male and female aspects, active and passive powers.

In this complex process of alchemical transformation, matter gradually attains perfection and becomes hot and dry and gaseous. The whole process of 'sublimation' is defined as an 'elevation' of matter (Salomon: 191). The prepared and heated female 'sperm' turns mercury (quicksilver) into a 'vegetative power capable of receiving the form of its spirit and silver which is the soul and which it receives by the operation of spirit' (190). Thus, in alchemy passive and 'sterile' matter (female) is worked on by an active spirit or substance that is linked to heat and sulphur (male). The alchemical model of creation is hylomorphic, so that 'essence' is secured by the operation of spirit (male) on *hyle* or matter (female) with the aim of producing the elusive pure being: the unity of opposites that Salomon defines as the androgyne, but which also sometimes appears in other texts as the bisexual hermaphrodite. The whole model works at macro- and micro-levels: at the level of the body (which is made analogous to the alchemist's still); in alchemy itself; and even at the level of the world which is also presented through models of heating and condensation. Thus, the 'philosopher's steel' is also linked to 'the menstruum of the world' (*le menstruë du monde*) in ways that pick up an Aristotelian understanding of the body and of 'menses' in particular (2).

To understand this curious model it is necessary to emphasise that the ancient Greeks understood the processes of production and creation in terms of the shaping of pre-existent matter which was conceptualised as chaotic and heterogeneous until unified and rendered harmonious by its relationship to form. Production was compared to reproduction, but birth itself was also thought of in hylomorphic terms. According to Aristotle, matter (*hyle*) was contributed by the female who was linked with becoming and the not-yet-perfect. Matter needed to be given shape (*morphe*) by a formative power that was exerted from outside, through the seed or sperm of the male that contributed the defining *logos* or formula that makes a species or genera distinctive (its essence). Only by such a process of hylomorphic moulding could continuity of form be passed on to subsequent generations (Allen 1985; Laqueur 1990).

The linking of the 'female' to 'matter' is evident in Aristotelian biology and in the subsequent neo-Aristotelian and Galenic accounts of the reproductive processes that came to dominate Europe until the eighteenth century. Of the four basic qualities—hot, cold, wet and dry—the female was said to be characterised by coldness and wetness, whereas growth and the attaining of perfection was seen as a product of maleness and heat. In the case of humans, menstrual bleeding was seen as evidence of female sterility and lack of formative force, and was interpreted as the expulsion of unheated and unshaped matter from within the womb. In the Renaissance this basically Aristotelian model of human embodiment mingled with more mystical notions of hermaphroditism and androgyny that entered alchemy through the influence of neoplatonism (Maclean 1980).

In the *Symposium* Plato had mythologised a perfect form or 'roundness' of being through an account of the origins of erotic love and of the creation of the world that is put into the mouth of the character Aristophanes (Plato *c*.385 BCE: 190b–193e). Although in Aristophanes' narrative the most perfect love was the search of the male homosexual for a lost 'other half' that was also male, Plato also indicated that there were original male–female dyads (the hermaphrodites) which engendered an inferior erotic quest that is heterosexual and procreative. In the Christian and neoplatonic take-up of Plato it was the search for a lost bisexual completeness that was privileged above the male–male and female–female searches. In the alchemical tradition the most pure matter (gold) and the production of a perfect and spiritualised type of being—the hermaphrodite or androgyne—was also the goal.

Within alchemy, neoplatonic mysticism combined with elements of Aristotelian biology in which the female was regarded as a deficient male. Further modifications to the Aristotelian framework came from Arab, Egyptian and Chinese input into the traditions of alchemy. Instead of Aristotle's four elements—

earth, air, fire, water—as the ultimate constituents of the cosmos, came an emphasis on naturally occurring elements and metals. These included mercury (also called quicksilver) and yellow sulphur (also called brimstone) which was originally collected from inside volcanoes. Alchemists recognized sulphur as a mineral substance that can be melted and burned so that it forms gases and extremely viscous amber-coloured liquid. By contrast, mercury is a fairly unreactive metal which was used, amongst other things, to dissolve numerous metals, and to extract gold dust from rocks by dissolving the gold and then boiling off the mercury. Thus, sulphur (hot, dry, associated with the inside of volcanoes, changed by fire) came to signify maleness, and mercury (cold, wet, formless, moveable, fusible, but unchanged in the fire) came to signify the female. It was the male element, sulphur, that the alchemists sought to change into a new compound through the introduction of heat. Indeed, it was only the male element that was capable of being 'sublimed' into gold.

This alchemical tradition fed into the aesthetic tradition of writing about the sublime. These links are especially prevalent within German Romanticism where we find a heady mixture of Kantianism, neoplatonism and alchemical symbolism, producing an emphasis on androgyny as a necessary condition for poetic creation and genius. It would be a mistake to suppose that, because German uses different terms for the aesthetic concept of the sublime (*das Erhabene*) and the process of sublimation (*sublimieren*), the alchemical background did not impact on German aesthetics and philosophy during the eighteenth century. The relevance of the alchemical associations of the term 'sublime' to the aesthetic literature on *das Erhabene* and *die Erhabenheit*—both signifying elevation as well as sublimity in the aesthetic sense—was well known to earlier generations of German-language writers. Indeed, in Chapters 8 and 9 I will comment on the way that Nietzsche also draws on this tradition, even as he rejects the Romantics' linking of the feminine to the sublime.

Novalis is particularly important in this respect. His notebooks are full of comments on minerals, and he earned his living during his (short) life as a Salt-Mine Inspector in Saxony. He regarded mining as a (mystical) art that kept him in touch with the stars and the planets and the old powers of the earth (Rommel 1998). Some of this is reflected in the song that the miner sings in his (unfinished) novel *Heinrich von Ofterdingen* (Novalis 1802: ch. 5). In this song, the miner is in love with the earth and descends deep into 'her womb' where be becomes 'fully intimate' and 'allied' with her: 'By her he is inflamed / As if she were his bride'. But the miner starts out as the masterful 'lord of earth' and in the last stanza the miner is back 'atop the mountains / The joyful lord of the world' once again. The miner's happiness comes not from material wealth, but from the fact that 'He guides the flow of gold / Into his King's abode' (Pfefferkorn 1988: 102–3 *corr.*). It seems at the start of the poem that the male I longs to merge with the feminine other that is the object of his desire, but, like the male poet, the miner reasserts his position of mastery, utilising the alchemical gold and feminine materiality for male ends. As in the case of

Novalis' desire to see behind the veil of Isis, there is a longing for the feminine 'other', but the feminine is incorporated so that it becomes an aspect of the male self. What is privileged is the androgynous male who attains femininity as the object of his mystical and alchemical quest, but this has nothing at all to do with the all-too-material and fleshy bodies of *women* who were denied the same kind of transcendence (Battersby 1989).

The pro-male bias in the language of sublimation can be seen more than a century later in the psychoanalytic writings of Sigmund Freud. As Norman Brown has pointed out, Freud adopts the language of sublimation (*Sublimierung*) to explain how some forms of neurosis can be culturally productive and enable the creative genius to produce great art. Although Brown is critical of Freud's theory, he registers that it was a 'sound instinct' that made Freud adopt the term 'sublimation' with all the connotations that attach to it from religion and poetry. Quoting Swift on religious enthusiasm Brown defines sublimation as a '"lifting up of the soul or its Faculties above Matter"' and claims that it involves 'an attempt to be more than man' and to become immortal: 'Sublimation thus rests upon mind–body dualism, not as a philosophical doctrine but as a psychic fact implicit in the behaviour of sublimators, no matter what their conscious philosophy may be' (Brown 1959: 143).

For Freud, sublimation is one of the means whereby the ego protects itself against illness and is also the means whereby an artist 'finds a way back to reality' through the displacement of sexual energy into creativity (Freud 1916–17: 390; 423). As Brown explains, there are tensions in Freud's account (Brown: 126ff.). However, one thing is clear, the healing aspects of sublimation are not open to all, but only to gifted individuals:

> Not every neurotic has a high talent for sublimation; one can assume of many of them that they would not have fallen ill at all if they had possessed the art of sublimating their instincts. ... It must further be borne in mind that many people fall ill precisely from an attempt to sublimate their instincts beyond the degree permitted by their organization ... .
>
> (Freud 1912: 119; quoted Kofman 1970: 159)

What also needs to be 'borne in mind' is that, according to Freud's theory, women are unlikely to be amongst the group of lucky individuals who are able to protect themselves against neurotic illness by sublimating their bodily instincts as literature or art.

Thus, in a passage where Freud repeats the accusation—discussed in Chapter 3—that 'women must be regarded as having little sense of justice', he goes on to add that 'We also regard women as weaker in their social interests and as having less capacity for sublimating their instincts than men' (Freud 1933: 432). Freud claims that culture comes from the re-direction of the instinctive forces, especially sexual drives, which are 'sublimated (*sublimiert*)—that is to say, they are diverted from their sexual aims and directed to others that are socially higher and no longer sexual' (Freud 1916–17: 47–48). From the conjunction of these two claims, it follows that the Freudian woman will be psychically unsuited for the tasks of cultural production as opposed to those of biological reproduction.

This is, indeed, what Freud (infamously) claims in the 1933 lecture on 'Femininity' (*Weiblichkeit*) in which he refuses mature women the same ability to sublimate their instincts as the males:

> Shame, which is considered to be a feminine achievement *par excellence* ... has as its purpose, we believe, concealment of genital deficiency. ... It seems that women have made few contributions to the discoveries and inventions in the history of civilization; there is, however, one technique which they may have invented—that of plaiting and weaving. If that is so, we should be tempted to guess the unconscious motive for the achievement. Nature herself would seem to have given the model which this achievement imitates by causing the growth at maturity of the pubic hair that conceals the genitals. The step that remained to be taken lay in making the threads adhere to one another, while on the body they stick into the skin and are only matted together.
>
> (1933: 430)

Women's 'shame' produces their own real cultural achievement—weaving—and even this is not ascribed to sublimation, but to the imitation of nature. Freud's women lack the bodily energies and drives that 'sublime' sexual energies into art.

There is an anti-female bias built into Freud's account of the origins of art, and this reveals itself in his deployment of the language of sublimation which involves a denigration of the merely bodily (and the bodies of women in particular). It was not that Freud delved deeply into the alchemical underpinnings for the language of sublimation—as Carl Gustav Jung did later, in ways that also combined a eulogy of the 'feminine' with a lethal bias against the merely female—but Freud inherited this vocabulary and bias from the German Romantic philosophers and poets whose anti-female ideal of 'feminine' androgyny incorporated the language and symbolism of alchemy (see Jung 1929–54; Jung 1944). For Freud, as for Kant, women are normatively trapped within immanence and debarred from transcendence—except that the Kantian woman was disqualified from enjoyment of the sublime, whereas the Freudian woman belongs to the culturally sterile sex and is refused the power of sublime creation. Freud, Kant and the alchemical tradition are in some respects surprisingly coincident. In all three *femaleness* is linked with materiality, immanence and the non-transcendent. Sublimation and sublime art are linked to the male. As we will now see, the psychoanalytic version of this framework that links great art to the displaced sexual energies of males still had resonance at the end of the twentieth century—even amongst some of the advocates of a 'female', 'feminist' or 'feminine' sublime.

The suffocated sublime

It is now time to turn to a consideration of women writers, to see how they negotiate the traps that the sublime presents to the female sex. I am not, of course, alone in doing this, and Timothy Gould is amongst those who, in recent years, have sought to bring feminist perspectives to bear on the Kantian sublime (Gould 1995: 66). Gould registers that accounts of the sublime have become 'entangled with masculinist ideology and sensibility', and seeks to avoid these snares whilst also registering that 'the theories and discourse of the sublime were initially the province of male writers' and that the accounts these writers gave of the sublime 'were marked by the masculine experience within which the accounts were arrived at' (70, 71). Using the theoretical frame of Eve Kosofsky Sedgwick (1986) and making reference to such writers as Charlotte Brontë (1816–55) and Emily Dickinson (1830–86), Gould suggests that the underlying experience of the sublime has the same content and structure in women and men, but that historically speaking there was a 'blockage' in the expression and underlying experience in the case of women writers.

For Gould, it would seem, the notion of a 'female sublime' involves a kind of internal contradiction, since the historical condition of being a woman and the experience of the sublime pull in different directions, so that historically the energies of women writers have been deflected away from the genre of writing the sublime. I am sympathetic to much of Gould's analysis—especially to his concern with locating the condition of being a woman in a historical and social context. As we will see, however, Gould continues to conceptualise the self and its experience in masculinist terms, and an influential psychoanalytic model underlies Gould's account of the necessary failure of female poets and writers with respect to the sublime. As we will see later, an oedipalised model of self-identity has also infected some other advocates of a specifically female sublime. The literary critics and cultural theorists whose theories I will consider here continue to think identity in terms of a model that takes the male subject as norm.

Gould argues that the intensity of the experience of the sublime—which 'was (and often still is) bounded by wonder, awe, and dread'—produces a need for a language in which to express it and an audience to address (68, 75). The need is so great and the feeling so forceful that without a means of communicating the response to the sublime to an auditor or a reader, the experience itself is blocked. Women writers of the sublime found themselves silenced through the lack of an audience, experiencing a 'sense of suffocation', with the drive for expression that would otherwise lead women to produce sublime works of poetry and fiction redirected elsewhere (76). The fact that women writers are drawn to 'the imagery of the Gothic, with its live burials and other uncanny terms of isolation' is, Gould suggests, not 'a merely "psychological" condition or an episode of taste possessing merely historical interest', but is bound up with the very condition of being a woman in our culture. This leads to the production of 'radically new forms of poetry and fiction' that cannot be categorised as either Romantic, modern or postmodern (76). Thus, Gould finds in the poetry of Emily Dickinson 'the Kantian sublime, without the instigation of nature—but also without much possibility of being communicated to an audience' (82).

Here, once again, it seems to me that there is much that is right about Gould's approach. However, his actual description of Dickinson's poetic achievements not only underestimates the communicative power of her verse, but also situates it in a frame that seems inappropriate to her textually subversive manoeuvrings. Gould recognises that Dickinson's poetry is not a direct response to nature in the manner of the Kantian sublime. But he does not register how Dickinson also disturbs the isolation of the Kantian 'I' and the way that it transcends terror and materiality through the intervention of reason. These deviations are so profound that it seems odd that Gould should situate Dickinson poetry as a kind of failed sublime, which chokes and suffocates in its failure to communicate the experience of the 'I'.

> One need not be a Chamber—to be Haunted—
> One need not be a House—
> The Brain has Corridors—surpassing
> Material Place—
>
> Far safer, of Midnight Meeting
> External Ghost
> Than its interior Confronting—
> That Cooler Host.
>
> Far safer, through an Abbey gallop,
> The Stones a'chase—
> Than Unarmed, one's a'self encounter—
> In lonesome Place—
>
> Ourself behind ourself, concealed—
> Should startle most—
> Assassin hid in our Apartment
> Be Horror's least.
>
> The Body—borrows a Revolver—
> He bolts the Door—
> O'erlooking a superior spectre—
> Or More—

(Dickinson 1975: 670, p. 333)

As we see from this poem written by Dickinson some time around 1863, there is no emphasis on an I that encounters an infinite and inexpressible otherness that is outside or beyond the self in the manner of the Kantian sublime. On the contrary, in this poem otherness is internalised and is within the embodied mind. Here, at least, Dickinson's poetic voice does not transcend fear, but self-consciously employs the literary devices of the gothic and the grotesque to manage fear actively—not in the cowardly fashion of a Kantian female who is banned from the sublime. Kant's account of the mastery of nature through a transcendent or disembodied I is not operative in this text. The poetic voice situates itself alongside materiality: its 'Brain' is the 'Chamber', which is haunted, and there is no transcendent or transcendental self looking out over the 'lonesome Place'. In fact there is no first-person subject anywhere in this text; instead there is a 'one' that moves into an 'our' since the one contains within itself the bodies and ghosts of the others that haunt it: 'Ourself behind ourself, concealed'. It is the unseen phantoms in the dark corridors of the brain that terrify, making the 'one' into an 'ourself'.

In the last stanza a (phantasmic) body acts by picking up the revolver, but it is impossible to tell if the 'he' who bolts the door has the same body as the one that handles the weapon. The number of spectres is indeterminate, as is also the problem of which body or ghost is 'superior' and 'O'erlooking' the others. The persistent use of spatial metaphors is reminiscent not so much of Kant's transcendent and transcendental subject that looks out over the sublime landscape from a position of mastery, but of Kant's use of, and comments on, the German term *Frauenzimmer* that links the condition of being female to physical sequestration (Kant 1764–65: 20/69; 1991: 55). Since *Zimmer* means 'room' or 'frame', the eighteenth-century German word (which is now regarded as derogatory) shrinks a woman to the place that she occupies and, in Kantian terms, confines her within the framework of the spatio-temporal. Appropriately enough, Kant registers this spatial confinement in *Remarks in the Observations of the Feeling of the Beautiful and Sublime* which comprises, as we have seen, the notes in which Kant most explicitly refuses women the capacity for the experience of the sublime. Dickinson's voice moves between the merely bodily—'the Brain'—and the spiritual, the 'Corridors—surpassing / Material Place'. But although the voice stresses spatial and material confinement, we find within the interior of the chamber new passageways and openings that are closed off to the Kantian subject in the experience of the sublime.

Gould wants to remain within a Kantian frame for handling the sublime, but he does not seem to recognise how inappropriate it is to align the Kantian model of 'universal communicability' with Dickinson's textual playfulness. For Kant the pleasure in the sublime originates in the defeat of human understanding. Integral to the enjoyment of this defeat is the imagination of a community of similarly isolated subjects: each alone with its pleasures, but each responding to the power of the infinite or the apparently boundless other with satisfaction, not terror or despair. Gould suggests that women's understanding, manner of expression and modes of experience are more cut off—less able to be communicated—than those of the males. But Dickinson's 'one' is not cut off from all others in the same way as Kant's. The poetic voice that speaks in 'One need not be a Chamber' is already an 'ourself'. As Ellen Moers long ago made clear, although Dickinson's life seems one of seclusion and confinement, she does not write in literary isolation. Her poetry involves a communication with other authors whose poetry and words have been internalised and made part of her poetic persona or self. Thus, many of her poems involve a kind of improvisation or an elaboration of the poetry of Elizabeth Barrett Browning, especially the heroine–poet whose life is narrated in *Aurora Leigh*—so much so Moers asserts that 'the Dickinson poems serve almost as arias in rhyme to break up the onrushing blank verse recitative of *Aurora Leigh*' (Moers 1963: 59).

Gould seems to suggest that the sublime is a universal experience that is—or that has the capacity to be—shared by all, if only women and other socially oppressed groups were less socially 'suffocated'. But it is worth stressing that this is not what Kant himself says. For Kant the sublime is a normative ideal and, as I argued in Chapter 2, the emphasis on the 'universal communicability' of the pleasure of the sublime is not a claim about the capacity of all to share the pleasure, but an implicit appeal to the judgement of the paradigm manly (and appropriately educated and racially superior) male. In contrast with Kant, Gould treats the communicability of the sublime empirically, perhaps because he has incorporated within his account a psychoanalytic reading of Kant's aesthetics of the sublime. Thus, in a revealing footnote, Gould expresses his debt to Neil Hertz, the influential psychoanalytic literary critic, as he notes: 'the most convincing recent accounts suggest that the sublime occurs in the first instance not as masculine power *tout court* but as paternal power' (Gould: 85 n.14).

Oedipal imaginings

Hertz had set out to interpret Kant, and the sublime more generally, in terms of underlying dynamic forces operating in the unconscious which can be traced back to oedipal power struggles that occur both between fathers and their sons and also within the emergent self. Asserting that all humans in our culture conceive power first and foremost in terms of a father's relationship with his offspring, Hertz treats the writer of the sublime as an ego who is locked in a struggle with death, and who in 'the sublime turn' is carried away from death, emerging as a unified, free and victorious entity. Thus, for example, in 'A Reading of Longinus', Hertz's first essay on the question of the sublime, he analyses the sublime in terms of an agonistic competition between self-unity, on the one hand, and death which would overwhelm the self and fragment it (Hertz 1973: 9). But this strong claim—which Hertz then seeks to generalise—relies on a detailed analysis of the ode by Sappho that exemplified the sublime for Longinus. Hertz's analysis does, however, simply ignore the fact that

Longinus offers us an example of a *woman* poet 'Lost in the love trance'. It is Hertz, not Longinus, who implicitly genders this emergent ego as male and treats the paradigmatic I as a man who is confronting his own death (Freeman 1995: 20–22). For Longinus, it is the woman poet's love for another woman that shatters the self into a collection of trembling, sweating, faltering elements: 'Do you not marvel how she seeks to make her mind, body, ears, tongue, eyes, and complexion, as if they were scattered elements strange to her, join together in the same moment of experience?' (Longinus: 17–18).

Hertz conflates Longinus with the Romantics as he sidelines the female–female and mother–child bondings that are operative within the Longinian sublime. Indeed, Hertz's blindness to the role of women in the Longinian scheme even stretches to describing another of Longinus' paradigm examples of the sublime—Euripides' treatment of Orestes—as the treatment of a 'parricide' (Hertz 1973: 9). Technically, this might be defensible, given the definition of parricide in the *Shorter Oxford English Dictionary*: 'One who murders his father or either parent or other near relative'. However, the refusal of the exact term—'matricide'—which could capture the specificity of Orestes' act is striking. Hertz provides us with a model of psychic relations which is, on the surface, gender neutral; but which, in reality, takes the son's antagonistic relationship with his father as the paradigm for all tensions, oppositions and bondings that exist between the child and others. A hidden matricide is the underpinning for Hertz's account of the sublime: Clytemnestra disappears. And what vanishes even more completely is the possibility of the mother symbolising power to the young infant or later on in the development of the child.

Hertz's 1973 essay on Longinus was an originary contribution to a sequence of writings by American psychoanalytic critics who use Freudian and Lacanian analysis to provide a rationale for Romantic understandings of the sublime experience. Thomas Weiskel extended the psychoanalytic implications of Hertz's argument in his influential volume, *The Romantic Sublime* (1976). Weiskel argued that in the negative sublime of the Romantics the self registers excess and the infinite, and forms itself against that moment of recognition of that which is transcendent. Using Kant's analysis in the third *Critique* as his model, Weiskel detects two sets of defensive gesture against excess:

> To put it sequentially: the excessive object excites a wish to be inundated, which yields an anxiety of incorporation; this anxiety is met by a reaction formation against the wish which precipitates a recapitulation of the oedipus complex; this in turn yields a feeling of guilt (superego anxiety) and is resolved through identification (introjection).
>
> (Weiskel 1976: 105)

For Weiskel, then, the mother/woman has a role in the story; but only as the underlying threat to the ego, and 'still only as a tributary of the Oedipal system into which it invariably flows' (Hertz 1978: 53).

This last phrase is taken from an important later essay by Hertz, 'The Notion of Blockage in the Literature of the Sublime' (1978). Here Hertz opens up his earlier position in the face of Weiskel's insights, and now explicitly asserts that there is a kind of primary matricide at the root of the sublime. Like Weiskel, Hertz now allows that it is only against the threat of feminine gaps, excess, formlessness and inundation that the boundaries of the male self are constructed. The sublime reveals the author confronting the blockages—the difficulties—in exerting his self: producing anxieties that are transformed to guilt as they manifest themselves at the secondary (mature) level of the adult self, locked into oedipal struggles of son against father. In this drama of confrontation there is once again no place for mother–daughter bondings, nor for an ego that is not sent into defensive anxiety by confrontation with excess.

Hertz extends his argument on gender and the sublime one more time: in the afterward to his collected essays, *The End of the Line* (1985). By now, Hertz has read some feminist criticism; he knows his Kristeva; and he also discusses a woman writer en route to an understanding of how femininity figures in the dynamics of the sublime. The example he chooses is George Eliot (1819–80), and he argues that in *Daniel Deronda* the Princess represents a 'double darkness'—that of the mother and that of pre-oedipal chaos—which is cast out as the female author stabilises her identity and places herself within the symbolic contract that exists between author and reader (Hertz 1985: 229). Hertz's model has as its underpinning the anxieties of an ego that is not born knowing that it is a unified self, but establishes itself as an ego through cutting itself off from the indeterminate and all-powerful other/the mother to which it is bonded.

Freud's and Jacques Lacan's accounts of the oedipal stage in the child's development provide the underlying logic for the analysis that Hertz proffers—even though Freud's narrative does not successfully deal with the psychic development of the young girl, and even though Lacan's claim that an oedipal economy of psychic relationships is necessary to the emergence of a stable ego is thoroughly controversial (see Kofman 1980; Irigaray 1974). For Lacan, there never could be a subject position which is that of 'woman' (Lacan 1972–73: 144). She is instead the unknowable unconscious of man (his 'Other'): an elusive absence that underlies the I, and which marks the limits of the knowable and the representable, whilst simultaneously acting as a continual allurement to the consciousness which it haunts. As such, 'woman' represents both the 'beautiful' object of desire and the ego's drive towards its own dissolution which is warded off via the structures of the sublime (Lacan 1959–60; Battersby 1998).

Like Lacan, Hertz implicitly denies the embodied female human a distinctive subject position. Like males, Hertz's female authors are also thrown into crisis by unclear boundaries, by excess, by emptiness, by the formless. Female authors now have a place in the scheme, but only—to use Luce Irigaray's language which puns on the French term for 'man' (*homme*) and love of the same sex—within a 'hom(m)osexual' economy of the same (Irigaray 1977: 171). Hertz's female authors mimetically reproduce the patterns of male authors, and differ only at the secondary (oedipal) stage. On Hertz's model, if a female author were to be sublime, it would only be by making herself a Promethean figure who both rebels against but also identifies with her father/ God, and cuts herself off from her mother/chaos/blackness/Nature. She would have to make herself masculine; and her pre-oedipal relationship with her mother would have to resolve itself into oedipal patterns of anxiety and competition.

Hertz's masculinist model of the sublime has been extremely influential. But even George Eliot—Hertz's preferred example of a 'matricidal' female writer— does not straightforwardly fit within his analysis. This is particularly clear if we look at an early novella by Eliot in which she knowingly plays with the tropes of German Romanticism and the sublime. *The Lifted Veil* was published anonymously in *Blackwood's Magazine* of 1859. In it, the male hero, Latimer, who relates the story in the first person, tells us several times that German lyric poetry is his favourite poetry, explicitly mentioning Novalis (Eliot 1859: 197, 194, 192). Latimer also recounts how he lost the happiness of childhood through becoming a poet and having a series of visions or dreams—described as a kind of 'brain disease'—that enabled him to 'lift the veil' and see into the future and into other people's consciousnesses, including knowing such terrible things as the time and agony of his own death or that Bertha, his wife, despises him and will try to kill him.

The relationships between the male characters in this story are certainly marked by antagonisms and oedipal rivalries. Thus Latimer had a brother who also loved Bertha, and the engagement only takes place after a period of intense competition which ends when the brother is killed by a fall from his horse (209). But the oedipal struggles and the horror of seeing behind the veil are contrasted with the earlier state of ecstatic joy that certainly does not fit with Hertz's description of femininity as a 'darkness' that needs to be cast out. Instead Latimer says, in a passage that draws directly on the imagery of Rousseau in *Reveries of a Solitary Walker*, but also on German Romanticism:

> My least solitary moments were those in which I pushed off in my boat, at evening, towards the centre of the lake; it seemed to me that the sky, and the glowing mountain-tops, and the wide blue water, surrounded me with a cherishing love such as no human face had shed on me since my mother's love had vanished out of my life. . . . I looked up at the departing glow leaving one mountain-top after another, as if the prophet's chariot of fire were passing over them on its way to the home of light. Then, when the white summits were all sad and corpse-like, I had to push homeward . . . .
>
> (pp. 189–90; and see Rousseau 1782: 85)

117

Here, the bond with the mother is presented in positive terms and as an irreparable loss, not as part of the script of a matricidal drama that must be followed if the I is to emerge as a unified and coherent self.

There is, however, another, darker, kind of femininity also operative in Eliot's text: the mask of femininity that is created by the male lover as the object of his desire. As far as everyday life is concerned, Latimer only manages to function normally and stay sane by practising a type of 'double consciousness' which enables him not to register one of 'two parallel streams' of consciousness which operate within him (Eliot 1859: 203). For most of the time, Latimer's relationship with Bertha does not require such a mode of self-deception. This is because his desire 'thickens' the veil and prevents him seeing into her soul. Thus, we are told that the reason that Bertha is attractive to Latimer is because she is the one consciousness that is hidden beneath a veil 'thick enough' to block Latimer's view into the 'truth' about the other's thoughts and feelings:

> So absolute is our soul's need of something hidden and uncertain for the maintenance of that doubt and hope and effort which are the breath of its life, that if the whole future were laid bare to us beyond today, the interest of all mankind would be bent on the hours that lie between; we should pant after the uncertainties of our one morning and our one afternoon . . . .
>
> (211)

Latimer does, however, have glimpses into Bertha's cruel and callous character in moments of dream or vision when he sees into the future. Then, eventually, the thickness of the veil that acts as a lure is entirely lost when Latimer feels a strong emotion that is not focused on Bertha. This happens only some years after marrying, and is caused by the grief generated by the death of his father. Then, at last, he is able to see past the veil and into Bertha's mind:

> The terrible moment of complete illumination had come to me, and I saw that the darkness had no hidden landscape from me, but only a blank prosaic wall: from that evening forth, through the sickening years that followed, I saw all around the narrow room of this woman's soul—saw petty artifice and mere negation where I had delighted to believe in coy sensibilities and in wit at war with latent feeling.
>
> (214)

Positioned between Romanticism and the gothic mystery tale, Eliot's novella acts as an ironic commentary on the young male 'enthusiast' who sits enraptured 'before the closed secret of a sarcastic woman's face, as if it were the shrine of the doubtfully benignant being who ruled his destiny', whilst he also plots the downfall of his 'rival', his brother (197). Eliot seems to suggest that even if the drive towards the absolute is a universal; even if we all require infinite mystery, it is only male desire that reads the absolute onto the body of a real-life woman; it is only the man's self-deception that transforms 'a blank prosaic wall' into an alluring phantom waiting to be unveiled.

Although Neil Hertz's account of Eliot makes it sound as if she fits the model of the oedipalised ego that can only attain selfhood by expelling the boundless and infinite (m)other to whom she was once bonded, *The Lifted Veil* seems to undermine this account. George Eliot evokes Latimer's (lost) bond with his dead mother who is not hidden behind veils, but located in nature and the heavens. Here there is a lapse in the overall irony of the narrative, and the tone is nostalgic, not matricidal. Furthermore, Eliot also juggles with the metaphorics of unveiling the absolute in ways that are symptomatic of female authors who cannot position themselves comfortably either side of the 'veil of Isis'. Eliot offers us not so much an oedipal tale, as a kind of dry mockery that deploys its narrative to oppose the 'eternal feminine' which, in one way or another, draws man onwards and upwards in so much of German Romanticism. Eliot seems to write in opposition to those who make the male's search for the elusive feminine ennobling (Goethe); or who equate the sublime Isis with a forever unobtainable truth hidden behind a veil (Kant); as well as gently satirising Schiller who romanticises the madness of the man who sees through the veil, and Novalis who lifts the veil of the goddess at Sais and finds truth in the face of the woman he loves. Eliot's irony in *The Lifted Veil* also distances her from Karoline von Günderode (1780–1816), the German Romantic poet whom I will now turn to consider, but the narrator's vision in the boat on the lake of his mother's 'cherishing love' that 'had vanished' out of his life puts Eliot closer to Günderode than is allowed by Hertz's oedipalised model of the struggles and blockages of the (male) sublime.

The sweet sublime

The poetic career of Karoline von Günderode (also spelt Günderrode) was brief. She committed suicide in 1806, aged 26, a silver dagger stabbed through her heart. Found on the banks of the Rhine, Günderode had tied stones in a cloth, clearly intending that her corpse should float free, but she remained on land, only her hair floating in the water. Günderode's suicide was not a transitory whim, but a long-considered objective of dying (gaily) at the right time. Deprived of the possibility of living with the (married) man she loved, she left the house laughing, calling her goodbyes, going back for the cloth in which to wrap the stones. She attempted to merge with the earth and the waters of the Rhine in ways consistent with her mystical and poetic writings. Although two small volumes of that poetry appeared during Karoline's lifetime, and some also appeared in the epistolary novel *Die Günderode* (1839) by her friend Bettine von Arnim (née Bettine Brentano, 1785–1859), most—including her drama

119

and prose works—remained unpublished for around 100 years. Much seems completely destroyed, including material that her lover, Professor Friedrich Creuzer—perhaps *the* most important German Romantic mythographer—committed himself to publish, and then withdrew at the last moment, for fear of compromising his reputation and his marriage.

Günderode's male contemporaries understood her as writing the sublime, and their responses mixed admiration with attempts to dissuade. Thus, for example, Clemens Brentano's enthusiasm for Karoline's poetry is excessive, but also poisonous. Encouraging her to develop further her gift for creating 'lyrics that are nothing but profound, truth-telling turtle-doves', in a letter of 2 June 1804 he complains of her first book:

> 'you must take care to replace the grey thoughts with bright, lively images. . . . The only thing that can be an objection to your entire collection is that you shift between the masculine and feminine . . . where, for example, words like "adept", "apocalyptic" etc are in the titles.'
>
> (Günderrode 1979: 190)

Friedrich Creuzer, by contrast, can accept Karoline's mysticism, as long as it is allied to the childlike or to intuitions into nature. He refers approvingly to her ability to position herself as a child 'lying in the lap of the great Mother'. However, he lectures her at some length against tackling 'systematic–heroic dramas' which have come to represent the sublime. Creuzer dissents from the traditional view concerning woman's relation to the sublime, but, nevertheless, comes out with some very conventional advice in trying to deflect his beloved from writing tragedies. Myths, romances, lyrics and oriental subjects, it seems, are suitable for women, but not Julius Caesar or other heroes of Western culture. Awkward enough for a male (unless Plutarch or Shakespeare), such histories are 'doubly awkward for a woman' he says in a letter of 20 February 1806 (Görtz 1991).

One of the things that is interesting about Günderode from a feminist point of view is that she is a theorist herself. Living contemporaneously with both Kant and Friedrich Schelling (1775–1854), she was deeply immersed in their systems and used her mystical poetry and dramas to appropriate the sublime for female writers (Günderrode 1991). This was a point not lost on her contemporaries, such as Bettine von Arnim, who tried in her novel, *Die Günderode*, to position Karoline in her life and tragic suicide as the epitome of the female sublime (Arnim 1839). As we will see, Günderode develops a female sublime, which refuses many of the oppositional categories of Kantian aesthetics that were so central to the Romantic sublime. In particular, she collapses the Kantian distinctions between mind and body; self and other; individuality and infinity. She does not abandon all notion of self; but she wants an individuality that is in harmony with, and permeated by, the opposing forces that together constitute Nature and the All. She rejects Kant's subject/object binaries, and suggests that the ego is an illusion produced by Western culture. Her longing to re-join the earth and simultaneously dissolve her identity into fluidity resonates throughout her poetry and prose, but cannot be equated either with Kant's sublime, in which ego is threatened and then recuperated, or with the sublime of Novalis who reduces the feminine to the counterpole of the male self. Instead, Günderode re-works the self–other relationship as a way of voicing *female* poetic transcendence.

Once I Lived a Sweet Life

Once I lived a sweet life
for it was as if I had suddenly become
but an airy cloud.
Above me I could observe nothing
except a deep blue sea
and I navigated easily around
on the waves of this sea.
Merrily I fluttered in the breezes
of heaven the whole day long,
then lay down happy and fluttering
at the edge of the earth
as, steaming and blazing,
she tore herself from the arms of the sun,
to bathe in the cool of the night,
to refresh herself in the evening wind.
Gripped by the sadness of parting,
the sun's arms went round me then,
and the beautiful, bright rays
loved all and kissed me.
Coloured lights
came spilling down,
skipping and playing,
airy partners
waving in the breezes.
Their garments
purple and golden,
like the deepest blaze
of fire itself.
But they became
fainter and fainter,
paler the cheeks,
extinguished the eyes.
Suddenly my playfellows

completely disappeared,
and as I looked
sadly after them,
I saw the great
hurrying shadow
who followed them,
to snatch them up.
Deep in the West
I still saw the golden
hem of their garments.
Then, flapping slightly, I rose upwards,
flitting first here and then there,
enjoying the lightness of life,
resting in the clear aether.
And in the deep, holy
unnameable space of the heavens
I saw strange and wondrous shapes
and figures that moved.
Eternal gods
sat on thrones
of glittering stars,
looked one at another,
blissful and laughing.
Ringing shields,
clanging spears
were borne by
powerful, warring heroes;
and running before them
were powerful beasts,
others moved
round earth and heaven
in broad bands,
following each other
in eternal circles.
Radiant with grace
a virgin stood
amongst this fierceness,
controlling all.
Loveable children
played amidst
poisonous snakes.—
I wanted to flit over
to the children,
to play with them

and then kiss
the virgin's feet.
And I was caught up in
a deep longing within myself.
And it was as if once I had
torn myself away from a sweet body,
and now for the first time
the wounds of this ancient agony bled.
And I turned towards the earth
as, sweet in drunken sleep,
she rocked in the arm of heaven.
The stars were tinkling softly
so as not to wake the beautiful bride,
and the breezes of heaven played
softly over her tender breast.
Then it was as if I had sprung out
of the innermost life of the mother,
and had reeled forth
into the aetherial spaces
like a child gone astray.
I had to cry,
dripping with tears
I sank down
into the lap of the mother.
Coloured calyxes
fragrant flowers
caught the tears,
and I permeated them,
all the calyxes,
trickled backwards
through the flowers,
deeper and deeper,
right down to the shoots,
to the hidden place
from which life springs.

(Günderrode 1979: 73–76, my translation)

On the egotistical sublime that is characteristic of many of the male post-Kantian writers, there is typically a narrative 'I'—entrapped in a mortal body—and an imaginative experience in which the finitude of the body is left behind in the confrontation with infinity. Sometimes the transcendent moment is framed as an imaginative tour of the heavens or the deep: technically, Kant's mathematical sublime. Sometimes, transcendence comes via a confrontation with the power of nature—storms, gaunt mountains, waterfalls, heroes, wars—

technically, Kant's dynamical sublime. However, there is also a move from body to transcendence, and then back to an (ennobled) self. The logic of Günderode's poem 'Once I Lived a Sweet Life' could not be more different. We start up in the heavens. And although there is an 'I' flitting like a cloud through the 'deep, holy/ unnameable space of the heavens', this 'I' is bodiless and ephemeral.

The repeated verb *gaukeln* that I have translated as 'fluttered' and 'fluttering' can mean both to move like an insect and to juggle, and is linked with sleight-of-hand, illusion and phantoms. Any sense of solidity in this narrative 'I' is produced only fleetingly, by pain and by loss. The first playfellows—no more substantial than coloured lights—are scared away by 'the great / hurrying shadow / who followed them, / to snatch them up'. Their replacements, the children playing with poisonous snakes, are more substantial, but remain tantalisingly distant. Indeed, it is the desire of the ephemeral 'I' to position herself among these embodied children, and kiss the feet of their protectress, that sets up the 'deep longing' that will lead to the ejection of the 'I', alone in the immensity of space 'like a child gone astray'. Günderode could hardly be more explicit about the role of the mother in this primary separation: 'And it was as if once I had/ torn myself away from a sweet body, / and now for the first time/ the wounds of this ancient agony bled'. The 'I' is temporarily presented as a Jesus crucified into selfhood: expelled from glory by god the mother. However, no sooner is the separation secured by the processes of loss and rejection than the 'I' turns back towards a state in which self and other interpenetrate.

The 'I' moves backwards: 'and I permeated them, / all the calyxes, / trickled backwards/ through the flowers, / deeper and deeper'. The way forwards is the way back into childhood, and then further back to a place that grounds life itself. Günderode's desire to re-join the mother's 'lap' or 'womb' is also a longing to move back into or through the earth's 'shoots': she plays on the German words 'Schösse' and 'Schoss'. The poet yearns to melt her identity into that of otherness. *Durchdrang*: permeated, penetrated—the connotations are sexual. There is interpenetration as the flowers catch the tears of the I which trickle back through all the calyxes or chalices (*Kelche*) to the Earth, the spring, source, fountain (*Quelle*) of life: the I fluidly melts into both self and (m)other. Although for a brief poetic moment, this disembodied 'I' had longed for a body—the body of the other—by the end of the narrative all sense of embodiment, or of stability to the ego is once again lost.

Günderode's sublime involves inversions of space, time and of identity itself. It involves no anxiety in face of the other/the mother, but a double position of reverence for and identification with the mother. There is no struggle for domination here, and no confrontations between an 'I' and an 'it'. Thus, the 'I' nowhere exalts itself by a process of overcoming matter, body or the earth. The 'I' flits 'first here and then there, / enjoying the lightness of life'—drifting through space, time and identity itself—without abrupt movements of perpendicular transcendence. Neither does this 'I' plummet back down to the earth in an ecstasy of domination. Active and passive combine as the 'I' responds to the draw of the earth; overspills in tears: 'I had to cry'. The subject sinks down; is permeated; and also penetrates. Since bodies and identities are not fixed, there is no master.

Although much of the language and metaphors that Günderode employs are strongly reminiscent of Novalis' *Hymns to the Night*, what Novalis does is subordinate life to death and the power of the 'loving, maternal goddess' to that of the Father god whom she foreshadows. Indeed, in the published version of his prose–poem, the poem ends by sinking 'us' into the 'Father's lap' (Novalis 1800: 25, 29, 43). By contrast, the ultimate power in Günderode's poem does not rest with the male. Neither the bridegroom (the heavens) who rocks the earth, nor the sun (a feminine noun in German), nor the 'blissful and laughing' gods exert the power of a patriarchal ruler. Rather, it is the virgin 'Radiant with grace' (Mary? Isis?) who controls (*beherrschend*) the 'fierceness', the 'warring heroes' and the 'powerful beasts'. Günderode evokes a force that is not terrorising: a power that protects children at play, and keeps snakes and threatening shadows at bay.   ◆

Elsewhere Günderode also deploys the 'veil of Isis' imagery which the last chapter explored, adopting a position that is neither straightforwardly that of the male Romantics who thought it possible to see through the veil, nor that of Kant for whom an infinite process of unveiling is made the task of the I. For Günderode, infinity becomes an aspect of materiality and also of the I itself. Thus, in her short, and apparently fragmentary story, 'Tale of a Brahmin', the narrator makes reference to the inscription on the gates of the Temple of Religion that he and his young friend wish to enter:

> its inscription is infinity and language is finite. But I will try to unveil the holy statue of Isis at Sais (beneath which stand the words, 'I am all that is and that was and that shall be'), but so that the inner meaning of the goddess is not exposed to you, so that you will not see her, either through reason, nor through your knowledge.
>
> It is an unending struggle, an entire life, that everything that is here, what is, was and shall be, that produces itself in a mysterious way, eternally remaining through all change and dying.
>
> (Günderrode 1979: 123–24)

Günderode's narrator is Almor, the son of a French merchant, who had converted from Christianity to Islam. Born in Smyrna (in present-day Turkey), Almor later travels round Asia and examines a variety of religions and moral codes, claiming to have learnt much from the Qur'an, and also from Zoroaster, Moses, Christ, and Confucius. Like Reinhold and Schiller, the narrator tells us that all religions transmit the myths of the Egyptian priests and Hindu mythology. Almor distances himself from Western philosophy which has become 'hateful to him' in its way of subordinating the individual to the totality, and instead claims that totalities are nothing but the sum of individuals:

'To me every individual is holy and is god's work' (124). However, Almor's understanding of the relationship between the individual and the whole is deepened by an encounter with a Brahmin who explains:

> how in each part of the infinite spirit of nature lies the sketch for eternal perfectibility; how the forces migrate through all the forms until they develop into consciousness and human thoughts; how onwards from the human there waits for the soul an endless line of migrations that always lead to ever higher perfection; how in the end in a mysterious way they will all be united in the original force from which they came, and will become one with it, and nevertheless remain distinct, and so the divinity and the universality of the creator is united with the individuality of the created.
>
> (126)

Günderode started out as a Kantian, but in 'Tale of a Brahmin' we see her undermining Kant's way of thinking the relationship between the universal and the individual and nature and man. Günderode's hero, Almor, does not transcend nature or master it, but is an aspect of the infinite, and the individual 'I' is also no more than one aspect of the infinite forces that act through him. Making an implicit reference to the title of Kant's *Toward Perpetual Peace* (1795), Günderode's narrator claims that this new insight into things brought him 'perpetual peace' (Günderrode 1979: 125). This new sublime is linked with spirit, but not to the Kantian universals of reason that involve thinking of the phenomenal and noumenal as separable spheres. The noumenal is now no longer tied to the moral sphere, but to a sublime infinity that starts with the earthly and the human and treats these as perfectible. Innocence and purity are states that do not involve transcendence of materiality, but can be attained whilst moving through the 'bright hurly-burly' of the earth and amongst the 'whirlpools of decay' (126). The individual does not represent an aspect of the universal, but is an expression of the universal forces that express themselves through his or her individual existence. What is envisaged is a kind of pantheism that necessitates a transformation of the matter/spirit and self/non-self divides.

In 'Tale of a Brahmin', these mystical speculations are delivered not in Günderode's own voice, but via a variety of embedded narrators, and so it is hard to be sure to what extent the author shares these views. However, in a letter that she writes to her friend 'Eusebio' (in reality, Friedrich Creuzer) similar views can be found expressed in her own voice, disguised only by the pseudonym 'Tiann' that she so often used:

> I have stood at the dividing point between life and death ... I am happy every night and prefer unconsciousness and dark dreams to bright living, why then should I be afraid of the long night and the

> deep sleep? ... That you could be lost to me is for me the most painful thought. I said your I and mine would become dissolved in the old, original material of the world. But then I comforted myself again that our elements are so allied that they would respond to the laws of attraction and seek each other out in infinite space and join together with each other again.
>
> (115)

Günderode goes on to speculate that it is possible to posit a perfected form of earthly existence when 'all appearances melt into a communal, organic whole; when spirit and body are so interpenetrated that all bodies, all forms are simultaneously thoughts and soul, and all thoughts have at the same time form and body'. Thus, Günderode does not want transcendence of body, but a transformation of the form–matter, self–other, spirit–body dualisms. She wants an attitude to flesh that makes it possible for bodies to be perfect, in a way 'that is very different from what we call form and body' (117). From her lover, she wants an intermingling (and completeness) of bodies that involves refusing separation into an 'I'—or, rather, valuing each 'I' as a unique element in the greater organic whole (124). Günderode manipulates the Kantian sublime so as to counterpoise 'male' positions of transcendence (up in the heavens) by an emotional interpenetration with the earth (which she describes as a womb). In so doing Günderode fundamentally subverts models of the self and its relation to materiality in ways that undermine the masculinist model of the 'I' as separate from nature and of the sublime as involving a transcendence of materiality and the earth.

Modes of the female sublime

In her essay 'Toward a Female Sublime', Patricia Yaeger has argued that three new modes of the sublime have emerged amongst women writers 'in recent decades', plus a further mode of writing that flirts with the 'mock sublime' before coming 'close to inventing a new mode of the sublime: what we might call "the sublime of nearness"' (Yaeger 1989: 195). The near-miss at the sublime is exemplified for Yaeger by the poet Elizabeth Bishop who 'wants to re-invent the sublime—not as a genre of empowerment based on the simple domination of others, but as a genre that can include the sociable, the convivial, as well as the empowering' (195). In terms of the analysis of Emily Dickinson offered above, I would argue that Dickinson should be seen as a precursor of this mode of the 'near sublime' that, Yaeger claims,

> begins to invent a new kind of self–other dialectic that allows the object ... to remain something other than the perceiving subject's conception of it, and that allows that perceiving subject, in turn, to become something other than a unified ego.
>
> (196)

Yaeger does register Dickinson as a possible precursor for Bishop, but is too quick to assert that there was no other nineteenth-century woman poet who is 'creating for herself a female tradition to join'—a tradition in which the female poet is accompanied by a 'fiery trail of language' suggestive of *hypsous*: 'of power and influence, of transport and height' (194). It is a shame that Yaeger does not recognise here Karoline von Günderode and Margaret Fuller (1810–50) who, as we will see, were part of a 'female tradition' of women poets and writers—even at the time that Dickinson was writing.

Yaeger's three modes of the female sublime that are not near-misses are (1) the 'failed sublime'; (2) the 'sovereign sublime'; and (3) the 'feminine sublime'. The 'failed sublime' involves the depiction or expression of 'a woman's dazzling empowerment followed by a moment in which this power is snatched away' (201). The 'sovereign sublime' involves an inversion of the type of oedipal sublime that Hertz and Weiskel describe: instead of the 'moment of blockage which is followed by a moment of imagistic brilliance' that we find in male writers, the woman writer 'expends or spills' the 'power' that the sublime moment had 'promised to hoard' through its 'structure of crisis, confrontation, and renewed domination' (202). The 'feminine sublime' is also described in psychoanalytic terms, and exploits the pre-oedipal space that Hertz's late model of the sublime registers as a 'darkness' and unbounded infinity that needs to be overcome:

> the agon typical of the Romantic sublime is retained as part of a narrative or poetic structure, but this oedipal conflict is rewritten so that the pre-oedipal desire for closeness and nearness with the other that the conventional sublime tries to repress, remains visible and viable; it hums pre-oedipal songs from the ruins of an agonistic and oppositional poetics.
>
> (204)

In it, the pre-oedipal desire to bond with the mother's body is not negated, and the author 'revels, for a brief poetic moment, in a pre-oedipal longing for otherness and ecstasy' (209).

If we compare Günderode's poetic strategy with Yaeger's account of the modes of the female sublime, we see that Günderode fits nowhere—except as a part of the background to Bishop and Dickinson that Yaeger cannot see. Of the three 'new' modes of the female sublime, the 'feminine or pre-oedipal sublime' comes closest in that in it the desire to bond with the mother's body is not repressed; the 'subject is infiltrated with the world' and 'otherness is carried to the very heart of selfhood' (205). However, Yaeger only seems to be able to think selfhood in oedipalised—masculinised—terms, so that the self only emerges via the negation of the other and 'the agon typical of the Romantic sublime is retained as part of a narrative or poetic structure'. For Yaeger, the pre-oedipal moment of pleasure and ecstasy of the 'feminine' sublime remains no more than a fleeting opening in the dominating structures of an oedipalised psychic economy, in which the 'other' is treated as a kind of indeterminate threat that needs to be negated. But this clearly does not fit the case of Gün-derode who eschews Yaeger's 'agonistic and oppositional poetics', who portrays the bond with the mother as 'sweet', and who works to make selfhood itself seem transitory. We misunderstand the dynamics of loss and longing in Gün-derode's work if we read them as simply opening a space for the sublime power of the oedipal father.

In the oedipal model that Yaeger inherits from Hertz and Weiskel, we are all trapped within the father's reality, and the power of the mother can only be understood in terms of that of the father. Yaeger opens a space within that model for a fragile—if compelling—pre-oedipal sublime. For Günderode, how-ever, the fundamental power is that of the mother, and it is a power very dis-similar to that exercised by the father. Yaeger links her feminine sublime with that of two contemporary theorists of *écriture féminine*: Hélène Cixous and Luce Irigaray. But I read the two French writers as in many ways opposed, and Yaeger as being much closer to Cixous than to Irigaray. Irigaray raises much more fundamental questions about the presuppositions of psychoanalysis than does Cixous. Indeed, Irigaray denies that mother–daughter relationships can simply be conceptualised by opening a gap within the economy of the male. Nor is she simply interested in a 'feminine' writing that is open equally to males and females. For Irigaray there is no gender-free pre-oedipal moment. Rather, she aims at a female symbolic that does not just treat 'woman' as 'the other' of 'the same' (Irigaray 1974: 321). For Irigaray, unlike Lacan, it is not the case that there is only one possible subject position, with 'woman' acting simply as the counterpole to the masculinised and oedipalised ego. Instead, she tries to think a mode of subjectivity that remembers natality. On Irigaray's model, a female symbolic would be one that is *non-oedipal*, and not simply *pre-oedipal*: in it, identity would emerge through a non-agonistic link with the other, rather than through a defensive gesture of refusal.

In Irigaray's alternative economy of psychic expenditure, the subject does not disappear, but is maintained by flowing excess. To explain this thought Irigaray spends some time describing a mechanics of fluids, rather than solids (Irigaray 1977: 106–18). This *other* economy—the economy of the gift—that Irigaray would say that Yaeger is refusing to think, involves quite different laws of exchange. In a gift economy, self and other are not oppositional; there are no 'blockages' that build up as the flows are dammed up; and, since there are no structures of domination, there is also no repression, and no sudden release.

> The greatest value would be at the same time the least kept in reserve. Nature's resources would be expended without depletion, exchanged without labor, freely given, exempt from masculine transactions: enjoyment without a fee, well-being without pain, pleasure without possession.
>
> (Irigaray 1977: 197)

129

This means that the very notions of 'ownership' and 'property', and therefore also the ego, would need to be re-imagined. By putting forward this explicitly 'utopian' dream, Irigaray is seeking to highlight how much is concealed in the metaphorics of exchange that structure Freudian and Lacanian thought about desire and its repression (197).

Like Irigaray, Günderode privileges fluidity over matter, and becoming over being. Both would also agree that what is necessary is to re-work the fundamentals of the Kantian scheme: space, time, the 'I am', God, and the relationship between the sensible and the transcendental. It is a shame, therefore, that Irigaray seems unaware of her as a foremother and that she seems to think it is not worth looking for female precursors within post-Platonic history. As we will see also in Chapter 8, Irigaray treats history as a monolithic unity in which only the male symbolic has found expression, but within which a female symbolic is waiting 'to be born' (Irigaray 1985: 13). What I am suggesting, by contrast, is that within modernity there never was a time in which women artists, writers and thinkers did not develop alternative models for thinking self and transcendence.

Through the flowers

Although the sublime has generally been portrayed as that which is 'beyond' language or as that which presents the 'inadequation of presentation' (Derrida 1978b: 131), the female sublime that interests me is not an absence, but a forgotten presence in the history of philosophy, literature and art—the forgetting of which has consequences for women working in the arts today. As we have seen in this chapter, what has been 'forgotten' is a model for subjectivity which is appropriate to the female subject who is capable of birthing the other within her own embodied self, and who thus fall outside the norms of oedipalised selfhood which represents the relationship between 'self' and 'other' in fundamentally oppositional terms. Looking at the self–other relationship in the case of the female sublime does not present us with oedipal agonistics, but instead threatens the 'truth' of the psychic (oedipal) 'universals' underlying our experience of nature, infinity and 'otherness'.

If we fail to see the characteristically female manoeuvrings around the problematics of the sublime—or if we cannot find any literary foremothers of the present-day 'feminist', 'female' and 'feminine' sublimes—it is because we are viewing the sublime from a perspective that treats male psyches, experiential histories and dynamic interrelations as norm and/or ideal. From this point of view, past female writers have to be understood as mimetically doubling—or, rather, as failing to perfectly match—the psychic dramas recorded by the males. There are, however, other ways of analysing women writers' relationships to the sublime in the eighteenth and nineteenth centuries, during which the category was being shaped and marked by gender distinctions. The poetry of Karoline von Günderode and Emily Dickinson provide useful starting points for investigating the way that women themselves have negotiated the sublime—and not just in 'recent decades', as Yaeger implies, nor merely in ways that mirror (whilst failing to exactly duplicate or match) the sublime experience of the males, as the psychoanalytic model suggests.

Although the literary critic Harold Bloom has maintained that literary history involves a dynamics that rests on an 'anxiety of influence', a 'battle between strong equals, father and sons as mighty opposites, Laius and Oedipus at the crossroads' (Bloom 1973: 26), the relationship between creative women and their foremothers is often much less agonistic. There has been a search for lost foremothers and a memorialising of their achievements through incorporating them as 'others' within the later woman's words or work. Irigaray could have found a tradition in which female art and the female sublime had already been born if she had not been too despairing to look. Indeed, the memory of Günderode's poetry and of her life and friendship with Bettine has been an important element in the matrilineal traditions of female creativity.

In the twentieth century Christa Wolf's important German edition of Günderode's poems and letters (Günderrode 1979) took over the task of cultural transmission performed more than a century earlier by Margaret Fuller and Bettine von Arnim. Wolf also edited Bettine von Arnim's novel *Die Günderode* (Arnim 1839) and she also fictionalised Günderode's life in her own novel *No Place on Earth* (*Kein Ort, Nirgends*) (Wolf 1979). Günderode became a kind of symbolic mother for Wolf as she did also—thanks in part to Wolf—for women artists such as Meret Oppenheim (1913–85) who entitled one of her large 1983 canvases 'For Karoline von Günderode' and another of the same year 'For Bettine Brentano' (Curiger 1989: Plates 90). Since the Günderode painting includes, beneath interlocking abstract squares, the dark silhouette of a boat or cradle part obscured by white clouds or waves, it reads as a visual evocation of 'Once I Lived a Sweet Life'. Oppenheim spent the last years before her death 'reading, or rather re-reading' the correspondence between Bettine and Karoline. Indeed, the Swiss surrealist artist died on the same day that *Caroline*, her book of poems and graphics dedicated to Günderode, was presented to the press (85, 89).

Although Karoline von Günderode did not fully enter the literary canon until her 'rediscovery' by the East German novelist Christa Wolf in 1979, she seems to have been widely read and discussed in America long before that, in part as a result of Bettine von Arnim's report on Günderode's suicide in her *Goethe's Correspondence with a Child* (1835) which was translated into English by Bettine herself in 1837, but also because of the efforts of Margaret Fuller who translated selections from Bettine von Arnim's novel *Die Günderode* (1839) in 1842, and included additional material in her translation of *Correspondence of Fräulein Günderode and Bettine von Arnim* in 1861. A feminist and also a philosopher, Fuller's own poetry and prose also seems indebted to Günderode, as well as to Novalis (whose imagery she tried to feminise). Fuller clearly had an effect. Thus, when the American theologian, Theodore Parker, visited Bettine in Berlin on May 23 1844 he recorded in his notebook that they discussed Margaret Fuller and the 'Letters from New York' which she kept in a scrapbook: 'She has many letters from all parts; was pleased when I told her that her books were much read in America. I told her also of Gunderode' (Sanborn 1909: vol. 2, ch. 23).

In Emily Dickinson's 'One Need Not be a Chamber', she writes of an 'Ourself behind ourself, concealed'. It seems that Karoline von Günderode was part of the hinterland behind Dickinson's 'ourself'. Like Karoline, Emily Dickinson also sent poems and letters to a close female friend, and eventual sister-in-law, Susan Huntington Gilbert Dickinson (1830–1913), who was herself a writer and mathematician. In a letter of 1890 to Thomas Higginson (the first editor of a selection of Emily Dickinson's poems), Susan Dickinson described her bond with Emily in terms of the Bettine–Karoline relationship (Martin 2002). Susan Dickinson possessed a copy of Fuller's translation of the letters between Günderode and Bettine and it seems likely that Emily herself read it, especially since a childhood friend records that she and Emily together read about Bettine and Karoline, not long after Margaret Fuller's 1842 translation was published (Barolini 1994).

Like Günderode, Emily Dickinson also marks out a subject-position in which 'otherness' and self intermingle. In the case of Günderode, however, this mingling is a part of nature (which is itself both material and spiritual); it is not inside the 'corridors' of the brain as it was in Dickinson's playful use of gothic imagery which produces a disequilibrium between the poles of the ridiculous and the sublime. Günderode remains a Romantic woman poet; Dickinson, whose 'One Need Not be a Chamber' was written more than 50 years later, seems already modern in her use of parodic and transgressive textual strategies. Whether we call the resultant literature and poetry by women sublime, mystical or gothic does not much matter, as long as we devise a theoretical frame that makes the specificity of their achievements visible by countering the supposedly universal structures of the imagination and the symbolic that render the women ghostly absences. I do, however, want to resist calling these women writers' strategies 'feminine' as opposed to 'female', for reasons that should by now have become clear.

When psychoanalytic literary critics represent the sublime object as an excess that is 'feminine' (the mother), but the genre of writing or creating the sublime as 'masculine' in the sense that was originally undertaken only by men, they are echoing the responses of Kant and the male Romantics who worked hard to maintain the gender boundaries around the sublime. As we have seen, for Kant nature and infinity have to remain elusive; excess (the sublime) is the object against which the fictions of the (male) transcendental self and phenomenal reality are formed. This dynamic has been taken over by many of the feminist critics who draw on Freudian psychoanalysis, and reinscribe an oedipal dynamics that would make a female subject just like a man. When a writer like George Eliot does not fit, what is distinctive about her voice is lost and she is fitted into the oedipal scheme. When Patricia Yaeger and Timothy Gould attempt to develop a feminist perspective on the sublime, they find their backward gaze into literary history blinkered by psychoanalytic assumptions. Not only are female authors who do not fit with the logic of the oedipalised subject seen as 'suffocated' or blocked out of that history, but also the radicality of the female sublime is diluted into that of the far less challenging 'feminine' sublime.

As we saw in the last chapter, the language of femininity that has been deployed by Kant, the male Romantics and some recent literary theorists has allowed a variety of male alliances with the sublime—all of which negotiated femininity, but downgraded the female. The 'feminine' principle idealised by the Romantics is not a feminist starting point, since it starts from the notion of a 'feminine' that is excessive to a self that is already gendered as male. Kant's respect for Isis as the sublime Mother of Nature suffers from a similar drawback. Although it is the feminine excess of the sublime that leads man's reason and imagination upwards and onwards in the Kantian system, it is barred to flesh-and-blood women who are positioned as deficient in the reason and imagination that enable male humans to transcend materiality. In the last chapter we saw how some deconstructive critics get trapped by the 'feminine' and come to identify an aesthetics of the feminine with a feminist aesthetics. Now it seems that much recent psychoanalytic criticism falls into the same trap.

If, in our society, both the ego and the transcendence of the ego are linked with the male subject position, then female responses to the infinite and overwhelming that do not simply mimic those of the males will tend to disappear from literary histories that use Kantian, Freudian or Lacanian markers to demarcate the contours of that contact with the unrepresentable that constitutes the sublime. In Freudian and Lacanian theory, the dialectical processes that have erased female authors and artists from history are given a spurious, timeless necessity. If we want to re-think aesthetics from a feminist perspective, we need to open ourselves up to this impossible past and examine the tactics employed by previous generations of creative women. We need a woman-centred history that judges women's achievements in their own terms, and not simply as 'deviant males'. We need a history turned inside out and upside down: a history that moves 'through the flowers', following the patterns of movement towards the future (via our female origins) that Günderode's poem itself evokes. In so doing, we can free ourselves from the oedipal blockages in notions of aesthetic transcendence of the self, and devise strategies for conceptual change. We can also register traps—as well as advances—in the current search for a feminine or female sublime.

By coincidence, *Through the Flower* was the title of Judy Chicago's 1974 autobiography and of the art-production company that staged her feminist art exhibition, 'The Dinner Party'. Chicago designed elaborate china and place-settings, and laid out a dinner table, for important women artists, writers and thinkers concealed in the historical past. Chicago did, however, view the relationship between female art and the female body in straightforwardly bio-logistic terms, with the calyx of the flower directly symbolising female sex organs. By contrast, I am arguing that there is no unmediated relationship between a woman and her body. Since our experience as women is socially, historically and culturally conditioned, it is variable and often conflicting. Female experience is, however, given overall patterning by the social, cultural and symbolic codes that position women as both excess and lacking in regard to the patterns of male development that serve as ideal and/or norm.

As will be seen also in the next chapter which considers the visual arts, my emphasis on a female sublime should not be read as essentialist or as implying that all women writers and artists respond to the paradoxes of the female sub-ject-position in the same way. Neither should it be thought that I am blind to the dangers inherent in Günderode's fate. Instead, I have used Günderode—a historical impossibility in terms of some recent theorists of the feminine and of the sublime—to show how psychoanalytic literary criticism too often provides an analysis of literary texts that is as blind to the potentialities of the female with respect to the sublime as was Kant himself. What seem at first sight to be universal and gender-free accounts of the moment of sublimity turn out, on closer inspection, to offer only historically specific and gendered analyses of the dynamics of the modern male self. Against such universalist accounts of the sublime and the limits of the expressible, I have wanted to show how differ-ently positioned are male and female writers with regard to the constructions of self and other, the sublime and the transcendence of self.

7

ANTINOMIES OF THE FEMALE

My own ontology that takes the embodied, *female* subject as the norm for identity has been developed in more detail in *The Phenomenal Woman* (Battersby 1998). There I pick out five features of the female subject position that are discrepant in terms of the dominant models for personhood and self in Western societies:

(i) *Natality* troubles the notion of identity as a fixed, permanent or pre-given 'thing' or 'substance', since it entails noticing a fact too often forgotten in philosophical and political accounts of the self—the fact that selves give birth and are also born out of the bodies of other selves.

(ii) *Physiological dependence* disturbs a model of political association and social organisation that treats all selves either as ideally equal and autonomous, since it emphasises the modes of dependency that are a necessary aspect of the human condition, both before birth and also during childhood and other times or states of physical dependence. What is also undermined is the claim that the only alternative to the equality model is one in which each self or entity seeks only to invade, destroy, subdue or capture other entities or selves.

(iii) *Pregnant embodiment* upsets any ontology that treats 'self' and 'other' as necessarily opposed. During pregnancy the relation between 'self' and 'other' is not sharply delineated, but changes over time. This does not imply that 'self' dissolves into 'not-self'. The 'other within' does not need to be conceptualised as always and only the 'enemy within'.

(iv) *Fleshiness* also troubles the notion of a free or autonomous and individua-lised 'soul' or 'mind' that merely inhabits the flesh, especially when in relation to female flesh which has historically been linked to 'mere' mate-riality and to immanence.

(v) *Cognitive dislocation* is a consequence of the other four features. Given the aberrant nature of the 'female' with respect to the 'normal' (male) modes of selfhood and personhood in Western modernity (and post-modernity), the female subject has to negotiate the monstrous, the inconsistent and the anomalous, especially with regard to freedom, flesh and the self–other boundary.

To insist that the subject position allocated to the *female* in our culture is bound up with conflictual values and frames of reference does not entail that there is an underlying or authentic 'female' or 'feminine' subjectivity that is always the same. Women's artworks are infinitely variable—and so are women's experiences. The identities of individual women are scored by a variety of forces and factors. Not all of these scorings relate to issues of sexual difference. Race, nation, religion, education, family background, neighbourhood, class, wealth: all contribute to configuring the specificity of the individualised self. However, given that the traditions of the sublime are primary sites of exploration both of the borderline between self and not-self and also of materiality and transcendence, and that women are peculiarly positioned with respect to each of these dualities, it will hardly be surprising if patterns of tension might be detectable in artworks by women, especially insofar as the sublime is concerned. I will call these tensions 'antinomies', adopting a term inherited from Kant.

For Kant human knowledge is marked by pairs of antinomies: beliefs that exist in apparent contradiction, but which can nevertheless be resolved as we register that the space–time world is merely a construct of the 'I'. As the poet W. B. Yeats put it in *A Vision*, elaborating on the language and imagery passed down from Kant: 'All things fall into a series of antinomies in human experience' (Yeats 1937: 193). Antinomies for Yeats are about two states or feelings that exist in apparent contradiction, but which nevertheless fit together as necessary oppositions that occur within the parameters of a life. These tensions occur when our sense of ourselves as unique, autonomous, controlling agents breaks open in the face of that which is infinitely great or mysteriously excessive and other. In Kant, this moment of breaking open occurs in the face of the sublime; but the fracture is healed over in that man must necessarily treat himself *as if* the self were free at a noumenal level—as if each self were a person—whilst simultaneously registering the merely bodily and deterministic reality of existing as a self at the level of the phenomenal.

In Kant's philosophy 'man' is given a double positioning: as the idealised 'person' of the noumenal realm who is a self-determining freedom; and as the purely logical 'I' that must be supposed to persist as a substance through the time of experience. However, as we have also seen, for Kant women are not to be treated as full persons (as noumenal selves), and the antinomies of the female subject position remain, therefore, unresolved. Historically, women have been treated both as if they were *not-at-all* bodily (as if the soul had no sex) and as if they were *more* bodily—and less capable of transcendence—than males. As such, what I will call 'the female sublime' departs from the Kantian sublime, but in ways that cannot be assimilated to the Romantic sublime which devalues the flesh.

Women in our culture are trained to think of themselves as not different from men: as unrelated to a body that can give birth and that is also born. But women are also taught to think of themselves as more bodily and as bound—

136

through relationships of care, childbearing and childrearing—to other selves that are also fleshy. As such, women are—whether they realise it or not—caught in a set of antinomies that are non-Kantian. Positioned somewhere between freedom and autonomy, on the one hand, and embodied and thing-like passivity, on the other hand, the female subject either registers—or conceals from herself—the 'peculiarity' and 'singularity' of her own difference from the norm (which is male) and from other modes of 'deviation' (which can be either female or male). Consequently, women artists who engage with the traditions of the sublime frequently draw attention to embodiment in a variety of (apparently paradoxical) ways. Space, time and embodiment are reconfigured, even as the centrality of the subject is displaced and even when the art seems to be undermining the notion of an autonomous person who remains in control of her destiny.

To illustrate some of the ways these tensions reveal themselves in practice, I will now turn to a consideration of women artists. As in the case of the female writers considered in Chapter 6, I am not arguing for an 'essentialist' understanding of artworks by women. But I am interested in the category of the 'female' artist in our culture, not with that of the 'feminine'—and 'female' entails a necessary reference to *embodied* human differences. By 'feminine' I mean a set of psychic or behavioural dispositions that are more commonly associated with women than men, but there is no contradiction in talking about a 'feminine male'. By contrast, 'female' involves a reference to the way that one is categorised on the basis of physiological characteristics, in a way that to be 'feminine' does not. In other words, I am interested in the way that those socialised in our culture as 'female' negotiate the 'sublime' which has been, since the eighteenth century, a zone of potential transformation of the borderline between self and not-self.

The spaces between

We know from interviews with the Welsh figurative Evelyn Williams (1929–) that she is very conscious of herself as a woman artist, and of failing to fit into traditions and conventions for painting and drawing inherited from the past. Indeed, she has expressed her sadness at failing to find female artists who could serve as role-models (McEwen 1990). This is surely not through lack of knowledge of previous women creators (such as Gwen John who was admired by Williams from a quite early age), but rather seems attributable to the lack of well-known foremothers within the northern and mystical traditions of visionary painting and drawing on which she draws. Thus, if I look for precursors for Evelyn Williams' own art, it is to such artists as William Blake (1757–1827), Henry Fuseli (1741–1825) or Stanley Spencer (1891–1959) that I would turn, as well as to early Dutch and Flemish masters such as Hieronymous Bosch (c.1460–1516) or Pieter Brueghel the Elder (c.1527–69).

137

Williams works in a variety of media: much of her recent work is oil painting on canvas; but her *oeuvre* also includes ink, charcoal and chalk drawings on paper, painted clay reliefs and wax sculptures. Although some of her pictures and sculptures are indeed sweetly (and, indeed, disturbingly) 'feminine', others are massive in scale and also dramatically 'unfeminine' in their content. Recurring *leitmotifs* include: anguished heads, arms or hands that reach out into the air or clutch other humans; crowds shuffling along with heads bowed or gazing up to the sky; thin and naked bodies racked with emotion; heaving, broken or pitted landscapes; violent lights; turbulent skies; boxes, prisons and a variety of spatial containers from which the stretching arms protrude. Many of the motifs overspill the picture plane: some jut forward towards the viewer; others continue past the edge of the image or are taken up on adjacent pictures that demand simultaneous display.

Evelyn Williams' art is not conventionally naturalistic, but neither is it abstract. Instead, it draws attention to its own status as art: exploiting tensions that occur within the pitted, bulky and hard surfaces of the material in the case of the painted clay reliefs. In her drawings and paintings the landscape is marked via a series of abstract contours, colours and shadows, with features such as hills, rocks or trees indicated via a minimum of lines. This is not a sign of primitivism: there are also vivid, realistic details in the features of heads and figures that occupy her unstable surfaces. Hovering between two and three dimensions, the emphasis on boxing, framing and the 'beyond' of an always unnatural landscape disturbs our framework for deciding what is 'real'.

In talking of her work up to 1990 when the dominant techniques and *leitmotifs* began to change, Williams described herself in terms of the 'northern European medieval tradition' of cathedral art and as having been born into 'the wrong age'. But Evelyn Williams' work is also distinctively modern: it is clearly marked by her experiences of the London Blitz, by cinematic representations of the Holocaust, and also by Cold War anxieties and terrors. Often, the figures in her artworks seem to be responding to an overwhelming force that has impacted on an entire people or on the whole human race. What this 'something' might be remains unspecified, mysterious, half-familiar, threatening. We are made to feel that something is about to happen or that it has already long ago happened. We seem caught by contradictions that erupt as moods, desires and fears impact on the mind and fuse the landscape of dreams with that of everyday vision.

Although not in any customary sense 'religious' pictures, many of her images draw on a lost (spiritual) past, suggesting a world in which God once lived, but is dead. In the six frames of *Sea of Faces* (1984, chalk on paper) the upturned faces and open mouths suggest the tormented rhythms of one of Dante's hells. In *Crowd* (1976, charcoal on paper) the massed people seem about to break into movement, impelled by some awful catastrophe that is left unrepresented. Only one small child looks up to the heavens, where the threat perhaps comes from; all the others reach forward as they contemplate either the object of the terror or the means of escape. Looking away from the source of the catastrophe features also in a number of other works featuring crowds. Thus, in the large painted relief of *The Valley* (1984, 143 × 226 cm) (see Figure 1), the danger clearly comes from the boiling clouds, and the rain that falls in chunks from the moonlit skies. But only three people stare upwards; and they are just small figures in the massed crowd of naked humans who trudge passively across the picture, making their slow way down into the valley, looking only at their feet.

In the Kantian version of the sublime the ego is, ultimately, strengthened by the encounter with, and the mastery of, an infinite or indefinite otherness powerful enough to annihilate the I. But this is not the mood generated by Williams' vision of apocalypse. It's not that the self disappears from Williams' images of the apocalyptic sublime, it is rather that the self is reconfigured so that it is portrayed as relational, fragile and dependent. Thus, in *Whirlpool* (1986, charcoal, ink and white on linen) the humans who have been sucked towards the centre of some great vortex are simultaneously divided into patterns and groups by the impact of the force that controls them. The whirlpool is simultaneously depicted as beautiful (with the humans functioning as individual petals of some great flower), but also as relentless and inhuman in its power. Some individual arms reach out desperately beyond the spiralling currents or clutch at other naked bodies in an attempt to gain comfort or some degree of control. Terror and need are recorded, evoked, almost celebrated— even though presented from an angle which decentres humanity, and which represents the individual human as lacking autonomy or power.

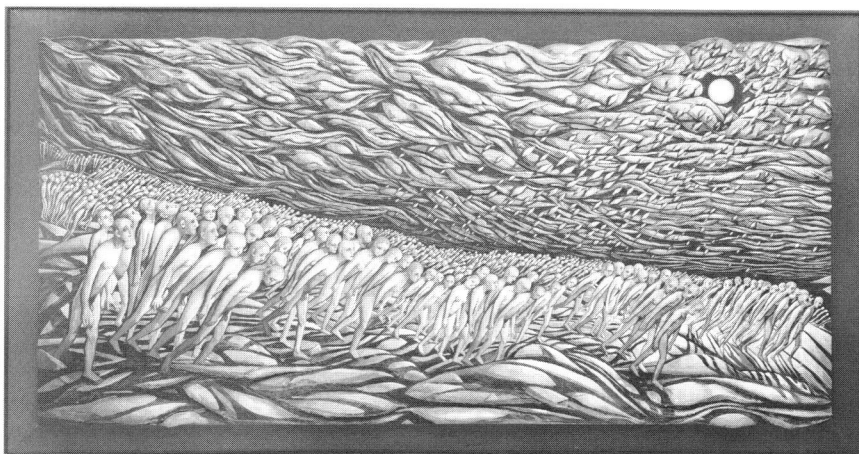

Figure 1 Evelyn Williams
The Valley, 1984 (painted relief)
Williams, Evelyn (Contemporary Artist) / Private Collection / The Bridgeman Art Library

In Williams' art we confront no strong ego reasserting its identity in face of threat or overwhelming infinity. Instead, in the eerie, almost radioactive, light of the astonishing series of drawings called *The Edge of the World* (1987), tiny people stand as if hypnotised by the glare of some natural—or supernatural—energy. This work comprises four huge drawings in charcoal, chalk and ink, each of which measures 94 × 122 cm. Portrayed from above, from a perspective that seems non-human, there is an almost cartoon-like sense of animation: of observing the world through the eye of some creature soaring and swooping through the air, taking close-ups and wide-angle shots of the pits and surfaces of the human predicament. The colour employed in these images is reminiscent of black and white films, and leads us to try and read the images in narrative sequence. But the instability of viewpoints and of scale, magnified by the uniform harshness of the lighting, makes it hard to read these images in this way.

Refused a single perspectival viewpoint, our attempt simply to contain the imagery via narrative strategies is brought to a jarring halt, as the perspective—and also the scale—changes across the individual 'panes' of the artwork. In the bottom left image of *In the Pit* (1987) (see Figure 2)—also four images, each 94 × 122 cm, in charcoal, chalk and ink—one minute human figure crawls

Figure 2 Evelyn Williams
In the Pit II, 1987 (charcoal & chalks on paper)
Williams, Evelyn (Contemporary Artist) / Private Collection /The Bridgeman Art Library

140

towards an abyss in the earth's surface, reaching out longingly towards the edge; but in the bottom right image we see what the isolated figure cannot himself see: a squash of faces of other humans who are trapped inside the rift. The viewpoint on the pit in the top right 'pane' of the artwork also conceals the humans from the spectator, and in the top left image the fissure in the earth's surface is so small that the upturned faces inside appear merely as dots. To make sense of the images, it is necessary to read them sequentially and then, once again, re-read them in terms of absence, concealment and presence, as well as the (in)significance of human expectation. Like the crawling and solitary figure, the spectator finds herself reaching towards certainties that could explain the abyss. But she is also made to feel that any such longing involves a form of illusion.

Unlike the Romantics who reach out for a 'truth' that is hidden behind the illusion, Williams' art locks us into space–time relationaties and ambiguities. As Williams herself has said, it is the space between the figures that provides the focus of her work (Williams 1998: 86). Although the recurrent *leitmotifs* and the lack of narrative closure would tend to render the images static and formalised, the actual content of the pictures is enlivened by tension. Her skill is to utilise this tension to draw us into the space and time *between*, and lock the spectator in a form of visual suspension which offers no optical or temporal resolution and no reassuring point of balance. Refused a unitary pictorial 'truth', the images function as symbolic depictions of emotion, rather than as representations of the real. The fact that the colour palette so often hovers between colour and black and white also increases the instability of the 'real' that is represented. And it is the tension engendered by these apparent contradictions that gives us the impetus to move through the perspectival puzzles and modalities of Evelyn Williams' world.

Until 1986, when a bad back put an end to her output as a sculptor, Evelyn Williams' preference was to use *papier mâché* or clay reliefs built on to the surface of her paintings and drawings to explore the limits of two- and three-dimensional form. Neither exactly painting nor sculpture, the reliefs burst out of their frames to undermine the conventions for representing surface and depth. In the 1970s she also constructed other fully rounded 'sculptures', but these are for the most part made out of dead white, moulded white wax. So realistic in their details that they seem like caricatures, the waxy flesh and the glass eyes of her faces and figures are psychically and artistically disturbing. Are they dolls or sculpture? It is hard to read this imagery except in terms of a female desire to blur the boundaries between doll making and sculpture making. These disturbing doll-sculptures constitute a disregard for conventional notions of both the beautiful and the sublime. Almost sentimental, they also parody the sentimental by their grotesque emphasis on (lifeless) flesh and (sightless) eyes. They constitute a distinctively female form of anti-art.

Just as Williams' use of materiality is characterised by tension, so also in her *oeuvre* we can detect two quite different approaches to human embodiment and also to flesh. In one of these approaches, human beings are transcendent, and not essentially embodied—souls that merely inhabit the flesh. In this respect it is noticeable that her figures seem almost androgynous, despite the genital organs and breasts that mark the distinctions between females and males when nakedness is portrayed. As in the case of William Blake and the traditions of Gothic and northern cathedral art, sexuality is downplayed—at least insofar as visual markers are concerned. Problematically, however, this can also switch over—as it does in the doll sculptures and some of the late oils—to portraying flesh as itself dead, and the soul as elsewhere.

In conversation, Williams has volunteered the description 'naked, not nude' to characterise her figure drawing—although this seems to change around 1990 when she moves to painting with oils. Kenneth Clark's famous (and famously gender-blind) accounts of Western civilisation can usefully be drawn on to contextualise this claim. For Clark, the 'nude' is clothed by his or her flesh:

> To be naked is to be deprived of our clothes and the word implies some of the embarrassment which most of us feel in that condition. The word nude, on the other hand, carries in educated usage, no uncomfortable overtone. The vague image it projects into the mind is not of a huddled and defenceless body, but of a balanced, prosperous and confident body: the body re-formed.
>
> (Clark: 1956: 1)

Epitomised by the Italian Renaissance artists and their heirs, Clark describes the nude male body in terms of a universal ideal that signifies power, rationality, harmony, beauty, proportion. For Clark, the nude female body should provide a suitable counterpart for such a mate. However, Clark also insists that, 'The shape towards which the female body tends to return is one which emphasises its biological functions; Venus is always ready to relapse into her first vegetable condition.' (87)

With barely concealed distaste, Clark also comments on the human figures in what he terms 'The Alternative Convention' for representing the unclothed human body. Dismissing Bosch and the Flemish masters whose art images Williams herself so strongly evokes, Clark complains:

> Roots and bulbs, pulled up into the light, give us for a moment a feeling of shame. They are pale, defenceless, unself-supporting. They have the formless character of life which has been both protected and oppressed. In the darkness their slow biological gropings have been the contrary of the quick resolute movements of free creatures, bird, fish or dancer, flashing through a transparent medium, and have made them baggy, scraggy and indeterminate. Looking at a group of naked figures in a Gothic painting or miniature we experience the same

sensation. The bulb-like women and root-like men seem to have been dragged out of the protective darkness in which the human body had lain muffled for a thousand years.

(301–2)

Williams' conflictual feelings about the human body—a body that she seems to grow more comfortable with only when she is well past childbearing age— seems consonant with Clark's account of the naked, but she revalues fragility and the 'slow biological gropings' of an entity that is 'pale, defenceless, unself-supporting'. Thus, significantly, the figure of 'Eve' is another of the *leitmotifs* to which the art of Evelyn Williams recurrently returns as she revalues the vulnerability of human flesh.

'Body' and 'flesh' are also not interchangeable terms. At the outset of the Hebrew creation myth in 'Genesis' (II, 23), 'flesh' (*bâsâr*) is linked to life and to blood, with Eve described by Adam as 'bone of my bones, and flesh of my flesh' (Welton 1998: 243). In Christianity 'flesh' is bound up with both evil and with good: with the 'sins of the flesh' and also with 'God made flesh'. The Hebrew texts do not at the start single out flesh as the source of moral corruption; it is only after the Fall that flesh is represented as debased and evil. As Leo Steinberg has demonstrated via his exploration of the imagery of Jesus' sexuality in Renaissance art, although Jesus was also represented as 'flesh' (with a disturbing emphasis often placed on the display of the penis both of the infant Jesus and even sometimes of the crucified Christ), Saint Augustine and his followers deemed the genitals of Jesus to be uncorrupted and, therefore, not a proper object of shame, in a way that simply did not apply to mankind after the Fall (Steinberg 1983). The emphasis on Eve's flesh and her role in the account of original sin does, however, provide one of the important roots of later representations of woman's flesh as more bound up with immanence, with the female portrayed as trapped by her biology in a way that the male was not.

Being a 'female' artist is not just a matter of biology, but involves occupying a position of marginality in terms of a history and a culture that has treated the fleshiness of male and female bodies in markedly different terms. Women artists cannot opt out of this history, but have to find a way of appropriating it or disrupting it. And this history is likely to produce tensions and fractures in their artworks, especially since the ideals of autonomy and self-sufficiency that are so emphatically inculcated remain masculine ideals, and are in many ways at odds with other ideals taught to women. Women learn to value bondedness to others: both in romantic love and via the processes of rearing and birth. Perhaps it is worth emphasising here that the education that Evelyn Williams received during her early years made her particularly ambivalent about the value of freedom, autonomy and the individualism of modernity.

At the age of three Evelyn was sent as a boarder to that most 'modern' of schools, Summerhill. The school had been specifically chosen by her father for its rationalist, secular principles. Summerhill aimed to allow children their own 'natural' development, treating them as equals, and allowing them to choose what lessons they were to follow. In a perverse refusal to recognise the need of a child for shelter and dependency, children were treated as mini-adults, so that the vote of a toddler had equal weight with that of the Director and teachers. Although Evelyn Williams still praises Summerhill for respecting the autonomy of the child, she has also described how unhappy she was, and how slow she was to read (or even talk). For the 'best' of reasons, her Welsh ex-Catholic father adopted principles which marooned her in an environment that she remembers as, above all, 'cold'.

It is hard not to look to this early emotional deprivation for the origins of the sense of loss that haunts so much of Evelyn Williams' work. As we discover from her 'Workbook', Evelyn Williams feels that she remains attached to another by an 'umbilical cord' that remains 'unsevered still' and squeezes her to death (Williams 1994: 13). But she also feels trapped in that very individuality that was the gift of her extraordinary education, like 'a fly in a glass box that the world knocks on from time to time' (Williams 1998: 60). Other passages in the 'Workbook' show how important the experiences of herself giving birth and of love have been for the artist in her own adult life. The tension between bondedness and separation appears even in her most tender imagery. Evelyn Williams seems to have experienced in its most extreme form the predicament of many women in our culture; she seems caught between masculine ideals of autonomy and feminine ideals of bondedness and collectivity.

Using Evelyn Williams as an example, we can see that 'being a woman' involves a double social positioning. On the one hand, women are supposed to be full members of this culture that takes individuality and autonomy as both ideal and norm. On the other hand, the fully autonomous and individualised 'person' of the democratic state (bearer of rights, carrier of duties and locus of individual and family responsibility) is not female, but male. Women find themselves locked into two different logics of self/other relationships. Being a woman is not a matter of simple biology. But that does not imply that there is nothing distinctive about the female subject position. Women in the past and present have already managed—consciously or unconsciously—to use the tensions within patriarchal modernity to open up different (female) ways of looking, different (gendered) spaces and distinctively female genres of art.

Reclaiming the life 'between'

The second artist I will consider has spoken out vehemently against the 'pigeonholing (or dove-coterie) of gender' as regards her mission as an artist (Caws et al. 1991: 228). However, as we will see, despite her claim that it is 'disgusting' to be considered as a 'woman artist' (Glassie 2002), the work (and words) of Dorothea Tanning (1910–) frequently exemplify the type of antinomies that I have associated with 'the female sublime'. In her memoir, Between Lives, Tanning tells us how, as a child in Illinois and then later in New

York, she was consumed by a love of books: Emily Dickinson, Edgar Allen Poe, Samuel Taylor Coleridge, Thomas De Quincey's *Confessions of an English Opium-Eater* are amongst those that would have familiarised her with Romanticism and the theory of the sublime (Tanning 2001: 42, 27). It was this background in reading that initiated her plunge into the world of surrealist art: 'I was the kind of feminine romantic whose romanticism feeds on random, obscure or forgotten texts and pictures that abound in musty books and documents' (90).

Amongst the 'extravagances' which filled her head and which were integral to her decision to become an artist, Tanning picks out Coleridge in particular (Glassie 2002). But Coleridge adapted German Romanticism when he insisted that 'a great mind must be androgynous', whilst differentiating the feminine lightness of thought which the poet requires for creativity from the heaviness of the merely material and also from the female (Coleridge 1835: Sept. 1, 183). Coleridge set out to revivify the vocabulary of 'the chymical technology', and used the metaphorics of alchemy to describe his own experience of poetic creation—as, for example, when he uses the language of 'flame', 'gold', 'quicksilver' and 'rising' in a letter to William Godwin of 25 March 1801 (Coleridge 1845: 204; 1991: 117–19). However, his advice to geniuses who require an 'active life' out in 'the stir of the world'—and their wives and sisters, for whom it is 'meritorious' to remain in the home—makes it abundantly clear that for Coleridge all genius is male. He compared the intellectual 'secretions' of the genius to certain 'physiological' secretions taken back into the blood, and it is clearly male bodily fluids and sublimated energies that he had in mind (Coleridge 1817: ch. 11).

Tanning's own autobiographical memoir shows how she had internalised this 'romantic' view of genius, and both in her painting and her novels she also draws on the imagery of alchemy to delineate creativity. It is certainly no accident that the main character of Tanning's 1946 novel, *Abyss*, is Albert Exodus, a painter who is 'hiding behind his colors like an alchemist behind his fiery liquids, his sulphurs, his loathsome fumes' (Chadwick 1985: 186). It is probably also of significance that this novel was written in the same year that Tanning married the painter Max Ernst—formalising the relationship which had started in 1942—since Ernst's own immersion in the philosophy, imagery and poetry of German Romanticism has been extensively documented (Spies 1991: 21ff., 341–50).

As we have seen in the last chapter, the metaphorics of alchemy used by the Romantics leave female fleshiness behind as the androgynous feminine becomes the goal. It seems scarcely surprising, therefore, that Tanning finds it easier to narrate the life of her artist-husband in terms of the norms of the 'great artist' than her own life. Constantly caught 'between lives' (his and hers), we feel her puzzlement as she intermittently returns to the question of how 'Dottie Tanning' from Galesburg, Illinois came to inhabit the world of celebrity artists and poets in New York and Paris, whilst producing a substantial *oeuvre* that both fits within the traditions of surrealism and oversteps that genre (Tanning: 291).

From analysing Tanning's visual imagery, it would seem that one of the Romantic pictures that inhabited her imagination was Caspar David Friedrich's *Wanderer Above the Sea of Fog* (c.1818) which functions as an appropriate and celebrated representation of the Kantian sublime. Perhaps Dorothea came to know Friedrich through Ernst who explicitly claimed that he had 'always had Friedrich's paintings more or less consciously in mind, almost from the day I started painting', and who felt 'profound spiritual ties' with his German predecessor (Spies: 341). However, it is much more likely that Tanning's awareness of Friedrich, like her affinity with Romanticism, preceded the meeting with Ernst, and contributed to the love and admiration that Ernst felt both for her and also her art. After all, her self-portrait, *Birthday*, was on her easel in 1942 when Ernst walked in to her studio, and in it her engagement with the imagery of Romanticism was already evident.

The painting which I will analyse here is a slightly later self portrait: dated to 1947 by Tanning in *Between Lives*, but more commonly listed as 1944 (Tanning: 128–29, photo). *Self Portrait* was, she says there, the title given to it by Ernst, who would certainly have recognised how it reworks the imagery of Friedrich's most celebrated painting, *Wanderer Above the Sea of Fog*. In the latter the Wanderer stands with his back to the viewer, poised on top of a rocky summit, looking out over the immensity of the abyss and over the indefinite contours of a landscape shrouded in fog. The Wanderer's upright posture, his severely cut frock-coat, and his dominating position, mean that there is no sense of the observer being overwhelmed or terrified by the landscape he scrutinises. The posture of the head, looking down on—as well as out to—infinity, indicates respect for the power of nature, but also a confidence in man's power over nature.

The stance of the Wanderer—left leg forward as if about to walk out into the abyss, walking-stick held confidently in his right hand—tells us that this is a man who has just attained the peak and who remains halted in suspended motion even as he remains still. Likewise, the uncovered head also suggests a man who does not bow down to the power of the infinite, even when he respects it. The line of the neat white collar marks off the slightly stocky neck and head, emphasising control, despite the slightly wind-blown hair. Central to the picture plane and dominating the scene, what we observe is not just a man, but an agent who arranges nature in his own mind, so that even the indefinite and the infinite are made subordinate to the human (male) frame. It is not that this picture does not convey emotion, but rather that the mood generated by the painting is mediated by the dominating presence and gaze of the dark and strongly silhouetted back—often referred to as the '*Rückenfigur*' (figure seen from the rear).

Friedrich's image fits with Kant's account of the sublime which insists that the sublimity does not lie in the landscape, but in both registering the terror and also transcending its power to disturb. By contrast, in *Self Portrait* (1944, oil on canvas, 61 × 76 cm) Dorothea Tanning positions herself back-to-the-viewer in an analogous position to Friedrich's *Wanderer*. Both the similarities and differences between it and Friedrich's *Wanderer Above the Sea of Fog* are so striking that this oil-painting seems like a deliberate reworking of the celebrated *Wanderer* motif, even employing a blue-green colour palette which echoes and softens the tonalities of the Friedrich, instead of reproducing the strong reds and ochres of Arizona where Tanning was based. Here again the figure is central, but whereas Friedrich's male is severe and well-clad in his frock coat, Tanning's 'self' is dressed in a backless garment—apparently a one-piece bathing costume—which leaves her legs naked and her shoulders and back exposed. Her shoulder-length hair falls in a soft curve, concealing the nape of her neck, and is given height by the curls that dominate the head. The hair is more tidy and more fashionable that that of the 'Wanderer', but the figure certainly seems fragile, unprotected—not naked, but semi-nude.

Friedrich's 'Wanderer' is large in scale in relation to the canvas, despite the looming crags and peaks beyond the abyss. He looks out over and down upon the landscape from a position of dominance: he stands as 'other' to and equal to the mountainous landscape that surrounds him. By contrast, Tanning's young woman is dwarfed by the canyons and desert of Arizona—and almost assimilated into that desert—even as she remains the central focus of the picture plane. Indeed, the centrality of the semi-clothed figure is secured through contrast: through vulnerability, rather than mastery of the landscape portrayed. The self is positioned as if in the womb of nature: the landscape of the desert opens out into immensity; but the vastness incorporates the fragile human body—without, however, merging into it.

Tanning's 'self' carries no walking-stick. Her position on a round raised rock makes her analogous to a statue in a museum or a pillar of the desert, rather than to the 'man of action' that is Friedrich's Romantic Traveller. But the modernity of the young woman's dress and the softness of the shoulder-line also prevent this image being read simply as another 'woman on a pedestal'. Although she is still, she is not lifeless. The image stresses the fragility and fleshiness of the female body, instead of idealising woman as an art-object. Neither fully object nor fully subject, this self-portrait fits neither the magisterial subject of the Kantian sublime, nor the 'emancipation' into 'pure knowledge' which, in the next chapter, we will see Schopenhauer associating with the sublime, including the desert landscape and the 'interior of North America' (*WWR*: i, 204). Instead, Tanning draws attention to herself as embodied and also as dependent, involving a kind of active passivity that seems intimately bound up with sense of herself as an artist who is always and forever embodied.

Tanning's image evokes a series of contrasts: activity/passivity; nature/culture; freedom/dependence; dream/reality; subject/object; immanence/transcendence. It is these tensions that give vigour and quirky particularity to this

147

remarkable piece. Tanning would rarely paint landscapes in subsequent years, but fleshy and female incongruities run through her later works and are especially evident in the 'soft sculptures' that she produced between 1968 and 1973. Here naked female forms merge with the shapes of furniture, and are given material shape through the textures of sewn fabrics—tweeds, felts, furs, velvets, synthetic furs, wool, cloth, often with the pinkness of flesh. Tanning describes them as 'fugacious' and 'fragile': 'living materials, become living sculpture, their life span something like ours' (Bailly and Morgan 1995: 301). Uncanny and often disturbingly erotic in their celebration of a materiality that cannot be mastered, they constitute a kind of counter-sublime. Furthermore, although many of Tanning's later images are more abstract—she says they 'splintered' into colours and light—and although she turned against relying on 'precisely painted elements of the natural world in order to present an incongruity', in her later canvases and drawings fleshy disturbances and female embodiment persist in the 'prismatic surfaces' in which she 'veiled, suggested, and floated' her 'persistent icons and preoccupations, in another of the thousand ways of saying the same thing' (Tanning 2001: 178, 213).

In *Between Lives* Tanning is very critical of those critics who privilege women artists or who wish to read her own art in feminised terms (334–35). On the other hand, she is also almost as scathing about the privilege of the 'mystery' and the 'muse' of femininity that typified the Surrealist circles of New York and Paris: the circles in which she and Max Ernst lived, and in which she registered herself as too often dismissed as Max's '*dependent*' (78–80). In *Between Lives* she records in detail how this produced a sense of a 'divided self', and how this both fed her art and also interfered with her work and her sense of being an autonomous self:

> When I began life with this famous man [Max Ernst] I was confident that I could continue as a separate, one-sided individual. Suddenly, from one moment to the next—the time it takes to fall hopelessly in love (I did), or face a firing squad—I was transferred from my unapproachable aerie to a nest on the ground.
>
> (277)

This fall from the heights of the soaring and autonomous sublime to material and physical dependence is ascribed, in part, to the problems of not being granted the status of an autonomous artist, and always being treated as 'subsidiary' to Max or to other male artists, but also to her own mode of embodiment:

> for a girl there is no greater handicap to creativity and self-fulfilment in the solitary arts than physical prettiness.
>
> Pretty is a two-edged sword, not only because of the way the world sees you. Oh, no. More insidious is your own divided self. Divided because, like a muscle without exercise, you have become soft, you

have diluted your dreams, and you have no one but yourself to accuse if you cannot deal with the resultant atrophy, if you cannot deflect the preferential treatment you get for the wrong reasons.

(278)

It is this tension between female physicality and the muscular hardness of the Romantic sublime that is so often present in Tanning's artworks—as well as a tension between being idolised as the embodiment of the 'feminine' and her own sense of being a material and fleshy self. As such, Tanning's sense of herself as a divided self is an apt illustration of 'the female sublime'. At the same time that she denies that there is anything special about being a woman artist, she nevertheless describes herself as caught in the tensions between spiritual transcendence, on the one hand, and fleshy materiality and dependence, on the other hand.

Multiple strategies

Surrealist women frequently represented reality from a 'male' perspective, whilst simultaneously undoing that perspective. Take, for example, the paintings of Kay Sage (1898–1963). This American surrealist was much influenced by the paintings and art theory of Giorgio de Chirico, but the latter had claimed that only males were capable of 'metaphysical painting', or of the transcendent melancholy that enabled them to confront the terribleness of lines and angles. Sage insistently and with great melancholy paints lines and angles in ways highly evocative of de Chirico. Yet these spaces are also corrosively feminised: fragile eggs scattered amongst the harsh lines and angles, or with swirls of empty drapery that suggest an absent female poised over and against de Chirico's harsh linear world. In *I Saw Three Cities* (1944) or *The Secret Voyage of a Spark* (1947), the flame-like movement of the hollowed-out female draperies has more dynamism and potentiality than the cold lines and angles of the metaphysical landscape that her paintings mimic. In her universe, space and time are dialectically structured; negation is not simple emptiness.

In her last self portrait, *Le Passage* (1956), we once again find the woman artist portraying herself, bare back to the viewer, looking out over a harsh and empty landscape which is divided into square and jagged planes and jutting, geometrical shapes. Bare to the waist, sitting, slightly slouched forward, with her bones clearly visible beneath her pale skin, Sage portrays herself as a frail counterpart to an uncultivated land that is alien to human life. Dominating the right half of the picture plane, right shoulder forward so as to reveal the curve of her bare breast beneath her left arm, Sage looks out from a position high above the monotonous plane, but without dominating it in the manner of the *Rückenfigur* in Friedrich's *Wanderer Above the Sea of Fog*. There is a clear refusal to assign either the human or inhuman halves of the picture a greater weight, and balance between the competing elements is only attained by the

149

muted grey-green light that suffuses the whole, and that comes from a sun that seems unearthly, but that is unshown.

Sage was a friend of Tanning's, and visited her and Max Ernst in the Arizona desert, together with her artist-husband, Yves Tanguy (Tanning 2001: 147). Another visitor in 1946 was Lee Miller who also picks up on the theme of the sublime in a photograph that she took of Ernst and Tanning during 1946. Here, once again, we see the Arizona landscape that features in Tanning's own *Self Portrait*; but Miller photographs Ernst from an angle that makes him seem huge, striding masterfully towards the camera, left leg forward and also his left fist clenched. Underneath his fist, the diminutive figure of the young Dorothea Tanning stands, sideways on to the camera, looking up to the towering figure of Ernst, the dominating artist–genius, with her right arm raised in a gesture that seems half salute and half protest. With her left hand outstretched and the top part of her body in partial recoil, the image strongly connotes Tanning's ambiguous positioning vis-à-vis her much older, much more celebrated, artist–partner. Here it is the male artist who is represented as sublime and as dominating nature; the softly feminine woman, and even the harsh landscape of the desert, as dominated by Ernst's transcendent self.

The sublime is also a recurrent theme in a number of the photographs that Lee Miller took elsewhere, including 'Revenge on Culture' and other photographs in *Grim Glory* (1940) that record the London Blitz, as well as subsequent photographs that document the after-effects in Europe of the 1939–45 war. It is, however, not only in representational photography and figurative painting that the thematics of the female sublime feature. Take, for example, *Current Disturbance* (1996) by Mona Hatoum (1952–) which is a large installation which includes wire mesh attached to a series of wooden frames through which one sees a tangle of wiring (see Figure 3). In each of the cages an electric light bulb pulses, surging on and off. One *hears* the installation as well as seeing it. Indeed, one hears the sound first before the cages are seen, and one hears the noise at a distance before anything is seen.

The amplified noise of the electric current surging on and off is an important part of the installation (which is site specific, so some details can vary). The noise is threatening, like a swarm of bees or, perhaps, a fog horn. It is an *electrical* noise. It makes a pulsing, invasive sound that takes over the body and invades the body boundaries. It is the sound, as much as the light that pulses on and off, that creates a sense of power or danger and leaves the viewer in a state of heightened attention and anticipation. The anticipation is all the greater because it is impossible to predict the patterning of silence and noise, and of light and dark.

In this installation the viewer has no position of visual mastery in respect to the pulsing sound and light. She cannot explore the artwork from a position that involves the visual mastery or the psychic transcendence of the Kantian sublime. Spectators who come into the room stand rooted, as if hypnotised. They walk round the large, pulsing structure; indeed, they often stop quite still as the lights go out. It is as if the pulsing object controls *them*; it is as if the *object* is alive and they are subjects/viewers only in relation to the object. The viewers gaze, but the gaze is not objectifying or controlling. Threatened by sounds and pulses of light that cannot be focused, contained, distanced or even ordered into a regular pattern, the viewer feels the boundaries between 'self' and 'not-self' to be under attack.

Those on the desk at Newlyn, Cornwall, when *Current Disturbance* was on display there in 1997, reported that members of the public were both physically and mentally 'broken down' by the pulses of light and sound. However, it is not that all identity disappears when confronted by Hatoum's installation; but rather that identity has to be understood as no longer 'free' or 'self-controlling'. *Current Disturbance* combines solidity—the wood and wire mesh that constitutes the cage—with fragility; closure with openness; the rigid framework of the physical structure with surges and leaks of energy; a porous boundary with impenetrability; and a fluctuating equilibrium between centre and periphery.

Figure 3 Mona Hatoum
Current Disturbance, 1997 (wood, wire mesh, light bulbs, electrical wire, computerised dimmer switch, amplifier, speakers)
Installation in 'A Quality of Light', St Ives International, Newlyn Art Gallery, Cornwall.
Photograph © copyright Bob Berry Photography Ltd., Studio 5, Treglisson Rural Workshops, Hayle, Cornwall

Current Disturbance makes us experience our selves as constituted through unstable patterns of movement and flows of energies. As such, the boundary between 'self' and 'not-self' is rendered unstable and matter is no longer something alien to us or 'other' to the 'I'.

Like many other of Hatoum's artworks, *Current Disturbance* plays with danger and makes us aware that we are embodied humans, not the disembodied energies of Lyotard's 'postmodern' and 'inhuman' sublime, which will be further discussed in Chapter 10, nor Kant's ideal of a transcendent 'I'. Instead, Hatoum's installation serves to make us more aware of ourselves as physical beings, whilst emphasising also the fragility of the body and the non-autonomy of the 'I'. And here it should be added that in the case of Mona Hatoum there are also cultural factors related to ethnicity that affect the art that she produces, since she comes from a society which does not envisage mind and body as sharply divided.

Born in Beirut in 1952, Hatoum came to the UK in 1975. She had intended to stay only for a brief time, but ended up living and studying in London because war had broken out in her home country. Commenting on this move, Hatoum reports:

> The first thing I noticed when I came here was how divorced people were from their bodies. ... Since my early performances, the body has been central to my work. ... I have always been dissatisfied with work that just appeals to your intellect and does not involve you in a physical way. For me the embodiment of an artwork is within the physical realm; the body is the axis of our perceptions, so how can art afford not to take that as a starting point? We relate to the world through our senses. You first experience an artwork physically. I like the work to operate on both sensual and intellectual levels. Meanings, connotations and associations come after the initial physical experience as your imagination, intellect, psyche are fired off by what you've seen.
>
> (Archer *et al.* 1997: 8)

Although Hatoum comes from a different culture, she faces many of the same paradoxes as the American and British women artists from an earlier generation. Like them, she fails to fit within the dominant models of the self of Western modernity—models that purport to be gender-neutral but that do, in practice, take the non-birthing, disembodied male subject as norm. I read Hatoum's work, just as I interpret Tanning's and Williams', as an imaginative and novel reimagining of the sublime—and in ways that relate directly to their positioning as 'female'.

The sublime of flesh

To illustrate how the ambiguities of flesh continue to impact on the imagery of the sublime, I will end this chapter with one final example, that of A K Dolven (1956–) who works between London, Berlin and the Lofoten Islands in

Norway, the country of her birth. Apparently unaware of the use of the female *Rückenfigur* by Tanning and Sage, there are nevertheless analogies between the imagery employed in her DVD, *between the morning and the handbag II* (2002), and Tanning's and Sage's oil paintings. Anne Katrine Dolven's installation places the viewer inside a walk-through structure, with two 35-mm films projected on to opposite walls. Filmed at five am during the 'white nights' of a Northern Norwegian summer, in one of the projections we observe the completely bare back of a shapely young woman—completely nude and bald—sitting on concrete, apparently staring out over a sea or a lake. Unlike Tanning who paints herself in miniature, the large female nude dominates the picture plane even as she sits, almost completely still, looking out over the gently moving waves. In the opposite projection, a slightly battered handbag lies on the concrete by the water's edge. The only movement comes from the waves and a visiting fly. Photographed in real time, neither film has been edited; but the curious lack of shadows—an effect of the midnight sun—makes the landscape (especially the figure) seem out of time and unreal. Only the slow breathing of the young woman's body, the ripples and the slight crawling of the insect show that the temporalities are, indeed, exact.

In a version of the image that involves a still photograph (see Figure 4), Dolven had placed the handbag beside the woman who sits on the same hard and rough ledge, but with the sky beginning to brighten in the arctic dawn. In 2003 Dolven returned once again to this theme, but this time she films and photographs multiple naked figures with their backs to the camera as they look out over the distant mountains and sea. Photographed at a distance rather than in the disturbing close-up that marks *between the morning and the handbag*, these images of hairless female figures were once again shot in the strange shadowless light of the summer Norwegian dawn. The later films, including *4 min at 2 am 22 of July 2003* (see Figure 5), remain troubling, but are visually less challenging than the *'handbag'* images which came dangerously close to voyeurism even as they undid the conventions for representing the female body as 'mere flesh'.

The work of Dolven, who is also a painter, often picks up and reverses a view of nature and of femininity that is characteristic of the Romantic or Expressionist artists (especially that icon of Norwegian painting, Edvard Munch), but then uses temporal, spatial or behavioural incongruities to render strange the framework which the observer instinctively employs to make sense of what she sees. In *between the morning and the handbag II*, the baldness and apparent self-composure of the young woman position her in the temporality of the twenty-first century, in which the earlier conventions for presenting the unclothed female body are being reconfigured. Like the handbag, which seems to symbolise the cultural baggage that attaches to women in Western modernity, the white body and hairless head of the young woman remind us of the precarious health of a cancer victim, but also of the possibility of allowing female baldness to function as a badge of defiance and of courage.

153

Figure 4 A K Dolven
between the morning and the handbag
C-print 2002
140 × 114 cm
edition: 5+2AP
camera: Vegar Moen
makeup: Siw Jarbyen
courtesy: carlier | gebauer, Berlin and Wilkinson Gallery, London
sponsored by Mead Gallery, Warwick

Whereas for Clark an unclothed female body was *either* defenceless and naked *or* 'clothed' into beauty by her flesh, Dolven manages to disturb the nature/culture boundary which has been so integral to the imaging of beauty and femininity and modernity—whilst also treating the (real) young women who have posed for her with respect. Although the strangeness of the pose and the coldness of the lighting make the white figures seem more analogous to mannequins or to dummies in a shop window than to 'real flesh', the gently breathing body of her model does emerge as 'living flesh' as the slow temporalities of the film of *between the morning and the handbag II* unfold. And in that sense it is significant that in conversation Dolven has claimed that one of the

154

Figure 5 A K Dolven
4 min at 2 am 22 of July 2003
film still
35mm film 2004
35mm projection, mute
4:00
size variable
camera: Vegar Moen
makeup: Siw Jarbyen
edition: 5+2AP
courtesy: carlier | gebauer, Berlin and Wilkinson Gallery, London
commissioned by Norsk Kulturråd

things that is most important to her as an artist is that she knows, on a personal basis, the various people who feature in her films and photographs. A regular visitor to the community of Lofoten Islanders, she wants the young women to feel comfortable as their bodies are posed in the unfamiliar dawning light.

The bodies of Dolven's models in these dawn images are sometimes described as androgynous, despite the ample hips and hourglass curves which are standardly read as markers for the mature female form. This is probably because we still find it difficult to think autonomy and personhood in terms of naked female flesh, and because Dolven's images seem marked as much by respect for persons as by the awed and respectful response to the sublime mountains and infinite horizons that these images also convey. The menace in the pictures comes as much from the hairless young women, who remind us of death, as from the magnificent landscape which they seem to survey. Dolven's female figures do not transcend or master nature in the manner of the Kantian sublime, but neither do they become one with the forces of nature as happens so often in late Romanticism and also in Munch. Disrupting the conventions for painting sublime scenery, the incongruity of the figures disturbs our sense of what is real, and also means that the images do not fit simply within the conventions of the picturesque in which all potential chaos or disorder is framed so as to fit with the expectations of the I. The human menace is, indeed, intensified by the fact that the pornographic image of the female nude is an ever-present danger when naked female flesh is placed on display.

Dolven's art deals with some more recent stereotypes of the feminine than were available for Williams, Tanning or Sage during their formative years, but the perils of voyeurism that haunt her work nevertheless suggests that to be female in our culture involves a relationship to the fleshy and the self that is still riven with tension. Sexual difference may not be a straightforward 'biological' category and is certainly not to be thought of as determining an artist's output in any reductively causal way, but nevertheless one's positioning as 'male' or 'female' is not (yet) escapable in our culture, however much the categories are changed by the emergence of transgendered individuals, by new norms for deciding biological sex, or by the rapidly changing gender norms which shape the framework for 'masculine' and 'feminine' characteristics or behaviour. For me, it is the most interesting women artists and writers who manage to both confront and convey the *dangers* of these fleshy, spatial, temporal, human and *female* antinomies in what they create. And the *female sublime* is, above all, a site in which the dislocations of the female subject position are explored and made visible.

8

NIETZSCHE AND THE GENEALOGY OF THE SUBLIME

For many feminist theorists who have drawn on psychoanalytic theory and structuralist and poststructuralist philosophies, the 'other' that is equated with the feminine—and allied to the sublime—lies outside the realm of representation. Like Jacques Lacan, such theorists would assert that there is only *one* symbolic and that the feminine 'other' encountered in the sublime either takes us into a 'beyond' that cannot be expressed in language, or constitutes no more than an irruption in a language and symbolic system that models identity always and only in terms of masculine identities and oedipal rivalries. Against such an understanding of the 'feminine' and the 'other', I have been concerned to argue that the *female* and *raced* subject that interests me with respect to the sublime is not outside history, nor outside the frameworks of language or representation. Instead, my interest has been in exploring modes of *embodied* individuality and *human* differences that lie hidden in the folds of history: folds which are themselves created by fractures and tensions that are historically based. As such, nothing could be more alien to my own position than that of Jacques Lacan who reads Sophocles' *Antigone* in terms of Kant's account of the beautiful and the sublime.

For Lacan, 'woman' is symbolised by the figure of Antigone, the daughter of Oedipus, who represents 'what it is man wants and what he defends himself against' (Lacan 1959–60: 240). Describing Antigone is the *beautiful* object which man desires; Lacan also asserts that she 'pushes to the limit the realization of something that might be called the pure and simple desire of death as such. She incarnates that desire' (282). Just as in Kant, the sublime involves fear of the infinite, and the transcendence of fear, analogously, for Lacan, Antigone represents the death drive and the warding off of the death drive. Antigone/woman signifies the threat of the dissolution of the self into the Otherness that bounds it. Like Kant, Lacan argues for universal and necessary limits to the horizons of experience; 'woman'—like 'death'—marks the lure of the infinite, whilst also signifying a threshold that cannot be crossed, in much the same way as the Kantian sublime.

Even some of Lacan's fiercest critics, such as Luce Irigaray, have continued to represent the history of Western philosophy and culture in a way that is too monolithic. As indicated also in Chapter 6, Irigaray develops a notion of a female symbolic which is non-oedipal, but which has remained fundamentally the same since historical records began. Thus, she asserts that the privilege of the masculine 'can be traced historically':

> Man became God, he became *He*. Man, He, the people(s) of men only kept the virgin-mother side of female divinity to express the necessity of a taboo concerning mother–son incest. . . . The divine is no longer even in the position of mistress to man, as it is in some more feminine cultures.
>
> (Irigaray 2004: 107)

Irigaray relies on Johann Jakob Bachofen and 'goddess' feminists such as Merlin Stone for evidence for this historical claim (Bachofen 1861; Stone 1974; Irigaray 1990a: 17, 24). However, nothing substantial can be proved on the basis of Bachofen's argument which included the claim that civilisation develops only once a more 'primitive' stage of human development, characterised in terms of 'the rule of the mothers', has been left behind. Bachofen established this conclusion only by being determinedly blind to women's contribution to cultural evolution in historical times.

Ironically enough, it was Bachofen's approach—which was initially designed to prove the inferiority of women—that was taken up, and then inverted, by those radical, cultural and 'goddess' feminists who look back to matriarchy and to the worship of a prehistorical 'universal' goddess. Here, too, there has been a tendency to write out the importance of women as cultural creators in 'patriarchal' times, and to treat 'matriarchy' and 'patriarchy' as homogenous units that occur in a linear historical sequence, so concealing differences within the two 'stages' of cultural evolution. Thus, all anthropological, archaeological and scientific evidence about a historical break needs to be looked on with suspicion, and certainly any simple appeal to Bachofen or to the 'goddess' historians will not be enough to prove that the historical reversal that Irigaray points to is anything more than a myth (Russell 1993). Of course the difficulties in interpreting the prehistorical evidence does not imply that there never was a pre-patriarchal society in which mothers either ruled or had greater power. It does mean, however, that there is no possibility of looking back—or beyond—the history of Western thought to an established 'fact' of mother-rule or to a period before the mother goddess was displaced.

The goddess feminists say that patriarchal cultures have 'forgotten' the goddess; but what Irigaray herself forgets to see is something much more concrete: the achievements of women artists and writers within modernity and the histories of Western culture. Thus, in 'A Lacuna of Birth', Irigaray meditates on the drawings and writings of Unica Zürn (1916–70), and in so doing indicates that 'woman'—and hence also a female art—'is still to come (or come again?) in its own forms' (Irigaray 1985: 13). Zürn fails, according to Irigaray, because

158

she lives in a culture which is threatened by fusion with the Other. The birth/ re-birth of women artists will only be able to come when women learn to represent women's bodies not as passive matter, but as 'the place where the universe was generated' (13). But at this time, art is too interested in 'our flaws, our tensions, the disordered perturbations of our partial drives'. Occupied with fragments, Zürn, Bellmer and 'others' have 'created something ugly', whereas 'truth in its entirety is beautiful or sublime' (12).

In 1953 Unica Zürn became Hans Bellmer's mistress and model. She is there in his surrealist photographs and drawings: naked, trussed, her body publicly fragmented and on display, with a vulva where her right eye should be. Later she would go mad, producing prose recounting trips in and out of insanity, eventually killing herself. What is disturbing about 'A Lacuna of Birth' is the way Irigaray treats Zürn and Bellmer as representative of all women and men within the artistic past. Irigaray's aesthetic model tends to make women artists tragic failures: both consenting and resisting victims. There is a suggestion that things might once have been different, but this eventuality is pushed onto other non-Western, pre-patriarchal ('goddess') cultures. Although Irigaray does not treat the symbolic in the straightforwardly synchronic way that Lacan does, she also cannot register change in the history of the West since the decline of the goddess religions. She wants to open a space for painting or speaking the female, but she first closes down the history of Western philosophy and art into a history of sameness.

Whose divine?

Clearly understanding something of the difficulties of using the terminology of the 'sublime' in relation to this alternative 'female' symbolic, Irigaray does in general avoid using the term 'sublime', preferring instead to describe her project in terms of a 'divine' that is appropriate to women (Irigaray 1984). Very occasionally, however, as for example in her engagement with Kant and Nietzsche, Irigaray makes reference to the 'sublime' to demarcate the position that she is seeking to undercut (Irigaray 1974: 206). Thus, of Nietzsche's interpretation of the figure of Zeus, she writes: 'Is not all that is lofty and sublime in him pressed out of the bodies of those mortal women who have been seduced by the all-powerful fire and carried away from their genealogies?' (Irigaray 1980: 151). Irigaray reads Nietzsche as complicit with an aesthetic that associates masculinity with sublimity, before herself reversing the polarity and displacing the divine onto some of the feminine figures and goddesses who inhabit the margins of Nietzsche's texts. Picking up Nietzsche's famous line from *Twilight of the Idols*—'I am afraid we are not rid of God because we still have faith in grammar'—Irigaray protests:

> And you [Nietzsche] have invented no grammar other than the one
> that creates the gods—and makes you god. And no other love but war

to the death against everything that surrounds you and holds you back
from climbing to that supreme illusion.

(Irigaray 1980: 66; Nietzsche, *TI*: 483)

Nietzsche's point in this section of *Twilight of the Idols* is that the subject–
predicate structures of the Greek and European languages have led man to
privilege 'being' over 'becoming', and 'substance' and 'atoms' over process and
change. But Nietzsche expresses this insight via a gendered metaphor:
'"Reason" in language—oh, what an old deceptive female she is!' (483). Irigaray's complaint is that Nietzsche pretends to think an alternative to the traditional gods, but can do so only by negating the female. Irigaray sets up a
dialogue between herself and Nietzsche with respect to the divine, but this
conversation misses Nietzsche's ongoing dialogue with himself as regards the
sublime. As we will see in both this chapter and the next, Nietzsche spent
much of his philosophical career engaging with—and seeking to resist—the
seductions of the sublime, and ended by reconfiguring sublimity in ways that
are radical and also profound.

Nietzsche's restless attempt to revalue all values (including aesthetic values)
led him to move from viewing art as a mode of access to a truth 'beyond'
appearance to a reconfiguration of the notion of surface and its relation to
depth, as well as to a re-imagination of the relationship between the 'now' and
the eternal, and also to a redescription of the boundary separating self from
not-self. Thus, to help me think how the sublime might be reconfigured in such
a way as to deal with embodied differences (sexual and racial), I will turn away
from Irigaray and instead look back to Nietzsche whose philosophical trajectory
led him to confront the problems of the sublime in a much more direct fashion.

I will sketch in something of the dialogue between Nietzsche and Schiller,
Schelling and Arthur Schopenhauer (1788–1860) with regard to the sublime,
and also provide an overview of developments in the work of Nietzsche with
regard to this concept. I have been surprised to discover just how central
thinking about the sublime seems to have been to Nietzsche and also how
little, amongst the extensive welter of secondary writing on Nietzsche in English, has addressed this theme (but see Rampley 2000: 81–109). Since this
could be the topic for a whole book, my account will be necessarily incom-
plete, but the outline of Nietzsche's developing thought on this topic will
nevertheless become clear.

We will see that, like me, Nietzsche rejects the notion of the 'feminine' as
the indefinite and elusive 'other' that the I encounters in the experience of the
sublime, but that he nevertheless does not give up completely on the language
of sublimity. Like me also, Nietzsche puzzles over the possibilities for reconfiguring the sublime so as to conjoin it with bodies. And the Nietzschean body is
very different from the metaphysics of matter that I explored in Chapter 6 in
relation to alchemy. For Nietzsche, matter is not merely inert or evil—what
Beattie called 'the *slime*, the *mud*, or the *mould* of this world'—that needs to be

rendered 'sublime' by the processes of heating or purification. Instead, Nietzsche—like the Romantic writers and theorists considered in Chapters 5 and 6—draws on the metaphorics and language of alchemical sublimation, but gives these a new meaning as the 'feminine' is rejected and the body given priority in the description of a new and 'great' health.

As we will also see, at the start of his writing career Nietzsche's criticisms of the sublime are muted, and in *The Birth of Tragedy* Nietzsche begins by explicitly situating himself within a Schopenhauerian framework for analysing the sublime (Nietzsche 1872/86). However, as will also become evident, from the very start Nietzsche's own account of the development of tragedy as the paradigmatically 'sublime' art was fundamentally at odds with the analyses of the sublime provided by Schopenhauer, Schiller and Schelling. But Nietzsche himself only seems to have fully registered this discrepancy some time after 1882, which was the year which saw the publication of the first edition of *The Gay Science* (Nietzsche 1882/87). Because of the complexity of the developing nature of Nietzsche's understanding of the sublime, I will consider his position first in relation to the 1872 edition of *The Birth of Tragedy*, but also make some references to the 'Attempt at Self Criticism' that he added to the 1886 edition of *The Birth of Tragedy* as a new Preface. Only then will I move on, in the next chapter, to consider Nietzsche's changed relation to the sublime in other texts published in the 1880s, including *Daybreak* (1881), *Thus Spoke Zarathustra* (1883–85); *Beyond Good and Evil* (1886); *On the Genealogy of Morals* (1887); the Preface to the second edition of *The Gay Science* which was written in the Autumn of 1886, shortly after writing 'An Attempt at Self Criticism'; and the expanded version of *The Gay Science* which was published in January 1887.

The extent to which Nietzsche deploys the language of the sublime in his published texts is not always apparent in the English translations—and is especially hard to see in the recent series of translations issued by Cambridge University Press. In a sense this stems from the difficulties posed by the way that Longinus' concept of '*hypsous*' (linked to height or elevation) was taken up in Germany. Although John Hall, the first English translator of Longinus' *Peri Hypsous*, selected 'Of The Height of Eloquence' for the title of his 1652 translation, subsequent translators tended to follow the example of Nicholas Boileau (in 1674), in using 'sublime' or 'sublimity' to translate the title of the Greek text. The same was true for all the other main European languages, except Russian and also German. In the latter the title for this Greek text was rendered by more exact equivalents: '*das Erhabene*', '*die Erhabenheit*' and cognate terms linked to the adverb '*erhaben*' (raised, elevated).

This means that English translators of Nietzsche are faced with a dilemma; Nietzsche loves to play with the figurative language of height, but when he uses the language of the '*erhaben*'—28 times in *The Birth of Tragedy*—we certainly need to read these references in terms of the aesthetic debates concerning the sublime. Later, Nietzsche would sometimes use the much less common German word '*sublim*', as well as the related verb '*sublimieren*' (sublimate) and the noun

'*Sublimierung*' (sublimation), which bring with them the connotations of purification (chemical and alchemical) and spiritualisation, as they do also in English, Latin and French. But Nietzsche does not use this word in *The Birth of Tragedy*, and it is part of his later solution to show what has gone wrong in modernity (and with Kant and Romanticism) in terms of our relation to the truth and which is 'other' to the I. Thus, for example, '*sublim*' is the adjective used to describe the pale, northern, Königsbergian (Kantian) 'Idea' of the 'true world' in 'How the "True World" became a Fable' in *Twilight of the Idols* (*TI*: 485). Nietzsche also uses the term with a similar set of connotations in the 1887 edition of *The Gay Science*, but now in relation to a particularly 'German' set of moral values and 'conscience' (GS: §357). As we will see in the next chapter, it is the language of the '*sublim*'—not that of the '*erhaben*'— that Nietzsche will ultimately deploy to reconfigure the sublime. First, however, we must explore Nietzsche's unstable position with regard to sublimity in *The Birth of Tragedy*, especially with regard to Romantic philosophies of the sublime.

Sublime beauty

The Birth of Tragedy can be read as a kind of genealogy of the sublime, and in terms of Nietzsche's struggle to find a language that will express the possibility of a 'sublime' that is not the Romantic sublime of Schiller, Schelling or Novalis, and also not the sublime of Kant, Schopenhauer or Hegel. As we have seen in Chapter 5, for Kant, the absolute remains an unattainable horizon towards which the I reaches, and the pleasure of the sublime comes through reaching rather than through the attainment of a realm that is 'other' to the understanding or to the I:

> Perhaps nothing more sublime has ever been said, or thought more sublimely expressed, than in the inscription over the Temple of *Isis* (Mother *Nature*): 'I am all that is and that was and that shall be, and no mortal has lifted my veil.' *Segner* made use of this idea by means of a vignette, rich in sense, placed at the beginning of his theory of nature, in order to prepare the mind of his apprentice, whom he was ready to lead into this temple, through a sacred shudder and ritual attentiveness.
>
> (CPJ: 316n. *corr.*)

But for Schiller the absolute is attainable; art is morally educative and the beautiful and the sublime are not fundamentally opposed. The sublime is defined in terms of that which either defeats '*our power of apprehension*' or involves a 'power against which our own dwindles to nothing'. In the sublime, Schiller says, 'Nature' employs 'a sensuous means of teaching us that we are more than merely sensuous' (Schiller 1801: 198, 199).

Like Schiller before him, in *The Philosophy of Art* Schelling also emphasises that the experience of the sublime acts as a moral educator of man: 'The sublime in nature, just as that of tragedy and art, cleanses the soul by liberating it from mere suffering'. Schelling employs Kantian terminology as he indicates that the intellectually 'flaccid', the morally weak and the cowardly will not enjoy the 'terrible image of their own nothingness and contemptibility' that seems integral to the sublime (1801–4: 87). But whereas Kant himself said that an appropriate moral education and disposition is necessary for the appreciation of the sublime, Schelling stressed its morally transformative power. And Schelling quotes Schiller's 'On the Sublime' (1801) as he claims that, through encountering the sublime, '"the mind is irresistibly driven out of the world of phenomena into the world of ideas, out of the conditioned into the unconditioned"' (89). Via 'the fundamental intuition of chaos',

> the understanding passes over to the perception of the absolute, be it in art or science. After unsuccessful attempts to exhaust the chaos of the phenomena in nature and in history by means of the understanding, ordinary perception or knowledge resolves to take 'the incomprehensibility itself,' as Schiller says, 'as a principle of judgment.'
>
> (88)

Schiller and Schelling start within a Kantian framework, but then transform it, particularly in relation to the role of the sublime in art and literature. Although we have seen Kant discussing a copperplate print by Georg Daniel Heumann as an image that evokes the sublime, for Kant it is primarily nature that generates the distinctive response of awed respect that sublimity entails. For Schelling, by contrast, it is above all art that generates the feeling, and he explicitly claims that 'only in *art* is the object itself sublime' and that 'Nature is not sublime in itself' (90). Schelling is also quite unlike Kant both in making the response to the sublime dependent on an 'aesthetic intuition', and also in claiming that this response is not fundamentally opposed to the intuition of beauty (86). In the sublime, he says, we encounter '*the informing of the infinite into the finite*' in a way that is coercive; in the beautiful the finite is presented in such a way as to be rendered infinite (85).

Schelling quite explicitly claims that the beautiful and the sublime belong together, and that not only does the sublime properly encompass beauty, but beauty also encompasses the sublime—even distinguishing between 'sublime beauty' (his example is Juno) and 'beautiful sublimity' (he cites Minerva) (90). For Schelling, tragedy and sculpture are the two art forms that most adequately exemplify the sublime. In tragedy, the tragic hero is constrained by the infinite (fate and the forces of nature), but retains his own specific character (his finitude): 'The genuinely tragically sublime depends for just this reason on two conditions, namely, that the moral person capitulate to the forces of nature and simultaneously be victorious through his *inner character*' (89). In sculpture also,

Schelling claims, we find 'the highest contact between life and death', the 'mortal and the immortal', and the 'infinite' and the 'finite' that is necessary to the sublime (193–94).

When we turn to look at Schopenhauer on the sublime, we can see yet another mixture of Kantian and non-Kantian elements. Although Schopenhauer is often explosively rude about the philosophies of Kant (and Schelling), it is Kant's account of the sublime that is salvaged as 'true and fine': 'Only a few things in his language and the fatal faculty of reason are to be overlooked.—If only he had seen that the beautiful is only something indirectly sublime!' (Schopenhauer 1809–18: 320 and ff.). It was, in effect, Kant's characterisation of the sublime (modified by some elements of Romanticism) that Schopenhauer drew on as he put together an alternative system of metaphysics, morality and art that melds together Kant, Plato, Hinduism and Buddhism in ways that are riven with tensions, but which have nevertheless exerted a powerful influence on art and aesthetics in the last 250 years. Not only was Nietzsche profoundly in Schopenhauer's debt, so also were Wagner, Freud, Wittgenstein, Bergson, Proust, de Chirico, Thomas Mann, Mahler and Rilke. The list could go on; and it has even been claimed that in the twentieth century Schopenhauer's aesthetics was 'the artist's favored philosophy of art' (Levinson 1998: 245). It is Schopenhauer's account of music, in particular, that has provided the clues for later avant-garde and surrealist theories of art that emphasised 'shock' and a change in subject–object relationships as integral to aesthetic experience and the sublime. In Chapter 2 we saw Stockhausen drawing on just such a model in his comparison of the events of 'September 11' with the transformative power of avant-garde music and art.

For Schopenhauer, as also for Schelling and Schiller, the sublime and the beautiful are only *qualitatively* different in kind; but Schopenhauer is in some ways closer to Kant in that he draws a sharp contrast between the realm of the unconditioned and the infinite (the thing-in-itself) and the space–time framework imposed by consciousness and the ego on phenomenal nature. Art, Schopenhauer claims, can take man through the 'veil' of illusion and deceit imposed by consciousness, the senses and the individual ego. Our responses to both the beautiful and the sublime can help us make this transition; it is just that the sublime involves a more forceful and abrupt transition to the non-phenomenal realm of Ideas and of Will as thing-in-itself. Like Schiller and Schelling, Schopenhauer makes art and also the sublime morally educative. But here Schopenhauer departs more radically from Kant insofar as he sharply opposes the ideals of (Kantian) freedom and duty that Schiller and Schelling privilege.

Schopenhauer's ethically good man rises above mere egoism or the desires of an individualistic will, but—taken over by the universal—he acts out of sympathy (*Mitgefühl*) or compassion (*Mitleid*: the word is generally translated as 'pity' in Nietzschean texts and given negative connotations). Tragedy, as Schopenhauer says in *The World as Will and Representation*, is admirable in the way that it triggers compassion (Schopenhauer 1819/59: vol. i, 375–76). But even more admirable is the fact that tragedy acts as 'a *quieter* of the will' and 'produces resignation, the giving up not merely of life, but of the whole will-to-live itself' (i, 253). For Schopenhauer, such resignation is not characteristic of the ethically good man, but the saintly man; and 'the summons to turn away the will from life remains the true tendency of tragedy' (ii, 435). Schopenhauer illustrates this ascetic resignation through the example of Hamlet's 'to be or not to be' monologue, claiming that *Hamlet* illustrates that life 'is so wretched that complete non-existence would be decidedly preferable to it'. Faced with the choice of living or not living, no 'sincere' man who is still 'in possession of his faculties' could, at the end of his life, 'ever wish to go through it again. Rather than this, he will much prefer to choose complete non-existence' (i, 324). For Schopenhauer, the superiority of Hamlet over any Greek hero is proved precisely by the fact that Hamlet's failure to act—or even will his own suicide—displays a pessimism which is at odds with Greek 'optimism' which is dismissed as 'not merely an absurd, but also a really *wicked* way of thinking' (i, 326).

Nietzsche also discusses Hamlet in *The Birth of Tragedy*, but even in this early work it is certainly not Schopenhauer's *moral* (or *saintly*) analysis that he provides—although he also does not oppose Schopenhauer so completely as to claim that the most sublime hero might indeed will that he should live the very same life again and again (*BT*: §7). Nietzsche does, however, differ sharply from Schopenhauer in terms of the relative value that each gives to ancient and modern tragedy. Complaining that resignation is 'rarely' seen or expressed 'in the tragedy of the ancients', Schopenhauer had noted that both Oedipus and Cassandra might seem resigned to death, but both are also comforted by the thought of revenge, whilst Euripides' *Bacchae* is ethically 'revolting'. For Schopenhauer, 'Shakespeare is much greater than Sophocles', and Euripides is 'crude and vulgar' in comparison with Goethe, and this is because 'the ancients displayed little of the spirit of resignation, little of the turning away of the will from life' (*WWR*: ii, 434–35). For Nietzsche, by contrast, it is precisely this failure to 'quiet the will' that constitutes the excellence of the Greeks. Although he will also agree with Schopenhauer that Euripides is more vulgar than Sophocles (or Aeschylus), his analysis will be different.

In the 'Attempt at Self-Criticism', published as a critical forward to the 1886 edition of *The Birth of Tragedy*, Nietzsche quotes Schopenhauer on the sublime in tragedy:

> What gives to everything tragic, whatever the form in which it appears, the characteristic tendency to the sublime, is the dawning of the knowledge that the world and life can afford us no true satisfaction, and are therefore not worth our attachment to them. In this the tragic spirit consists; accordingly it leads to *resignation*.
>
> (*BT*: 'Attempt' §6 *corr.*, quoting *WWR*: ii, 433–34)

Adding his own emphasis to the word 'resignation', Nietzsche then carries on: 'How differently Dionysus spoke to me! How far removed I was from all this resignationism!' In 1886 Nietzsche signals his unease with his own position in the 1872 edition of *The Birth of Tragedy*, but indicates that the strength of that book is that it provides an alternative to a '*moral* interpretation and significance of existence' ('Attempt' §5). Schopenhauer's move from the aesthetic to the moral and to the 'unconditioned' is utterly unlike the movement that Nietzsche himself makes, which provides the sublime and the tragic with an *aesthetic*—and not a *moral*—justification. As we will see, what Nietzsche also ends up refusing is any notion of an 'absolute' truth or moral law that can be uncovered via the experience of the sublime. *The Birth of Tragedy* is, however, not altogether clear on this point, and it seems that Nietzsche did not himself fully grasp it until he had left behind his intellectual and spiritual love affair with Schopenhauer and also with Richard Wagner who was, at the time of writing *The Birth of Tragedy*, Nietzsche's 'master', but who later came to emblematise for Nietzsche much of what was wrong with Christianity, Germany and also 'Romanticism'.

'An impossible book'

The Birth of Tragedy is—as Nietzsche himself says in the Preface to the 1886 edition— 'an impossible book' ('Attempt' §3): one that struggles to express an attitude that is fundamentally non-Schopenhauerian within a vocabulary and a metaphysical scheme that he takes over from Schopenhauer. For Kant, as we have seen, we can never actually experience the supersensible or intuit the unconditioned; instead the enjoyment of the sublime is bound up with the process of reaching towards an infinite Otherness (Mother Nature/the absolute) that must forever elude us. In the case of Schopenhauer, however, the experience of the sublime allows us to penetrate the veil. He retains the language of veiling that we have seen Kant utilising in the case of the sublime, although he substitutes the Hindu 'veil of Maya' for the 'Egyptian' (in fact, Greco–Roman) trope of the 'veil of Isis' employed by Kant and Schiller *et al.* Schopenhauer also turns to the *Upanishads* to rewrite the sentence 'I am all that is and that was and that shall be, and no mortal has lifted my veil' that had been linked to Isis by Kant and the other Idealist philosophers and writers. For Schopenhauer, the truth hidden behind 'the veil of Maya' translates as, '"I am all this creation collectively, and beside me there exists no other." It is an elevation [*Erhebung*] beyond our own individuality, a feeling of the sublime [*Erhabenen*]' (*WWR*: i, 205–6n. *corr.*).

Schopenhauer had argued that through the mathematical sublime we come to confront a magnitude that 'reduces the individual to nought' and allows the self to be lost 'in contemplation of the infinite greatness of the universe in time and space'. As we confront 'the ghost of our own nothingness', we also realise how time and space 'exist only in our representation', and that the 'vastness of

the world, which previously disturbed our peace of mind, now rests within us'
(i, 205). In aesthetic experience Schopenhauerian man reaches through to a
dimension that is non-individuated. Through art and aesthetic enjoyment
subject–object boundaries fall away, all individuality is lost, and the I becomes
no more than a *'pure, will-less subject of knowledge'* (i, 195). All arts (except
music) provide us access to a realm which he identifies as that of the Platonic
universals or Ideas in which individuality is surrendered to that which is
'essentially one and the same' (i, 195). But Schopenhauer also asserts that 'Idea
and thing-in-itself are not absolutely one and the same', and that behind these
Platonic Ideas lies something yet more unindividuated: underlying forces or
powers (*Wille* or Will) which struggle for expression (i, 174, 145ff.). It is these
inchoate energies that he aligns with Kant's thing-in-itself, and it is music that
provides the most direct expression of Will in this pre-individualised sense:

> music, since it passes over the Ideas, is also quite independent of the
> phenomenal world, positively ignores it, and, to a certain extent,
> could still exist even if there were no world at all. . . . Therefore, music
> is by no means like the other arts, namely a copy of the Ideas, but a
> *copy of the will itself*, the objectivity of which are the Ideas. For this
> reason the effect of music is so very much more powerful and pene-
> trating than it is of the other arts, for these others speak only of the
> shadow, but music of the essence.
>
> (i, 257)

Although in the first (1819) edition of *World as Will and Representation*
Schopenhauer seemed reluctant to describe music as 'sublime', it is clear that
he thought that music provides us a direct expression of the realm of the
unindividuated thing-in-itself in ways that the other arts do not, and in a
manner which can also bypass consciousness and the ego. In the 1844 edition
music is described as having an 'essential beauty, purity, and sublimity' (ii,
449). But this does not mean that for Schopenhauer music is not linked to the
body and its desires. On the contrary, Schopenhauer describes the effects of
music in terms of 'a constant succession of chords more or less disquieting, i.e.,
of chords exciting desire, with chords more or less quieting and satisfying' and
also with a kind of pleasurable pain (ii, 456, 451). For Schopenhauer, the world
as we intuit it and represent it to ourselves in space and time is a construct of
the mind, but that mind is bodily—it is located within a brain which is itself
described as a 'parasite' of the body, its individualised will and drive to survive.
In music, what is bypassed is this individualised ego and its will (the will in its
everyday mode of serving and servicing the needs of the self), not Will (*Wille*)
as such. What music enables us to do is experience that unindividuated power
that comes from outside the body and its ego. Music is bound up with pleasure
and pain, desire and satisfaction. But music also remains linked to the universal: it does not express particularised moods or desires, 'but joy, pain, sorrow,

horror, gaiety, merriment, peace of mind *themselves*, to a certain extent in the abstract, their essential nature, and so also without the motives for them' (i, 261).

One of the things that makes *The Birth of Tragedy* so different from Schopenhauer on the sublime is that Nietzsche stresses the role that *music* plays in the origins of tragedy, as well as to its decay and subsequent transformation. For Nietzsche, tragedy is as non-conceptual as music was for Schopenhauer; but now it is no longer the case that in music individuality is surrendered to an underlying essence of the human, or to a mood or affect that is always 'essentially one and the same'. Instead, Nietzsche describes the changing relations between the actors, the chorus and the audience in ancient Greek tragedy, and the gradual emergence of theatrical spectatorship out of music, dancing and other modes of performative participation (*BT*: §s 8, 11). For Nietzsche, in the most ancient Greek tragedy, there are shared desires and passions that link the actors, chorus and spectators together via a pre-individual (Dionysian) force that is as unconceptual and overwhelming as Schopenhauerian music. But Nietzsche denies that the ancient Greek audience can be described as individualised spectators who are taken out of themselves via the mechanisms of compassion and empathy; instead he argues that the ancient audience participates in the drama—and in a way that must now seem entirely alien and strange to us.

In Nietzsche we find an entirely unSchopenhauerian emphasis on the historical specificity of the changing art forms of tragedy and also of music, so undermining Schopenhauer's claim that 'our' response to the tragic always leads to the surrender of individuality in the same kind of way. This means, in effect, that Nietzsche can also be read as offering a historically specific account of the sublime: something analogous to the 'genealogy' of morals that he would trace later. Thus, Nietzsche does not simply offer a 'history' of tragedy, but a diagnosis of the present which seeks to explain how our present response to tragedy and music came to be cut off from the original power of the Dionysian. By placing music—and not the arts that simply 'copy' unchanging essences—as central to his analysis, Nietzsche finds a way of treating art not as a 'copy' of a more universal and pre-individual reality, but as a transfiguration of the unindividuated—Dionysian—power that is expressed through it.

There is, however, something even more unSchopenhauerian about Nietzsche's comments on art and the sublime in *The Birth of Tragedy*. Nietzsche equates the power of Dionysus with the unindividuated pre-individual will that Schopenhauer termed *Wille* and that expresses itself in the phenomenal world as will-to-life. But, surprisingly, Nietzsche links the sublime and the power of Greek tragedy not simply to the unindividuated Dionysian, but also to the way that this pre-individual energy is masked or transfigured in terms of the Apollinian and the principle of individuation (Schopenhauer's *principium individuationis*). This is there right from the start of the text—and, oddly, precisely in those passages that are condemned in the footnotes to Walter Kaufmann's translation as most Schopenhauerian.

In §1 of the text, Nietzsche quotes Schopenhauer (*WWR*: i, 352–53), making reference to that which is most sublime (*erhabenste*). Via Schopenhauer, Nietzsche describes man as 'wrapped in the veil of máyá' (illusion). It is as if man were a boatman sitting in his small boat, out on a stormy, unbounded sea, sitting imperturbably, '"in the midst of a world of torments the individual human being sits quietly, supported by and trusting in the *principium individuationis*"'. Nietzsche goes on to link this unruffled sailor to the beautiful—giving a gloss which is his own, and certainly not Schopenhauer's:

> In fact, we might say of Apollo that in him the unshaken faith in this *principium* and the calm repose of the man wrapped up in it receive their most sublime expression; and we might call Apollo himself the glorious divine image of the *principium individuationis*, through whose gestures and eyes all the joy and wisdom of 'illusion,' together with its beauty speak to us.
>
> (*BT*: §1)

Nietzsche links the Greek god Apollo first to the sublime and then to the beautiful, so would seem to agree with Schopenhauer's assertion that 'the beautiful is only something indirectly sublime'. However, from a Schopenhauerian perspective, what is surprising about Nietzsche's description is the way that it focuses on the pleasures and security of beautiful illusion. Schopenhauer himself had claimed that all that has meaning for the boatman is his 'vanishing person, his extensionless present, his momentary gratification' which is only an outward manifestation ('the phenomenon') of an underlying 'objectivity of the one will-to-live'. For Schopenhauer, the boatman is faced by an 'ineradicable *dread*', a 'sudden presentiment' and a 'fearful terror' which—like the sublime—reveal the fragility of the illusion of the space–time world that man inhabits (*WWR*: i, 353, 351). Nietzsche does register that Schopenhauer links the breakdown of individuation with a 'tremendous terror' (the terror of the sublime), but he immediately goes on to mention a 'blissful ecstasy' which is associated not with loss of individuation or resignation, but with the masking or transfiguring of that loss.

Thus, the opening of *The Birth of Tragedy* uses a Schopenhauerian framework, but reverses the implications as Nietzsche privileges beauty, masking and appearances. This is evident elsewhere in Nietzsche's text as, for example, where Nietzsche draws on Schiller to describe Homer as both sublime and as an example of what Schiller called 'naïve' art. The latter is quite explicitly linked by Nietzsche to 'Apollinian culture' and to the illusion of beauty that is engendered by a deep underlying will which uses its creatures for its own ends by trapping them in an illusion. The Apollinian is linked by Nietzsche, quite explicitly, with Schopenhauer's *principium individuationis*, but we are also told that the 'unutterably sublime' Homer can 'be understood only as the complete victory of Apollinian illusion' (*BT*: §3). On the other hand, elsewhere in *The*

Birth of Tragedy, Nietzsche seems more conventionally Schopenhauerian, and allies the pre-individual power of the Dionysian also to the sublime. Thus the satyr is described both as Dionysian and as 'something sublime and divine'. He has 'sublime satisfaction' from his vision into an 'unconcealed' nature, so that the satyr chorus 'represents existence more truthfully, really, and completely than the man of culture who ordinarily considers himself the one true reality' (§8). Nietzsche quite explicitly compares the satyr vision with that into 'the eternal core of things, the thing-in-itself', with the gaze of the man of culture aligned to 'the whole world of appearances'. By insisting that there was in early Greek drama no division between public and chorus—and that 'everything is a sublime chorus of dancing and singing'—he argues that the Greek chorus is not merely the 'ideal spectator' of the play, but looks out over his surroundings and *beyond* his own self (§8).

Despite such passages as these, it is clear that Nietzsche's most stable use of the sublime in respect to early Greek tragedy—that of Sophocles and Aeschylus—locates the sublime in terms of the masking, breaking in, healing or transfiguring of the Dionysian. Thus although we are told that 'Dionysian man resembles Hamlet—both have once truly looked into the essence of things, they have *gained knowledge'*—we are also told that this produces a 'nausea' and knowledge which 'kills action; action requires the veils of illusion'. Here Nietzsche once again reverses Schopenhauer's account of the sublime which privileges resignation—and hence 'nausea'—as an ascetically and morally educative experience. Turning the Schopenhauerian framework back upon itself once again, Nietzsche defines the sublime as 'the artistic taming [*Bändigung*] of the horrible, and the *comic* as the artistic discharge [*Entladung*] of the nausea of absurdity' (§7).

Antigone and Cassandra

For Nietzsche, the 'sublime and celebrated art of Attic tragedy' involves a 'mysterious conjugal tie' (*Ehebündnis*) between two warring drives (*Triebe*) that together produce a child who is 'at once Antigone and Cassandra' (§4 *corr.*). The reference here is obscure, but Antigone is linked to Dionysus via her father, Oedipus, who is described by Nietzsche as one of the 'masks for this original hero, Dionysus' (§10). Oedipus' 'excessive wisdom' leads him into exorbitant crimes that are alien to Apollo who is an 'ethical god' in his demand for measure and order, and Antigone herself is born out of excess and disorder (§4 *corr.*). Cassandra is, by contrast, linked with Apollo. It was in Apollo's temple that she was said to have fallen asleep, waking up with the gift of prophecy after having been licked by a serpent who cleans her ears. For the Greeks, the word for prophet—'*antiphas*'—means 'one who speaks instead of a god', and it is Cassandra's curse to speak on behalf of Apollo (on behalf of order), but to have been cursed by Apollo (because she went back on a promise that she made to him) so that the truths that she told would never be believed.

Nietzsche's powerful image—Greek tragedy as doubly tragic (both Antigone and Cassandra)—once again stresses the double role of the Dionysian and the Apollinian in the 'sublime' birth of tragedy.

As far as Greek tragedy is concerned, Nietzsche indicates that the sublime can be represented by a woman (Antigone/Cassandra) as much as by a man. But Nietzsche also distinguishes between the 'active' sublime (Prometheus) in which wrongdoing and disorder are represented via the figure of a male (*der Mann*), and the wrongdoing that comes to typify non-Aryan—i.e. Semitic— peoples and which is symbolised by a woman (*das Weib*) and the myth of The Fall (§9). The relationship between the Aryan myth of Prometheus (who stole fire from the gods) and the Semitic myth of The Fall (which involves sin, seduction and deception, not active defiance) is said to be like that 'between brother and sister'. It is the *active sin* of Prometheus (not that of The Fall) that Nietzsche links to the Dionysian and counts as the pinnacle of the tragic sublime. Using the metaphor of 'the sublime and terrible Memnon's Column' (§9)—which produces musical notes as it is touched by the sun—Nietzsche invokes an image of Greek myth as intrinsically masculine in terms of the energies that are tapped. Antigone masks Dionysus (via Oedipus), whilst Cassandra is the ear and mouthpiece for that other male God, Apollo, who is associated with order and beauty. Although Nietzsche, like Schopenhauer and the ancient Greeks, associates beauty above all with the idealised male body (Apollo), there are also clearly places in his work where the sublime is associated with sexual and ethnic differences in ways reminiscent of Kant and Hegel.

Recently Catherine Constable has explored the place of the sublime in Nietzsche's writings in her *Thinking in Images* which engages with Film Theory and with the seductive—and frequently veiled—image of Marlene Dietrich (Constable 2005: 87–92). Constable seeks to draw on Nietzsche for the rehabilitation of beauty, femininity and 'the play of appearances', especially in relation to Hollywood cinema and filmic images (190). Constable's conclusions are, however, rather different from mine and this is, in part, because for her reading of Nietzsche she looks back at the tradition of the sublime in Kant and Burke in which 'beauty' aligns with the 'feminine' and the 'sublime' with the masculine, instead of to Schopenhauer who subsumes the beautiful under the sublime and who explicitly claims that women do not deserve to be called '*the fair sex*'. For Schopenhauer, women are so malformed—with their narrow shoulders, broad hips and short legs—that they instead deserve the title 'the unaesthetic sex' (Schopenhauer 1851: 107). Schopenhauer (who was famously misogynistic) also genders the sublime, claiming specifically that the genius must be male; but he does this not by opposing the beautiful to the sublime, but by aligning women solely with reproduction, as opposed to the godlike productive powers of the sublime and also beautiful male (Battersby 1989: 107–15).

In *The Birth of Tragedy* the sublime can be associated with the female, but the highest types of the sublime remain masculine as we see also from

171

Nietzsche's account of the decay and transformation of tragedy after the death of Sophocles and Aeschylus. Specifically, Nietzsche's claim is that tragedy declines with Euripides, and that part of what has gone wrong in the case of the latter is that Euripides has brought the spectator onto the stage. For Nietzsche, Euripides represents the transition into modernity; in the 'New Comedy' that succeeded him, there was 'a womanish [*weibisch*] flight from seriousness and terror', and hence also from the sublime. (*BT*: §11). What the 'New Comedy' celebrated was the 'cheerfulness of the slave' or the woman who has no responsibilities. Nietzsche's charge against the 'New Comedy'—and against Euripides whom the new comedians praised—was that it was this kind of drama that led the early Christians (and all subsequent writers) to regard the Greeks as *naturally* cheerful, and to fail to notice the Dionysian grounding for the tragedies of the sixth century BCE. What has been forgotten, Nietzsche claims, is Heraclitus and Pythagoras, along with the transfiguration and masking of the irrational and the excessive in the plays of the more ancient Greeks.

Sublime decline

Nietzsche becomes more ambivalent about the sublime as he moves closer to modernity, and this means that he associates it also with the 'feminine'. In the case of his analysis of Euripides, the term '*erhaben*' starts to take on new (and negative) connotations. Nietzsche tells us that Euripides never sees into the Dionysian abyss, never experiences ecstasy, and is never taken out of himself (§s 10–13). Although the plays of Euripides produce strong emotions in his audience (rather in the manner of the modern sublime), these 'fiery *affects*' are 'replacing Dionysian ecstasies' (§12). Furthermore, these strong emotions combine with 'cool, paradoxical thoughts', and show that it is not the Dionysian that is being masked in Euripidean drama, but something else. Nietzsche uses the language of the '*erhaben*'—lofty, elevated, sublime—to explain what is being masked here. Euripides feels himself '*erhaben*' in respect to his spectators, and when the masses idolise him he also rebuffs them with a defiance that is '*erhaben*'. But there are two members of his audience with respect to whom Euripides does not feel '*erhaben*': one is himself 'as *thinker*, not as poet'; the other is Socrates who has also closed his mind to the gods and for whom "'To be beautiful everything must be intelligible"' (§s 11, 12).

Nietzsche suggests that after Euripides the sublime will come to be linked to intelligibility—and to the limits of the understanding—and not to a god who speaks into one's ear or who takes one outside oneself (in ecstasy) via a vision into the pre-individual Dionysian. Now the sublime will become attached to 'mystery' and to the other of the self: 'Thus Euripides as a poet is essentially an echo of his own conscious knowledge'. Furthermore, 'Euripides was, in a sense, only a mask: the deity that spoke through him was neither Dionysus or Apollo, but an altogether newborn demon, called *Socrates*' (§12). For Nietzsche, Socrates is the 'typical *non-mystic*' in whom instinct and his inner voice appear only in order to block or hinder conscious knowledge; but Nietzsche does register two redeeming aspects. The first is related to a recurrent dream which Socrates had, and which did eventually—before dying, in prison—prompt him to set a fable to music (§14). Socrates' other redeeming feature links back to Nietzsche's underlying Schopenhauerian framework. Without Socrates, we are told, the energies of the world would not have been deflected away from the preservation of our (illusory) selves onto the acquisition of knowledge. Without Socrates, the perpetual struggle between individual egos and peoples would have led to a weakening of the life-force and produced the kind of mass suicides, parricides and ascetic renunciation that Schopenhauer's account would seem to threaten.

It is at this point in *The Birth of Tragedy* that Nietzsche seems closest to Schopenhauer (and Wagner), and seems almost to be recommending a new kind of 'sublime' based on 'compassion [*Mitleid*], self-sacrifice [*Aufopferung*], heroism, and that calm sea of the soul ... which the Apollinian Greek called *sophrosune* [temperance]' (§15, *corr.*). But Nietzsche also represents these virtues as 'second best', and necessary only because we find ourselves in modernity living in the ever-growing shadow of Socrates (§15). What Nietzsche suggests is that in modernity the 'other' that is encountered as an apparent infinity is only a mask for the conscious self, for logic or systematic knowledge (*Wissenschaft*). What is hidden behind the veil of illusion becomes too tied up with the self and the horizons of intelligibility. The sublime becomes nothing but a kind of blind spot for consciousness and is equated with that which understanding cannot grasp. The identification of the sublime with the incomprehensible is quite explicit in Schiller, and Schelling makes the additional step of identifying it with the chaotic. So it seems to me that Nietzsche is right to complain that what is veiled in the Romantic discourse about the sublime veil of Isis is no Dionysian 'beyond', but the 'I', the understanding (Socrates) and the (Kantian) limits of conceptual thought.

As we saw in Chapter 5, for Schiller, the young man with his 'hot thirst' for knowledge can unveil that which is hidden behind the veils of his understanding, but then goes mad and cannot communicate it (Schiller 1795). For Novalis, what the young apprentice sees when he raises the veil of Isis is his own face (Novalis 1978: 234). As Schopenhauer put it, in the experience of the sublime the 'vastness of the world, which previously disturbed our peace of mind, now rests within us; our dependence on it is now annulled by its dependence on us' (*WWR*: i, 205). In other words, whereas Schopenhauer represented the 'crude and vulgar' Euripides as inferior to Goethe in terms of teaching us the 'resignation' that is essential to our moral education, for Nietzsche Goethe remains in the tradition of Euripides, and what Goethe masks is the principle of intelligibility that is symbolised by Socrates and also by Kant.

In Sections 14 and 15 of *The Birth of Tragedy* Nietzsche provides a condensed but perceptive commentary on the varieties of false infinities that might be said to characterise the modern—as opposed to the early Greek—sublime. The false sublimes that Nietzsche describes in these sections of *The Birth of Tragedy* all relate back to the privilege given to consciousness, intelligibility and the self. And, as such, all relate back to Socrates. We are told that from the Socratic point of view—from the point of view of an eye that has never experienced artistic inspiration (*Begeisterung*)—what Plato called 'the "sublime and greatly lauded" tragic art' was merely,

> Something rather unreasonable, full of causes apparently without effects, and effects without causes; the whole, moreover, so many coloured [*bunt*] and manifold that it could not but be repugnant to a sober mind, and dangerous tinder for susceptible and sensitive souls [*reizbare und empfindliche Seele*].
>
> (§14, *corr.*)

In discussing Socrates, Nietzsche lapses into the language of Kantianism. And the engagement with the Kantian tradition continues as Nietzsche goes on to represent three types of false relationships to nature, all of which involve blind spots and veils.

The first false relation to nature is that of 'the *theoretical man*' whose 'desire finds its highest goal in a process of unveiling which he achieves by his own efforts and which is always successful'. This criticism applies to Schiller who thought it possible to penetrate the sublime 'veil of Isis' and see (but not speak) 'the truth' of the 'all' (§15, *corr.*). Nietzsche's second criticism is of the modern artist who fixes 'his ecstatic eyes' on 'what still remains veiled, even after the unveiling' (§15, *corr.*). Nietzsche cites Lessing as an example, but this criticism would seem also to apply to Kant for whom the unveiling of sublime nature remains a constant duty, rather than something that could be accomplished. Nietzsche explicitly registers the importance of the 'unveiling' model of nature when he remarks in this passage: 'There would be no systematic knowledge [*Wissenschaft*] if there were only one naked goddess and there were nothing other to be done' (§15 *corr.*).

Nietzsche's third criticism is of the 'sublime metaphysical illusion' that accompanies all knowledge systems (*Wissenschaften*) after Socrates for whom '*philosophic thought* overgrows art and compels it to cling close to the trunk of dialectic' (§s 15, 14). This illusion is the 'unshakable faith' that understanding, guided by the principle of cause and effect, 'can penetrate the deepest abysses of being, and that thought is capable of not only knowing being but even of *correcting* it' (§15). As apparently systematic knowledge systems get caught within their own illusions, Nietzsche suggests that a kind of false infinity arises as the circle of knowledge (which aims at completeness) conceals an 'infinite number of points' which could not possibly all be surveyed. The blind spot now becomes no more than these 'boundary points from which one gazes into what defies illumination', so that now noble and gifted men 'see to their horror how logic coils up at these boundaries and finally bites its own tail' (§15, *corr.*). Like Hegel, Nietzsche seems to be accusing Kant and the Romantics of equating the sublime with a false infinity; but his criticisms of treating nature in terms of the dialectics of reason also tells against Hegel himself.

What Nietzsche refuses is not the sublime of Sophocles and Aeschylus in which the Dionysian is masked by the Apollinian, but the sublime of all those who have lost their instincts, and their access to the Dionysian (and pre-individual) 'other'. Using as a clue to his problems with the sublime the emphasis that was placed on strong *affect* in writers after Euripides, Nietzsche does, in effect, provide a genealogy of tragedy that allows us to see the limitations of the modern framework for evoking the 'other' in the aesthetics of the sublime. That longed for and 'incomprehensible' other has been reduced to what Irigaray would later call 'the Other of the same'. Through losing access to a more alien kind of 'otherness'—the Dionysian that takes one outside oneself via *ek-stasis*—the sublime has been perverted and has become no more than the Other of consciousness, of space–time (causal) understanding, and the ego or self. Via contact with this kind of Otherness, we confront merely that which has been excluded as the I positions itself as free, as a unity or as the 'master' of nature and the space–time which it imposes on the world.

In these passages in *The Birth of Tragedy* we see the origins of Nietzsche's profound distaste for the modern language of the sublime—a revulsion that seems to have emerged gradually, and which was expressed most forcefully in a speech in *Thus Spoke Zarathustra* (1883–85). Headed '*Von den Erhabenen*' ('On the Sublime Ones'), in this section of Part 2 Zarathustra mocks the asceticism of those who portray themselves as sublime (*Erhabenen*), exalted (*Gehobenen*), and spiritually elevated (*erhoben*), claiming that such men need to learn 'laughter' and 'beauty', instead of 'almost starving themselves to death' through their 'expectations' which involve a kind of 'contempt' and also betray 'nausea' with the here and now (Z: 228–31, *corr.*). Here the man who sets himself up as sublime is portrayed as having a 'gloomy' disdain for nature and for living. Explicitly linking this discussion with the question of 'taste', Zarathustra privileges the taste for the beautiful over the sublime. But Zarathustra also indicates that learning to be beautiful is difficult for the one who has a taste for the sublime; he has to move beyond his love of 'monsters' (*Untiere*) and 'riddles' and relax into the beautiful once again. This will involve leaping 'over his own shadow'—and the shadow of Socrates and Kant, it would seem—and moving 'truthfully inwards into his *own* sun' (Z: 228–30, *corr.*).

At the time of writing *The Birth of Tragedy* Nietzsche was himself not yet ready to take this leap. Impossibly (and infuriatingly) the text does not stop after §15 and neither does Nietzsche seem to have registered to what extent he is subverting the Schopenhauerian language that he is employing. And this is what makes *The Birth of Tragedy* such an 'impossible book'. In the subsequent sections on Wagner and the rebirth of German music, nine further references to the sublime remain. Some of these pick up the new and negative connotations that the term 'erhaben' has attained in the course of the text (BT: §19); but some are distinctly Schopenhauerian and Wagnerian as Nietzsche tells of the 'sublime ecstasy' that comes from 'listening to a distant melancholy song that tells of the mothers of being: Delusion, Will, Woe' (§20). At the end, Nietzsche tries to pull the argument back, returning from Schopenhauerianism to the insistence that the pleasure of tragedy should be located in 'the purely aesthetic sphere, without transgressing into the region of compassion [Mitleid], fear, or the ethically sublime [Sittlich–Erhabenen]' (§24, corr.).

Here, in the concluding moments of The Birth of Tragedy, Schopenhauer's emphasis on the tragic as a copy of the universal is refused, and the emphasis on music not as mimetic but as transfigurative is also once again stressed. But still Nietzsche clings to the terminology and the metaphorics of the 'erhaben'. Thus, in the penultimate sentence we are told that it is with the 'sublime eyes of Aeschylus' that an old Athenian invites the young stranger—'du wunderlicher Fremdling'—to follow him to the tragedy and make a sacrifice in the temple of both Apollo and Dionysus. Nietzsche suggests that we need to go back to the temples of ancient Greece, rather than into the non-spatio-temporal noumenal. He replaces the metaphorics of the sublime Temple of Isis with that of the temple dedicated to Apollo and Dionysus. But as in the narratives of Schiller and Novalis, there is still a young novice—'the wondrous stranger'—who is following a master into a temple as towards a lure. It is still a long way from the radicality of Thus Spoke Zarathustra and other later texts which offer us not merely a rejection of the sublime, but also its reconfiguration.

176

9

NIETZSCHE'S NAKED GODDESS: RECONFIGURING THE SUBLIME

In 1882 the first edition of *The Gay Science* was published. It ended at §342 which marks the point at which the character of Zarathustra first made his appearance in Nietzsche's published *oeuvre*. This section starts with the sentence '*Incipit tragoedia*'—'The tragedy begins'—thus looking back to the analysis of tragedy in *The Birth of Tragedy*, and also forward to *Thus Spoke Zarathustra* (1883–85) which Nietzsche started writing in February 1883, and which opens with a prologue in the voice of Zarathustra which is almost identical with §342 of *The Gay Science*. That the problem of the sublime is also in play in the additions to the 1887 edition of *The Gay Science* is evident from the very first words of the added section. This opens with a quotation from a seventeenth-century French General addressed to his own body—'thou trembling carcass'—as the I transcends merely bodily terror and sets out to confront the great dangers ahead (GS: Book 5, *corr.*). Then Nietzsche's first sentence in his own voice in §343—'*The meaning of our cheerfulness*'—picks up 'On the Sublime Ones' from *Thus Spoke Zarathustra* in which Nietzsche had counterpoised laughter to the gloomy sublime.

Despite the explicit and implicit criticism of sublimity, Nietzsche's tactic in *Thus Spoke Zarathustra* as a whole is one that reconfigures the notion of sublimity through giving depth to surfaces and the moment, so that the 'now' is deepened as it intersects with the eternal (Z: 328–33, 389–90). Zarathustra experiences the 'nausea' of existence, but nevertheless overcomes the sickness that is at first completely disabling. In a state of convalescence, Zarathustra says 'yes' to life, and joyfully wills to live the same life again and again, in all its particularity, into eternity. Nietzsche is clearly revisiting—but also utterly transforming—the kind of pessimism that Schopenhauer found exemplified in *Hamlet*, and the 'to be or not to be' soliloquy that Schopenhauer had used to illustrate the sublime; the utter misery of existence; and the impossibility of any 'sincere' or sane man ever willing to repeat his own life (WWR: i, 324).

As we have seen, in *The Birth of Tragedy* Nietzsche had also associated Hamlet with 'nausea', and with looking into 'the eternal nature of things' in ways that do not respect the 'veils of illusion' that are necessary for effective action (BT: §7). But Nietzsche's challenge to Schopenhauer's 'resignationism' was overly cautious, as he himself pointed out in the 'Attempt at Self Criticism' of 1886. In *Thus Spoke Zarathustra*, Nietzsche seems to be looking back to Schopenhauer's analysis of tragedy, but he now turns it completely around, as 'optimism' displaces 'pessimism' and Schopenhauer's analysis of *Hamlet* is much more radically undermined. As in *Beyond Good and Evil*, which also alludes to *Zarathustra*, Nietzsche binds the doctrine of the eternal recurrence to the capacity to think 'pessimism through to its depths' and still take an optimistic joy in the infinite repetition of life, however terrible the pain and the suffering:

> whoever has ... looked into, down into the most world-denying of all possible ways of thinking—beyond good and evil and no longer, like the Buddha and Schopenhauer, under the spell and delusion of morality—may just thereby, without really meaning to do so, have opened his eyes to the opposite ideal: the ideal of the most high-spirited, alive, and life-affirming human being who has not only come to terms and learned to get along with whatever was and is, but wants to have *what was and is* repeated into all eternity, shouting insatiably *da capo* [from the beginning]—not only to himself but to the whole play and spectacle, and not only to a spectacle but at bottom to him who needs precisely this spectacle—and who makes it necessary because again and again he needs himself—and makes himself necessary—What? and this wouldn't be—*circulus vitiosus deus* [a vicious circle made god]?
>
> (BGE: §56)

Schopenhauer's 'Buddhist' counter to Christianity is displaced by the new character of Zarathustra—the Greek name for Zoroaster who was the ancient Persian hermit who founded Zoroastrianism—who is modernised and reinvented by Nietzsche, but in ways that look back to the counter-Christian significance of Zoroaster for Voltaire and other Enlightenment philosophers. The infinite is now no longer some kind of nirvana, nor a timeless Christian eternity, nor a sublime 'truth' concealed 'beyond' the veils of Isis or of Maya. Instead, it is the moment, the 'now'; it is the circle itself that has become 'god'—there is no 'beyond' and also no concealment—so what is sublime is the will to repetition, and the 'I' emerges from the process of repetition and not from encountering an 'other' to which it is opposed.

In the Preface to the second edition of *The Gay Science*, the links to the philosophies of the sublime are just as evident. Picking up the imagery of Schiller, Reinhold and Novalis who link the 'sublime' to the figure of the 'veiled Isis' and to a truth revealed 'beyond' the veil, Nietzsche comments acerbically: 'And as for our future, one will hardly find us again on the paths of those Egyptian youths who endanger temples by night, embrace statues, and put into a bright light whatever is kept concealed for good reasons' (GS: Pref. §4). Since this passage follows one in which Nietzsche quite explicitly distances himself from the aesthetics of the sublime, and links the latter to his former self, it is clear that in the 1886 Preface to *The Gay Science*—as also in the 1886 Preface to *The Birth of Tragedy*—Nietzsche is wanting to signal how much his position has changed, and that a reworked attitude to the sublime is central to that change:

> How the theatrical scream of passion now hurts our ears, how strange to our taste the whole romantic uproar and tumult of the senses has become, which the educated mob loves, and all its aspirations after the sublime [*Erhabenen*], lofty [*Gehobenen*] and weird [*Verschrobenen*]! No, if we convalescents still need art, it is another kind of art—a mocking, light, fleeting, divinely untroubled, divinely artificial art that, like a pure flame, licks into unclouded skies.
>
> (GS: Pref. §4, *corr.*)

In this passage from the 2nd edition Preface to *The Gay Science* we find an extended commentary on the failure of 'this youthful madness in the love of truth'. And it is clear that Nietzsche is criticising his own younger self, as well as at earlier accounts of the sublime, when he says that 'we' are now 'too experienced, too serious, too merry, too burned, too *deep*' to believe that 'truth remains truth after the veils are drawn back'. Indeed 'we' now consider it indecent to 'wish to see everything naked or to be present at everything, or understand and "know" all' (Pref. §4 *corr.*). Nietzsche then proffers an important new metaphor which takes up the imagery of the 'sublime' truth hidden behind the veil of Isis and undercuts it with a kind of 'holy' laughter:

> Perhaps truth is a woman who has reasons for not letting us see her reasons? Perhaps her name is—to speak Greek—*Baubo?*
> Oh those Greeks! They knew how to live. What is required for that is to stop courageously at the surface, the fold, the skin, to adore appearance, to believe in forms, tones, words, in the whole Olympus of appearance. Those Greeks were superficial—*out of profundity.*
>
> (Pref. §4)

Baubo was an old crone who acted as comforter to Demeter after Persephone (Kore) had been snatched into the underworld. In the all-female mystery rites of Eleusis in which Demeter's 'running for help' was annually re-enacted, Baubo acted as a kind of clown. Not only did she personify the obscene songs that the women sang, but she seems to have provoked laughter by lifting her skirts and showing her naked sexual organs beneath, in a way that mimicked the action she performed to amuse Demeter. Nietzsche deploys laughter as a counter to the sublime, and the need to stop at the 'fold' of the surface as a block to depth and a metaphysics that locates truth 'beyond' appearances.

In *Ecce Homo* (written 1888, but published posthumously in 1908), Schopenhauer is lumped together with Fichte, Schelling, Kant, Leibniz, Hegel and

Schleiermacher as mere 'veil makers' and 'unconscious counterfeiters' of knowledge (Nietzsche 1908: 321). As in the passages from the Preface to *The Gay Science*, Nietzsche is clearly signalling his opposition to the tradition of German philosophy that spiritualises the body and hides 'truth' behind a veil. However, it was not really until *Daybreak* (1881) that Nietzsche seems to have started to make the move that would turn him away from the language of 'veiling' towards those 'roundabout ways' (*Umwegen*) that would lead him to privilege laughter over tragedy, and surface over depth. Here, instead of the depths and veiled 'beyond' that is so characteristic of the imagery of the sublime, Nietzsche starts to emphasise a drive for the superficial and for the fleeting:

> for gentle sunlight, for light and moving air, for southern plants, the breath of the sea, the fleeting nourishment of meat, eggs and fruit ... in short for all those things that taste best to me and are for me the most bearable.
>
> (*D*: §553, *corr.*)

In an interrogative mode, Nietzsche asks whether these surface drives are no more than a translation of the deep drives of reason. And the questioning tone continues as the passage moves on to ask whether other and 'much higher sublimities of Philosophy' aren't in the end 'nothing other than intellectual ways around (*Umwege*) personal drives of this kind'. Nietzsche answers his own question by reference to 'the secret and lonely craziness [*Schwärmen*] of a butterfly' which is happy to fly round, 'unconcerned that its life will last only one day'. 'For it too a philosophy could be found, although it might indeed not be mine' (§553).

This celebration of surfaces, laughter and the moment towards the end of *Daybreak* remains, however, intertwined with the language of depth and of melancholy in ways that remain puzzling and uncertain. Nietzsche still praises those 'losses that communicate to the soul a sublimity'. Praising the snake that is transformed as it loses its skin, Nietzsche privileges those types of bodily and psychic expenditure that prevent the soul from wailing, and makes it go around in silence 'as if beneath black cypress trees' (§s 573, 570 *corr.*). Describing himself as piloting the 'air-ship of the spirit', Nietzsche dreams of new ways of moving towards the infinite: ones that are not the same as those of his 'great teachers and predecessors' who 'with noble and graceful gestures have come to a weary stop' (§575, *corr.*). And, indeed, *Daybreak* ends on an interrogative note—caught, as it were, between surface and depth, between the finite and the infinite, in the '*inzwischen*' (the 'in-between-time'), a term that Nietzsche uses as he contemplates the butterfly that flaps crazily by the sea (§553 *corr.*).

In the very final section of *Daybreak* Nietzsche's own metaphors flutter on past the butterfly to birds that 'will fly farther' than 'you or me', and then on to the figure of Columbus who is referenced in the riddling question that ends the book: 'Will it perhaps be said of us one day that we too, *steering westwards, hoped to reach an India*—but that it was our fate to be wrecked against infinity? Or, my brothers? Or?' (§575). Columbus is clearly an important figure for Nietzsche—as he was also for Kant and the German Romantic poets, especially Schiller—and he seems to have composed three poems on this theme. The first, 'Colombo', is a childhood poem from 1858, in which we encounter not only the seductions of the infinite, but also the birds that figure at the end of *Daybreak*, and that lure Columbus onwards as his spirit 'wrestles with doubts':

> ... Duped by
> A mirage, seduced into the distance,
> Already the sun rises high, dazzled and burnt
> My courage deserts me.
>
> But then I see a sprightly pair of birds
> That in song swing through the air,
> O leave your black mood, you wild flock
> Since this sign of hope never deceives
> Land is not far away, and even today,
> We shall reach our goal, where all doubts will fade
> Away! Rush, ship, through the tide
> Only have courage, have courage.
>
> (Nietzsche 1854–61: vol. i, 443)

The other two poems on Columbus were written in 1882, shortly after the completion of *Daybreak* and when Nietzsche was living in Genoa, the place of Columbus' birth. Both were inspired by Nietzsche's relationship with Lou Salomé, and a version of 'The New Columbus' was sent by Nietzsche to Lou in November 1882, along with the first edition of *The Gay Science* (Grundlehner 1986: 129–42, trans. *corr.*). Here, once again, Nietzsche allies Columbus with the man who is seduced towards the distant horizon, but in 'The New Columbus', there is a new, and less straightforwardly Romantic, tone: 'My Lady Friend!, said Columbus, Trust / The Genoese man no more! / He always looks out into the blue— / Distance entices him too much!'. In 1884—two years after Lou had rejected Nietzsche, and had moved away to be with his friend, and rival in love, Paul Rée—Nietzsche added a new stanza in which 'Columbus' declares, 'What is most foreign is now dear to me! ...', implicitly registering how the 'Lady Friend' (*Freundin*) has herself moved into the blue horizons that tug at the mind of the philosopher–sailor.

Again and again in Nietzsche we see him associate 'woman' with the seductions of distance. Thus, in *The Gay Science* there is an extended passage linking 'woman' to a 'spiritlike intermediate being' who moves like a boat with 'white sails' and also 'like an immense butterfly over the dark sea', and which explicitly states: 'The magic and most powerful effect of women is, in philosophical language, action at a distance, *actio in distans* ...' (GS: §60). As

Nietzsche explains in *Ecce Homo*, *Daybreak* offers a critique of philosophers 'as *crypto*-priests' (1908: 291). But *Daybreak* nevertheless ends with an open question that concerns the seductions of the infinite. Columbus, Nietzsche's Genoan alter-ego, is still lured onward by the wish to discover '*a new India*' in much the same way that Goethe's 'Eternal Feminine leads us onwards' and upwards towards the infinite—'*Das Ewig-Weibliche zieht uns hinan*' (Goethe 1833). At the end of *Daybreak* we see Nietzsche wondering whether he has yet solved the 'problem' of the infinite, or whether it may yet 'wreck' his philosophical endeavours. Evidently, in 1881, the way to reconcile the pleasures of immediacy and infinity were not yet clear. *Daybreak* opens with a motto from the *Rig Veda*: 'There are so many days that have not yet broken'. Thus it would seem that by the time *Daybreak* was finished, one of the days that had not yet broken is that of the 'one *naked* goddess' who was mentioned in §15 of *The Birth of Tragedy* and who would reappear as Baubo in the §4 of the Preface to the 2nd edition of *The Gay Science* which he worked on in 1886.

By 1886, however, Nietzsche had found a way to reconcile surface with depth which was not yet there in *Daybreak*, except as a kind of longing for 'a new infinity'. But if the move to Baubo and to the joy in surfaces still seems some way off, in *Daybreak* Nietzsche does seem to be moving on from the 'depths' and 'distances' of the sublime towards cheerfulness and the brief ecstasies of the butterfly in the here-and-now. *Daybreak* constitutes an important step along the way: it laughs in the face of the metaphorical language that links 'truth' with that which is hidden behind the veil and which represents the infinite in terms of morality or a *goal* to be reached. But it will not be until *Thus Spoke Zarathustra* that Nietzsche learnt to think the infinite *otherwise* (in terms of the eternal recurrence) and it is not until *Beyond Good and Evil* (1886) and also in the Preface to the 2nd edition of *The Gay Science* that the 'depths' of the infinite would be reconfigured as surface with folds, repetitions and multiple perspectives which mean that surface is neither simply a plane nor a façade, and neither is it fully accessible to the understanding or the eye. *The Birth of Tragedy* and *Daybreak* are, however, important steps along the way back to the laughter of Dionysus (and of Baubo) in the face of the (Kantian) tradition of the sublime that Nietzsche found so seductive, and so difficult to resist.

'Three hundred foregrounds'

As part of his strategy of resistance, Nietzsche revisits the vocabulary of the sublime, evidently uncomfortable with the connotations of spiritual—and anti-material—'elevation' that attach to that which is '*erhaben*'. By the time Nietzsche published *On the Genealogy of Morals* in 1887, the language of the '*sublim*' had taken over from that of the '*erhaben*'. The logic of Nietzsche's usage is clear, and fits with his contention that the 'self' is a fiction: a bundle of instincts and drives that act in temporary accord. 'Health' is when this 'bundle' acts as an effective unity (*TI*: 494; *BGE*: §259). But health is not stasis; instead it is the warding off of disease. Identities that are living and healthy thrive on opposition: 'whatever does not destroy me makes stronger' (*TI*: 467). For entities that are diseased or 'decadent' (degenerate) opposition causes a dispersal of energies, so that what seems to be a whole breaks down into an anarchy and acts as a multiplicity rather than as an (apparent) unity. Nietzsche identifies the *'great* danger' to mankind with 'its sublimest [*sublimste*] enticement and seduction' towards nihilism, nirvana and a 'Buddhist' renunciation of life which is the spiritual manifestation of a kind of physiological degeneracy (GM: Pref. §5). Picking up on the Kantian analysis of the sublime as involving a conflict of the faculties, for Nietzsche what is *sublim* is a symptom of a self in conflict with itself—but this inner conflict has now become a symptom of disease and a drive towards death.

As well as criticising this type of physiological degeneracy that is chemically purified or sublimated into the 'sublime', later in the same text Nietzsche also posits a kind of counter-sublime: a 'sublime (*sublim*) wickedness' which is not yet possible, but which will be available to the 'man of the future' of whom Zarathustra speaks (GM: Essay 2 §24). This new type of sublime involves the displaced bodily energies of one 'for whom conquest, adventure, danger, and even pain have become needs'. For this 'different kind of spirit'—who has become habituated 'to the keen air of the heights, to winter journeys, to ice and mountains' (and who, thus, inhabits the regions of the Kantian and Romantic sublime)—what is required is not the 'elevation' of reason or morality, but a physiological condition: 'an ultimate, supremely self-confident mischievousness in knowledge that goes with great health; it would require, in brief and alas, precisely this *great health!*' (2 §24). In other words, Nietzsche does not give up entirely on the language of the 'sublime', but makes his new '*sublim*' a product of bodily energies, rather than a question of the self and its transcendence. Furthermore, the Nietzschean self becomes itself through expending its bodily energies, and is not a unified ego that simply encounters an infinite or indefinite 'other' that functions as the horizon of the knowable.

Beyond Good and Evil (1886) seems to be the transitional point. Here the language of the *sublim* (used ten times) gradually displaces that of the *erhaben* (used only five times) as Nietzsche coins a new label, '*sublimer Hang und Drang*'—a 'sublime inclination and urge'—to counter the '*Sturm und Drang*' ('Storm and Stress') tag that has been applied to the period of German Romanticism (BGE: §284). Nietzsche started drafting *Beyond Good and Evil* in 1885, but he carried on making amendments into 1886, and it thus belongs with the new Prefaces to *The Birth of Tragedy* and *The Gay Science*—which were both completed in 1886—as well as with *Thus Spoke Zarathustra*. Thus, Nietzsche remarked that *Beyond Good and Evil* 'says the same things as *Zarathustra*, but differently, very differently'— (BGE: introd., p. x). Famously, the Preface to *Beyond Good and Evil* also starts with a reference to woman as 'truth': 'Supposing truth is a woman—what then? Are there not grounds for the suspicion that all philosophers, insofar as they were dogmatists, have been very inexpert about women?' Less often noticed is Nietzsche's reference to the 'sublime' (*erhaben*) a few lines later as Nietzsche links the edifices of the overly dogmatic philosophers to superstitious belief (*Aberglaube*)—and, in particular, to the 'superstitious belief' of the 'subject' and the 'I' which still leads us astray (*BGE*: Pref.).

In *Beyond Good and Evil* Nietzsche explicitly accuses the Romantics of a kind of dishonesty in respect to the sublime (the *erhaben*) that draws the soul 'further and higher', but also criticises a mode of relation to surfaces that simply displaces the Romantics' urge for the 'beyond' onto 'that sublime inclination', '*jener sublime Hang*', that simply negates all that is other or strange (§s 256, 230). Here Nietzsche registers a kind of 'will to appearances (*Wille zum Schein*), to simplification, to masks' which drives the spirit to treat every surface as 'a cloak'. This Nietzsche links to the logic of the Romantic sublime which wants to 'mask' the darkness of that which eludes the understanding or, alternatively, assimilate it to what is already known. The Romantic sublime serves to 'appropriate the foreign', to reduce the threat of the new, and to 'overlook or repulse whatever is totally contradictory'. It also, however, drives the seeker after knowledge into a kind of 'satisfaction with the dark' as a means of performing the self-protective masking function (§230, *corr.*). Here Nietzsche's analysis once again fits with the critique of the sublime that *The Birth of Tragedy* had opened up, but that Nietzsche seems only to have fully registered in these late texts.

Referring to Mozart, who deploys the imagery of the 'veil of Isis' and the bird catcher in his opera, *The Magic Flute*, Nietzsche argues that we need to become 'deaf to the siren songs of old metaphysical bird catchers who have been piping at him too long, "you are more, you are higher, you are of a different origin!"' (§230; Chailley 1971). However, here again Nietzsche does not altogether give up on the vocabulary of the sublime. Instead, towards the end of *Beyond Good and Evil*, Nietzsche once again makes reference to a 'sublime inclination and urge'—'*sublimer Hang und Drang*'—that displaces the Romantics' drive for a truth or value 'beyond' man onto the 'inclination and urge for cleanliness' (*BGE*: §284). What this involves is a less appropriative relation to surfaces and the 'foreign'; a joy in a multiplicity of surfaces—'three hundred foregrounds'— and the adoption of 'dark glasses' that will block the view into 'our eyes, still less into our "depths" ["*Grunde*"]' (§284, *corr.*). Nietzsche continues to oppose the Romantic philosophers of the sublime as he seeks to reconfigure 'the beyond', whilst also referring with evident approval to the 'four virtues' associated with the sublime in the German post-Kantian tradition of aesthetics and morality: 'courage, insight, sympathy [*Mitgefühl*], and solitude' (§284).

In this section Nietzsche is not arguing—as did Schopenhauer—that the man who experiences the sublime is taken via a kind of insight to the level of the 'universal' in which the ego vanishes and 'pity' or compassion (*Mitleid*) takes over. Nevertheless, in retaining 'sympathy' or 'empathy' (*Mitgefühl* means literally 'feeling with') and the other three virtues, Nietzsche indicates the need for the individual—and also the historical period—to be open to the other in a non-appropriative way. What this might entail is described in the very next section of *Beyond Good and Evil* in which Nietzsche reconfigures the notion of a truth or a value that lies 'beyond' the 'I' or beyond man via an emphasis on time:

> The greatest events and thoughts—but the greatest thoughts are the greatest events—are understood last. The sexes, generations or races— [Nietzsche uses the single term *Geschlechter* which can mean all three]—that are simultaneous with them do not live through [*erleben*] such events—they live right past them. What happens there is something, as in the realm of stars. The light of the most distant star comes latest to mankind; and before it reaches him man *denies* that there are—stars there. 'How many centuries does a spirit need to be understood?'—that is also a measuring stick with which one can create an order of rank and of etiquette as is necessary: for spirit and star.
>
> (§285, *corr.*)

As we have seen, Nietzsche's *Beyond Good and Evil* starts out with the complaint that philosophers have not devised a satisfactory etiquette for approaching 'truth' which has been treated as a veiled and feminine counterpart to the philosopher's own self. One remedial strategy would be to insist that the philosopher should impose his values and vision on the world in a way that is more open and honest than that found in the post-Kantian philosophies of the sublime in which the 'I' keeps control, even when it appears to surrender all mastery via the encounter with the 'other' in the experience of the sublime. But, as we discover by the end of *Beyond Good and Evil*, this is not Nietzsche's own eventual solution to re-imagining the self's relation to the infinity, the 'other' and that which lies 'beyond' the self. Instead, Nietzsche displaces the 'I' from the centre of the knowable space–time universe, and argues for an encounter with an 'other' where this other is not simply a construct of the I (as in the Kantian tradition of the sublime) but is so alien that the I 'lives right past' it. This radical otherness is, however, not negated, and has the capacity to re-emerge as the self looks back at the past from the perspective of the future and a differently oriented 'now'.

Nietzsche multiplies perspectives and folds surfaces into multifaceted complexities and also complicates the present, so as to render the 'now' and 'the given' into inexhaustible multiplicities that can never be grasped via an 'objective' god's-eye viewpoint; but this does not entail that there is nothing out there apart from the projection of the I. In some ways Nietzsche appears to be closer to Kant—for whom 'truth' and also 'nature' were forever elusive infinities that acted as lures to reason—than to post-Kantian philosophers such as Schiller, Schelling or Schopenhauer who believed it possible to penetrate the veil of Isis (or of Maya). What makes Nietzsche so utterly different from Kant, however, is his insistence that 'nature' is not simply a creation of the I, and that there is an 'event' (*Ereignis*) and a 'something' (*Etwas*) awaiting the encounter. For Nietzsche, the correct 'etiquette' for dealing with 'truth' is to reconfigure it as 'an event'—as an indefinite 'something' already there—waiting to be registered. This 'event' is not simply the 'other' of the I but both so distant and also so near that its significance only emerges in what Nietzsche called in *Daybreak* the *'inzwischen'* (the 'in-between-time').

But whose flesh?

I will come back to the *inzwischen* and also Nietzsche's notion of the 'event' below and in the next chapter, when considering how useful Niezsche's strategy might be for developing a philosophy that can deal with difference. First, however, I need to register a caution. Given the profoundly anti-female bias in the language of sublimation which was explored in Chapter 6, it is perhaps unsurprising that Nietzsche seems to be unable to associate this *productive* bodily energy with creators who are *female*. He thus describes the kind of 'spiritual pregnancy' that is necessary for creativity as an attribute of 'male mothers', and also argues against any notion that women should become 'free-thinkers and scribblers' or 'unlearn' the 'womanly' instinct of fear (GS: §72; BGE: §239). Furthermore, Nietzsche seems to endorse the voice of Zarathustra who asserts that 'Man should be educated for war, and woman for the recreation of the warrior; all else is folly'. For Zarathustra, a woman cannot have the great health of the 'overman', and should hope only to 'give birth to the overman' (Z: 178). Nietzsche sets out to 'revalue all values', but it would seem that—like the German Romantics before him—he continues to devalue femaleness, which is associated with immanence and procreativity, rather than with sublime creativity.

At a deeper level, the problem is that the 'health' and the 'life' that Nietzsche so values is conceptualised in ways that seem entirely inappropriate for thinking of the female body or the physiological capacity for birth. For Nietzsche, health is not stasis, but involves a war against disease, and he claims that antagonism 'belongs to the *essence* of what lives, as a basic organic function; it is a consequence of the will to power, which is after all the will to life' (BGE: §259). Arguing that 'life itself is *essentially* appropriation, injury, over-powering of what is alien and weaker; suppression, hardness, imposition of one's own forms, incorporation and at least, at its mildest, exploitation' (§259), Nietzsche deploys language that negates the fact that a foetus is ontologically dependent upon an other (the mother), as well as the long period of infancy that makes modes of non-conflictual dependency integral to *human* growth. Granted that the mother/foetus relation can go awry—and that problems of the immune system, such as preeclampsia, can occur—in the case of a *normal* (healthy) pregnancy, the body of the mother tolerates the growing foetus inside her, so that 'self' and 'baby' gradually develop their own separate identities and immune systems. In this case the bacterial economy of war and opposition is replaced by an altogether more gentle placental economy through which bodily fluids and markers are gifted and also exchanged.

Nietzsche's reconfigured sublime is physiologically based, but he continues to think the privileged physiology of the man with 'great health' as that of a *male* creator whose autonomy emerges only insofar as he is victorious in the unending struggles that occur both inside and outside the embodied self:

> Even the body within which individuals treat each other as equals . . .
> if it is a living and not a dying body, has to do to other bodies what
> the individuals within it refrain from doing to each other: it will have
> to be an incarnate will to power, it will strive to grow, spread, seize,
> become predominant—not from any morality or immorality but
> because it is *living* and because life simply *is* will to power.
>
> (§259)

As in a 'well-constructed and happy commonwealth', within the healthy body it is all a matter of 'commanding and obeying', Nietzsche says, and he employs the metaphorics of the 'governing class' and the 'feelings of delight as commander' to explain how the well-functioning body behaves (§19). Thus, although Nietzsche also explicitly claims that there can be many different kinds of healthy body— dependent on 'your goal, your horizon, your energies, your impulses, your errors, and above all on the ideals and phantasms of your soul' (GS: §120)—his new physiological model of the sublime nevertheless relies on a combative model of 'great health' which negates the materiality of the *female* self.

For Nietzsche, the 'I' is not given as a unity—'*L'effet c'est moi*'—but emerges as an 'effect' from the entities (the 'souls') that are at war within the apparently homogeneous self (*BGE*: §19). Identity is no more than a temporary and fleeting structure that lasts only as long as all the conflicting forces within an organism are captured and directed towards the same end. In his critique of the 'decadent' and 'degenerate' individual who is already decomposing into the multiplicity of incompatible elements within, Nietzsche privileges unity and totality whilst simultaneously acknowledging the micro-forces and sub-groupings that have the potential to pull apart the entity or embodied self (*TI*: 477–79, 490–91). A negative evaluation is implicitly placed on discordant agencies, drives or instincts that operate within the 'unity' of the self. By contrast, my own emphasis on the *female* and *raced* subject position involves treating fractures and irreconcilable tensions within the social unity or self in an altogether more positive way. The interlacing of self with otherness that is characteristic of the pregnant female who is *healthy* should help us reconfigure the self–other relation in ways that allow us to think of the richness and the potentiality of the 'others within'. There are other structures that can embrace difference, apart from commanding and obeying; power and capture; or the type of uniformity of goal that produces the illusion of Nietzschean 'individuality'. And oddly, as we will see, it is Nietzsche himself who provides with the resources for re-imagining this self.

Remembering difference

To help us think otherness afresh, it is useful to turn to other aspects of Nietzsche's philosophy. And here it is possible to draw positive lessons from Nietzsche, and leave to one side his overly oppositional ontology, as well as his inability to think matter and health in terms that allow women the same transformative energies as men. For Nietzsche, one of the necessary conditions for the emergence of the fiction of an 'individual' as a homogenised unity is the forgetting and negating of differences:

> Every concept arises through the equation of unequal things. Just as it is certain that one leaf is never totally the same as another, so it is certain that the concept 'leaf' is formed by arbitrarily discarding these individual differences and by forgetting the distinguishing aspects. This awakens the idea that, in addition to the leaves, there exists in nature the 'leaf': the original model according to which all the leaves were perhaps woven, sketched, measured, colored, curled, and pain-ted—but by incompetent hands, so that no specimen has turned out to be a correct, trustworthy, and faithful likeness of the original model. ... We obtain the concept, as we do the form, by overlooking what is individual and actual; whereas nature is acquainted with no forms and no concepts, and likewise with no species, but only with an X which remains inaccessible and undefinable for us.
>
> (Nietzsche 1873: 83)

Here Nietzsche suggests that when the mind 'forgets' material differences in the formation of a concept (such as that of a leaf), material differences are not simply negated but remain on the fringes of consciousness. As the knowing subject encounters the world, 'there are frightful powers that continuously break in upon him, powers which oppose scientific "truth" with completely different kinds of "truths"' (88). Since it is only '*by means of this unconsciousness and forgetfulness*' that the inherited and simplified 'truths' of science emerge, there remains the possibility of an encounter or an intuition that, when it comes, 'smashes this framework to pieces' (84, 90). This shattering of conceptual understanding via the remembrance of forgotten differences—dif-ferences that don't relate to a truth hidden beyond the veil, but that concern the forgotten 'other' within—is, in effect, the role that Nietzsche gives to his reconfigured sublime in his late works. And it is this aspect of his theory of the 'sublime' and of the 'event' that can help us think more productively about those 'others' who are not outside the symbolic order, but who nevertheless vanish inside its folds.

188

Like the Kantian sublime, Nietzsche's reconfigured *sublim* disarms conceptual understanding; but, unlike Kant, Nietzsche links the sublime to 'difference' and to those aspects of an event, a subject or an object that are registered at the level of the pre-conscious, but that our framework of assumptions stop us from seeing. Whereas the Kantian sublime will forever escape conceptual understanding and bring the 'supersensible' into the frame, for Nietzsche human understanding is again and again reconfigured by the shock of difference. Furthermore, whereas Irigaray overlooks diversity within sexual groupings in her eagerness to provide a counter to Lacan's oedipal economy, Nietzsche's model of difference pushes us to pay attention to multiplicities that act as (temporary) unities, but which have the capacity to explode—and to transform the present and the past in the *inzwischen* (the in-between-time) in which conceptual, imaginative and visual frameworks collide. As we have seen, for Nietzsche, 'The greatest events and thoughts—but the greatest thoughts are the greatest events—are understood last' (*BGE*: §285, *corr.*). As such, the 'event' that inaugurates understanding does not take us through to the realm of the noumenal (even as a hope or a dream); instead what is opened up is the folds, surfaces and multifaceted complexities of 'this world' which is, according to Nietzsche, the only world that there is (*TI*: 485–86).

Nietzsche's reconfigured *bodily* sublime involves an encounter that does not take us outside the realm of representation. Nor is there simply a disruption to a single linguistic or symbolic reality that is a 'truth' that is always, everywhere the same. In §382 of *The Gay Science*, Nietzsche uses the language of the 'overhuman' and '*inhuman*' in relation to this new sublime; but he also suggests that these modes of the other-than-human are already here—forgotten, visible and audible but at the same time unregistered, existing in fragments—in both the present and the past. The contours of the 'real' are transformed as our concepts are unfrozen via an encounter with difference.

In Chapter 8 we saw Irigaray pointing towards a feminine subjectivity that lies *beyond* the histories and geographies of patriarchal thought. But the *female* and *raced* sublime that I have explored in this book does not involve anything so unheralded or strange. As Nietzsche's account of difference helps us grasp, the familiar can be reconfigured and hidden 'others' can suddenly emerge from *within* the histories of Western culture, as a 'rabbit' or a 'duck' might suddenly loom out of a duck–rabbit shape. As such, the female and raced sublime is not simply ineffable, and is also more material and more historically specific than might be supposed.

10

TERROR NOW AND THEN

In Chapter 1 I raised the question of the politics of the sublime, and in Chapter 2 we also encountered Lyotard's claim that such a politics could not exist: 'It could only be terror' (Lyotard 1988c: 71). On the other hand, Lyotard also registers 'a much earlier modulation of Nietzschean perspectivism in the Kantian theme of the sublime', and also provided resources for a respectful encounter with difference(s) via his analysis of the postmodern sublime (1982: 77). For Lyotard, the value of the competing and incompatible narratives of postmodernity is that dissension 'refines our sensitivity to differences and reinforces our ability to tolerate the incommensurable' (1979: xxv). And here it is necessary to note once more both the similarities and dissimilarities between my position and that of Lyotard who also describes the postmodern sublime in terms of difference and 'an event'.

In the series of essays and presentations on temporality and the sublime that are collected together under the title of *The Inhuman*, Lyotard added to his earlier analysis which made the postmodern sublime not temporally successive to the modern or Romantic sublime, but an irruptive moment within modernity and also, consequently, within history. Here Lyotard tells us that in the sublime of avant-garde painters what we are confronted with is an 'event, an occurrence'; something that is 'infinitely simple' and that involves 'a state of privation' through which all thought is 'disarmed' (Lyotard 1988a: 90). Using the example of Barnett Newman, Lyotard indicates that the painter of the postmodern sublime evokes the possibility of 'nothing happening' and a feeling of 'anxiety', but instead of anxiety taking on a 'negative value', it is transformed to pleasure and even 'joy'—specifically 'the joy obtained by the intensification of being'. Furthermore, this joy is not located in the 'beyond' of the Romantic sublime, but in the 'here and now' (91–93).

Lyotard is here referring to the 'zip' or the '*Tzim-tzum*' which is Newman's name for the rough stripe of colour that so frequently runs down his Abstract Expressionist canvases, allowing the eye to successively divide and draw together the colour planes into wholes and parts. Making reference to the often bare canvases, the still-evident masking tape and the rough lines and thick unevenness of the paint that were all features of Newman's work, Lyotard remarks:

It is chromatic matter alone, and its relationship with the material (the canvas, which is sometimes left unprimed) and the lay-out (scale, format, proportions), which must inspire the wonderful surprise, the wonder that there should be something rather than nothing. Chaos threatens, but the flash of the *Tzim-tzum*, the zip, takes place, divides the shadows, breaks down the light into colours like a prism, and arranges them across the surface like a universe.

(85–86)

Lyotard refers to Martin Heidegger for the notion of an 'event' that takes place in Newman's postmodern sublime, but he clearly knows that Nietzsche lies there in the background for Heidegger (90). In his late works Heidegger describes an artwork as 'a happening of truth': an 'event' (*Ereignis*) whereby Being discloses itself to man (*Dasein*) and a world unfolds (Beistegui 2005: 139, 141). What is put to one side is the response of the individual human whose life is shaped by everyday temporalities and anxieties, by bodily differences and by history itself. Heidegger's own solution to philosophy and the saving power of art sidelines the response of the individual human and, above all, the response of the embodied human caught in his or her everyday (ontic) concerns. Heidegger is critical of the Kantian notion of beauty, and Nietzsche is also criticised for linking art to a type of rapture which is an expression of life (129–37). And here Heidegger's criticism of Nietzsche is not the one that I offered in the last chapter—namely that Nietzsche has an overly restrictive model of health and of life that ignored the differently human—but that Nietzsche has not described art in terms that are sufficiently impersonal.

Lyotard describes the 'event' of a Newman painting in broadly Heideggerian terms which focus on a pre-personal and non-individualised response. Thus, he seems insensitive to the effect of an artwork on specific (historically located and embodied) persons and groups, even whilst being highly sensitive to the material and tonal differences that operate across the surfaces of Newman's canvases. Like Nietzsche, Lyotard emphasises differences that are masked by sameness, and sees the function of sublime art in terms of 'the occurrence of a thought as the unthought that remains to be thought' (Lyotard 1988a: 103). However, whereas Nietzsche's model allows us to find singular, material and 'forgotten' differences in the '*in-between-time*' that can be a forgotten moment *within* history, Lyotard remains suspicious of history—especially 'the grand narratives of legitimation that characterize modernity in the West' (1988c: 33–34). What is privileged instead is the bursting open of linear time in an *inhuman* way.

Lyotard emphasises the way that Newman's paintings strip away any temporal anticipation or evocation of an other that cannot be fully represented (1988a: 78–79). Here Lyotard contrasts Newman's artistic project with that of two artworks by Marcel Duchamp: *The Large Glass* (1915–23, also known as *The Bride Stripped Bare By Her Bachelors, Even*) and *Étant Données* (1945–66) which Lyotard analyses in more detail elsewhere (Lyotard 1977; and see Krauss 1993: 110ff.). *The Large Glass* depicts a fantastic, elaborate, but ineffectual, desiring machine involving males (the 'bachelors') who toil away, around and beneath a 'hanging female' (the *femelle* 'bride'). Duchamp's own notes on this (unfinished) painting on glass belong with the work, and show him exploring the temporalities of erotic labour (especially 'delay') and the alchemical purification of matter. By contrast, *Étant Données* positions the viewer as a voyeur, peering through a peephole to discover, on the other side, a naked and apparently headless female body, legs splayed wide, her pudenda directly in the line of the gaze.

Lyotard contrasts the 'fugitive' temporalities of pursuit in Duchamp ('not yet' and 'no longer') with the temporalities of Newman who 'is not representing a non-representable annunciation; he allows it to present itself' (Lyotard 1988a: 79). Duchamp's artworks 'refer to events, to the "stripping bare" of the Bride, and to the discovery of the obscene body'; in them, 'The event of femininity and the scandal of "the opposite sex" are one and the same' (78). But Newman's canvases involve a different kind of 'event' which eradicates the lure of the hidden (the feminine 'other'), and all sense of linear histories and time. They do not reach through to a 'beyond', but to a different configuration of the 'here and now'.

Elsewhere in *The Inhuman* Lyotard claims that all avant-garde art is linked to the sublime in that it 'is not concerned with what happens to the "subject", but with: "Does it happen?", with privation' (103). In *Peregrinations* Lyotard even goes so far as to say that Kant's account of taste in the third *Critique* is feeling-driven, and in a way that could bypass the 'I' altogether. The imagination, he tells us, is in the *Critique of the Power of Judgment* assigned the task of presentation (*Darstellung*), not representation (*Vorstellung*), and

> the work of presentation no longer requires the 'I think,' which was necessary for making phenomena understandable. If what is at stake is the multiplication of the ways of gathering data in order to present new forms and enjoy them, then something like a 'It is felt that …' would be sufficient to guide the imagination through the flood of possible forms. Is it possible to imagine the following? In the stream of sensitive clouds, no 'I' swims or sails; only mere affections float. Feelings felt by no one, attached to no identity, but making one cloud 'affected' by another.
>
> (1988b: 34)

This is a clear misreading of Kant who is, in effect, turned back into Kant's empiricist predecessor, David Hume, for whom the 'I' is no more than a resonance of affects, impressions and ideas. But one of the weaknesses of Hume's psychology of man is that he treats all humans as always the same in terms of the laws of association that bind together the chains of thought and of feeling into the 'bundle' of the self. Clearly, Lyotard would not wish to make any such move, but in sidelining the differently human and privileging the inhuman, Lyotard makes specific bodily, cultural and historical differences disappear.

My own reading of Kant on the sublime has similarities with Lyotard's. Like Lyotard I argue against a simple reading of Kant as an 'Enlightenment' philosopher who is a defender of reason. Like Lyotard I also argue that Kant's account of the sublime is politically useful, and that in it we can see some of the slippages that occur within the Kantian system. However, whereas in the Lyotardian reading of the Kantian sublime the subject eventually disappears into an 'inhuman' 'cloud' of direct feelings and 'affect', in my account what emerges is that Kant's apparently purely logical 'transcendental subject' takes as norm a particular kind of Westernised (and gendered) psyche that fears the 'other' and the infinite power of nature. My reading of the Kantian sublime thus emphasises the role of the Kantian subject before going on to radicalise that subject. So in the end nothing could be more different than our two interpretations of Kant on aesthetics, and especially the sublime. My concern is to read Kant's account of the sublime as opening up a way to rethink the subject in modernity and postmodernity, whereas for Lyotard we find in Kant's account of the sublime the beginnings of a move that renders the subject either otiose or no more than a set of reactive responses to affects and ideas.

For Lyotard, 'Thoughts are clouds' which are immeasurable and indefinite, and they are 'pushed and pulled at variable speeds' (1988b: 5). Aesthetic experience, and especially the sublime, puts us 'in touch' with these clouds and is 'the prime mode in which Being is "given" (and ungiven) in the frame of mind we call modernity' (40). The subject responds to 'thoughts' in a way that makes the thoughts not something that belongs to the subject, but something altogether 'more fragile, insubstantial, flimsy', like 'gossamer' (39). 'What we call the mind is the exertion of thinking thoughts' (6). Difference has been rendered entirely ahistorical and 'inhuman'; materiality has been deprived of its relation with human embodiment; and the 'subject' has been entirely displaced so that the question of the 'what is happening?' concerns only the energies of the non-sexed and non-raced body as the 'object' impacts on its senses.

That this impact—and, indeed, the whole 'exertion' of thinking—is curiously disembodied is particularly clear in the essay that opens *The Inhuman* which comprises a dialogue between an unidentified 'He' and a 'She' on the question of 'Can Thought Go on without a Body?'. Here, 'She' is given the last word, but it is 'She' who argues that 'post-solar thought' needs to prepare for 'the inevitability and complexity of this separation' of mind from body. In contradistinction from 'He' who had argued that the body is the 'indispensable hardware' for thought, 'She' insists that although thought cannot be separated from the lived (or 'phenomenological') body, it is already separate from the 'gendered body'—except insofar as the latter 'launches thought'. For 'She', after our sun has burnt out, thought can go on but bodies will be dissolved into unconscious forces and desires (1988a: 23, 16, 22).

Lyotard's fantasy about the possibility of thought continuing after the death of our sun seems to pick up the passage from Nietzsche about the 'event' being a something that happens 'as in the realm of stars' (*BGE*: §285). But insofar as Lyotard is seeking to connect Nietzsche's notion of the 'greatest event' and the 'greatest thought' to the theme of the sublime, it is a curiously eviscerated Nietzsche who is summoned. Lyotard looks not to the 'differently human' but to 'the inhuman' for the kinds of radicalisation necessary for thinking the sublime in respect to avant-garde art. But this depoliticises Lyotard's analysis insofar as racial, cultural and sexual difference are concerned, with the consequence—as we have also seen in Chapter 2 of this book—that modes of embodied difference disappear into linguistic and representational clouds, and cannot be spoken, or heard, in ways that enable bodily differences to be registered or understood. Like me, Lyotard is also moving 'back from beyond', and is concerned to re-imagine difference and the other. However, for Lyotard, 'the event', the 'other' and also thought itself have been deprived of any link to lived embodiment. And this means that embodied human differences also disappear.

Derrida and the 'event' of 'September 11'

Politically speaking, what might be lost if the 'event' is conceptualised via a Heideggerian framework, rather than in terms of the more historical model of embodied and forgotten differences that Nietzsche's leaf example suggests? The answer seems to be that we forego the possibility of political and historical transformation, as well as the possibility of registering a multiplicity of embodied viewpoints and affective responses that will, in the future—as well as in the present—be different from our own. Take, for example, Derrida's discussion of the attack on the World Trade Center on 11 September 2001. In response to various questions from Giovanna Borradori, Derrida elaborates on the question of what it might mean to claim that 'September 11' is a '*major event*' (Borradori 2003: 90). Borradori interprets Derrida's answer in Heideggerian terms, according to which an 'event' is a transformative encounter that can never be totally understood or assimilated. She even interprets Derrida as claiming that terrorism '*is* irreducibly ineffable and enigmatic', and that this is why it is 'hard to meaningfully attach any concepts to it' (153). Borradori does, in other words, make 'September 11' function as the equivalent to the sublime.

However, whereas Derrida does indeed talk about the 'terror' of 11 September 2001 in terms of a transformative event, what he seems to mean by this seems far closer to Nietzsche than to Heidegger. Thus, he does not position the 'event' of 'September 11' as forever outside the horizons of understanding or imagination, but instead ascribes our inability to come to terms with it to our location in historical time. He indicates that a re-interpretation of history and of the conceptual apparatus of the present is possible, if we start from within history and work to show what our conceptual apparatus prevents us from registering, noticing or saying *now*:

> it is if I were in fact content to say that what is terrible about 'September 11,' what remains 'infinite' in this wound, is that we do not *know* what it is and so do not know how to describe, identify, or even name it. And that is, in fact, what I'm saying. But in order to show this horizon of nonknowledge, this nonhorizon of knowledge (the powerlessness to comprehend, recognize, cognize, identify, name, describe, foresee), is anything but abstract and idealist, I will need to say more. And, precisely, in a more concrete way.
>
> (94)

This more 'concrete' way does, in fact, push Derrida towards a historical analysis of the stages of the Cold War and its end, including some extended comments on 'the possibility of another discourse and another politics' that might emerge once it is recognised that the European Enlightenment offered more than one conceptual framework for negotiating our relation to the 'other' (118, 115ff.). Perhaps he was thinking here of what I recorded in Chapter 4 of this book: the fact that Islam was positioned on the side of Modernity by Enlightenment thinkers such as Voltaire and Kant. Derrida does himself make reference to both these philosophers as he talks of the need for a 'historical genealogy of the concept of tolerance', and envisages a time in which a new mode of cosmopolitanism and tolerance will have emerged as we reorient ourselves towards the past (126, 120).

Derrida links this new politics to a mode of philosophical deconstruction that is not only discursive and conceptual, but also *historical*. For him, 'the event' involves a moment of temporal irruption that might seem reminiscent of Lyotard's postmodern sublime; but this disruption is given historical potential in a way that Lyotard's analysis of the sublime was not. Thus, in response to Borradori's questions, Derrida suggests that the trauma of 'September 11' is produced by the way that temporalities collide, but also says that it would be too simple to describe this in terms of a collision between the realities of the present and the expectations of the past:

> The ordeal of the event has as its tragic correlate not what is presently happening or what has happened in the past but the precursory signs of what threatens to happen. It is the future that determines the unappropriability of the event, not the present or the past. Or at least, if it is in the present or the past, it is only insofar as it bears on its body the terrible sign of what might or perhaps will take place, which will be *worse than anything that has ever taken place*.
>
> Let me clarify. We are talking about a trauma, and thus an event, whose temporality proceeds neither from the now that is present

nor from the present that is past but from an im-presentable to come
(à venir).

(Borradori 2003: 96–97)

In contrast with Freud, who claimed that anxiety about the future protects
the ego against the type of physiological and psychological shock that produces
trauma, Derrida maintains that 'Traumatism is produced by the *future*, by the *to
come*, by the threat of the worst *to come*, rather than by an aggression that is
"over and done with"' (97; Freud 1920: 222–24). Like Nietzsche, Derrida seems
to locate an 'event' in terms of the *inzwischen*, the in-between-time within
which temporalities collide, but he redescribes the moment of shattering. What
splits apart is 'the conceptual, semantic, and one could even say hermeneutic
apparatus that might have allowed one to see coming, to comprehend, interpret, describe, speak of, and name "September 11"—and in so doing to neu-
tralize the traumatism' (93). What Derrida suggests is that the 'double *crash*' of
'September 11' does not simply come from an event that makes us notice features in the past that we had previously 'forgotten' to see; there is also a shock
linked to anticipation and to other (possible) futures that are opened up by the
sudden shift in perspective (93).

According to Derrida, 'September 11' has, in other words, the potential of
what Nietzsche would term an 'event'—except that its power is, for the time
being, deflected into repetitive patterns of incomprehension, rather than
towards the change in conceptual and imaginative frameworks that the Nietzschean event instigates. In this late interview—first recorded in October 2001,
and published a year before his death in 2004—Derrida's own philosophical
position seems to have undergone a marked change. Here, he seems to be
imagining the 'event' in terms of historical blinkers, rather than in terms of
necessary and forever existing blind spots within philosophical and conceptual
thought. In this respect, Derrida's analysis of the 'event' and of 'terror' is more
useful than that of Lyotard for developing a politics of the sublime that might
enable us to deal with the breakdown in our frameworks of interpretation that
occurred with the Twin Towers attack.

Arendt: 'in-between' past and future

The other twentieth-century philosopher who wrote on political terror, on the
'event', and of being situated 'in-between' the past and the future, was Hannah
Arendt, whom Derrida also makes reference to when talking about the ideal of
a new 'democracy to come' (120). Arendt faced head on the collapse of standards of interpretation as she sought to make sense of the historical period that
she was living through, in particular the rise of totalitarian governments which
she described as 'the central event of our world' (Arendt 1953: 377). For her,
the task of judging the specific and unique nature of mid-twentieth-century
terror was made more urgent by Auschwitz, the discovery of which provided

the most profound 'shock' to the framework of values, meaning and understanding that she had acquired. Learning about Auschwitz only in 1943, as a German Jew living in exile in America, Arendt speaks of the difficulty that she and her husband had in believing the stories of the camps, and how even after 'proof' came six months later, a conceptual 'abyss' still remained:

> That was the real shock. Before that we said: Well, one has enemies. ... But this was different. It was really as if an abyss had opened. Because we had the idea that amends could somehow be made for everything else, as amends can be made for just about everything at some point in politics. But not for this. *This ought not to have happened*. And I don't mean just the number of victims. I mean the method, the fabrication of corpses and so on—I don't need to go into that. This should not have happened. Something happened there to which we cannot reconcile ourselves. None of us ever can.
>
> (Arendt 1964: 13–14)

'*This ought not to have happened*.' In the *Critique of the Power of Judgment*, Kant also remarks that we are all compelled to register that there should have been a different outcome in the way the world and actions unfold ('*es müsste anders zugehen*'; 'things must come out differently') (*CPJ*: 458). Kant uses this judgement as evidence of a moral sensibility that compels us to believe in a theistic God who is a moral legislator. By contrast, for Arendt, the judgements that we make about individual events are made without objective standards, and by the historian rather than by a God:

> Imagination alone enables us to see things in their proper perspective, to put that which is too close at a certain distance so that we can see and understand it without bias or prejudice, to bridge abysses of remoteness until we can see and understand everything that is too far away from us as though it were our own affair. This 'distancing' of some things and bridging the abysses to others is part of the dialogue of understanding (Arendt 1953: 392).

For Arendt, it is through the 'unending activity' of *human* understanding that is ideally disinterested, but never outside history, that we seek to 'reconcile ourselves to reality, that is, try to be at home in the world' (377).

Thus, Arendt claims that it is the task of the spectator—and the historian, the poet, the storyteller, in particular—to make judgements about human action and human goodness and evil, not by reference to necessary or universal values that are known in advance and clearly signalled as objective truths, but via strategies of narration and of comparative judgement. For Arendt, furthermore, the narrator who is engaged in the interpretation of history is not simply concerned to record a truth; instead she is an agent who is actively engaged with reconfiguring the present and also the past. However, with the conceptual 'abyss' of totalitarian terror always haunting her thoughts, Arendt was also always concerned to make a distinction between entirely arbitrary hypotheses and those who engage with past events and human actions in ways that are intersubjectively valid.

Arendt made 'total terror', as implemented in Auschwitz, the 'essence' of totalitarianism, but she equated the latter neither with tyranny nor with a top-down and authoritarian model of government (Arendt 1951: 466; 1961: 99). Arguing that totalitarianism was a distinctively new political system that emerged only when twentieth-century man lost his hold on a common tradition and a communal life, she described it as crushing all sense of human individuality, and presenting its own arbitrary (and often quite mad) hypotheses as inevitable 'truths' (87). Those caught up within its structures are offered 'the total explanation of the past, the total knowledge of the present, and the reliable prediction of the future' (1951: 469–70). Separated from traditional practices and from 'common sense', Arendt argued that the terrorised individual comes to believe that his or her subjective experience is insignificant in comparison with that which *must* happen (Canovan 2000).

Like Lyotard, Arendt can be read as a philosopher who is concerned with analysing beginnings. However, whereas Lyotard focused on historical irruption and those modes of 'inhuman' response that detach us from all identity, the major philosophical problem that Arendt addressed throughout her published work is the problem of describing, understanding and evaluating *human* actions and, specifically, the type of 'beginning which is man' (Arendt 1958: 177n.). She takes as central the problems of human agency or 'natality': a term which she defines as 'the capacity for beginning something new'. For Arendt, 'natality, and not mortality, may be the central capacity of political, as distinguished from metaphysical, thought' (9). And clearly natality is understood by her in terms of a specifically *human* type of agency that is not divorced from the past, but which also cannot be reduced to a prior causal chain: 'Only when something irrevocable has happened can we even try to trace its history backward. The event illuminates its past, and can never be deduced from it' (1953: 388). As such, an 'event' cannot be reduced to a causal type explanation because it involves a break—a new and radical beginning—in time. Its locus is the agent whose actions have an 'inherent unpredictability' (1958: 191). As a consequence, 'Action reveals itself fully only to the storyteller, that is, to the backward glance of the historian, who indeed always knows better what it was all about than the participants' (192).

Trying to explain how the human agent opens up a gap between the present and the past, Arendt quotes one of Kafka's parables from 1920 which appeared as a part of a collection of aphorisms entitled 'HE' (Kafka 1920). Correcting the English translation slightly, Arendt records Kafka's words:

He has two antagonists: the first presses him from behind, from the origin. The second blocks the road ahead. He gives battle to both. To be sure, the first supports him in his fight with the second, for he wants to push him forward, and in the same way the second supports him in his fight with the first, since he drives him back. But it is only theoretically so. For it is not only the two antagonists who are there, but he himself as well, and who really knows his intentions? His dream, though, is that some time in an unguarded moment—and this would require a night darker than any night has ever been yet—he will jump out of the fighting line and be promoted, on account of his experience in fighting, to the position of umpire over his antagonists in their fight with each other.

(Arendt 1961: 7)

Because of the context, she does not correct the translation of the noun 'Richter' as 'umpire'; but she could have noted that its primary sense in German is that of a 'judge'.

Arendt quotes this passage in full also in *Part 1: Thinking* of *The Life of the Mind*, so it clearly meant a lot to her, and second time around she compares it to Nietzsche's vision of the gateway of the 'Moment' [*Augenblick*] at which the infinite paths leading from the past and forward into the future 'contradict each other' as they meet (Z: 270; Arendt 1978, i, 202, 204). Commenting on both the Kafka and Nietzsche passages—and distinguishing her own interpretation of Nietzsche from that of Heidegger—Arendt argues against any simple notion that there is simply a crash of two temporalities in the 'now' where the temporalities intersect. 'He'—Kafka's nameless human—is the point of intersection, and it is only insofar as the 'he' (or what she elsewhere describes as a distinctively human 'who') intervenes that the present is distinguishable from the past: 'Without "him", there would be no difference between past and future, but only everlasting change' (i, 208). Since 'he' is the locus of the meaning and the values that are read onto the 'now', Arendt argues for a new 'diagonal' which emanates from man himself: 'For this diagonal, though pointing to some infinity, is limited, enclosed, as it were, by the forces of past and future, and thus protected against the void; it remains bound to and is rooted in the present—an entirely human present' (i: 209, and see 1961: 12).

Arendt was profoundly influenced by—but also writing in opposition to—Heidegger, her one time teacher and former lover, who had been a very public defender of Nazism in the years leading up to the 1939–45 war. And she is clearly negotiating a conceptual space between Heidegger's entirely impersonal analysis of the 'event' as 'a happening of truth', on the one hand, and the type of analysis of history that simply makes 'truth' a matter of subjective interpretation. Against Heidegger, what Arendt emphasises is the role of the human—Kafka's 'he'—as an 'umpire' whose task it is to judge and interpret the world in the 'in-between' of the past and the future. There are no longer merely two antagonistic forces, but a threefold intersection, in the 'press' of the 'now'. At the juncture of the 'crash' of temporalities, Arendt inserts man since, she says, it is only in respect to the human that beginning can be plotted. But Arendt's 'man' does not simply invent the real out of nothing. As she insists in the very last page that she wrote before her death, 'beginning is rooted in *natality*, and by no means in creativity' (1978: ii, 217). Her judging humans are located in history and are agents in this world.

Arendt's 'he' does not invent history, but is also not simply acted upon by inhuman forces; he 'remains bound to and is rooted in the present' she insists in both the 1961 and 1978 texts. But Arendt also dreams, along with Kafka, of a jump 'out of the fighting line', and finding 'the place in time which is sufficiently removed from past and future to offer "the umpire" a position from which to judge the forces fighting with each other with an impartial eye' (1961: 12, and see 1978; i, 209). Arguing against traditional metaphysical analyses of thinking and willing, Arendt positions the human as an idealised umpire in the 'gap' that opens up between past and future, and as such she 'humanises' Heidegger and Nietzsche's notion of the 'event'.

As far as Nietzsche's approach to temporality is concerned, Arendt is clear that 'A philosophy of life that does not arrive, as did Nietzsche, at the affirmation of "eternal recurrence" (*ewige Wiederkehr*) as the highest principle of all being, simply does not know what it is talking about' (Arendt 1958: 97). But she also argues that Nietzsche's thought of the eternal return is in the end fatalistic and closes down notions of agency 'and a future that is unknown and therefore open to change' (1978: i, 166). Arendt also, with good reason, accuses Nietzsche of being unable to analyse a specifically *human* life: 'the time interval between birth and death' of which a 'story' and a 'biography' can be told (1958: 97, 313n.). Like Nietzsche, Arendt rejects the notion that a person is an autonomous, self-determining agent (Kant's noumenally free person or self); but she nevertheless wants to keep hold of a notion of freedom and of beginning afresh.

Arendt and the politics of aesthetic judgement

Towards the end of her life Arendt turned to the account of judgement provided by Kant in the third *Critique*, and to the latter's account of aesthetic judgements of the beautiful, in particular, in order to try and figure out how judgement—as opposed to reason, understanding or willing—operates. Pondering the role of the 'umpire' of history—and, thus, in attempt to deal with the conceptual 'abyss' of Auschwitz—Arendt looked at how reason operates when it proceeds in a bottom-up and piecemeal fashion, as it does in respect to matters of aesthetic taste. Her claim is that Kant's aesthetic philosophy provides us with a model for political judgement insofar as judgement is by no means identical with 'the lawgiving faculty of reason' which idealises a principle of agreement with oneself, but involves instead a comparative act of judgement: a type of 'enlarged mentality' which consists of being able to imagine what other humans must feel (1961: 219, 220). For aesthetic judgement, Arendt insists, what is above all important is 'the ability to see things not only from one's own point of view but in the perspective of all those who happen to be present', and this entails 'sharing-the-world-with-others' (221).

In her published writings—especially in her political essays, and in the two parts of *The Life of the Mind* that she managed to complete (although not see through the Press) prior to her sudden death in 1975—we can see Arendt pointing to Kant's analysis of aesthetic taste for a potential solution to the conceptual 'abyss' of totalitarian terror that was her own 'central concern'. She thought Kant could help her understand how reason can still operate, even though totalitarian terror 'has brought to light the ruin of our categories of thought and standards of judgment' (Arendt 1953: 388). Arendt traced the history of this moral devastation back to the eighteenth century, and to writers like Montesquieu who suggested that our ethical standards are no more than custom and convention. By the nineteenth century, according to Arendt, 'the very framework within which understanding and judgment could arise is gone' (386).

In his influential interpretative essay on the third part of Hannah Arendt's unfinished—or, rather, almost completely unstarted—*The Life of the Mind: Part III Judging*, Ronald Beiner sets out to reconstruct the book that Hannah Arendt had in mind when she died. Beiner publishes the full text of Arendt's *Lectures on Kant's Political Philosophy* (Arendt 1970), and also adds an appendix in which he persuasively extends the sketch on Kant and judgement which closes *Part II: Willing* of *The Life of the Mind*. What Arendt was aiming for was a political philosophy that could enable us to give meaning and value to the suffering and evil that the past brings in its tow. As Beiner puts it, Arendt regarded the function of the judging spectator to be that of rescuing from the 'oblivion of history' certain 'unique episodes' that demand judgement:

> Events of this kind possess what Arendt, following Kant, calls 'exemplary validity.' By attending to the particular *qua* particular, in the form of an 'example', the judging spectator is able to illuminate the universal without thereby reducing the particular to universals. The example is able to take on universal meaning whilst *retaining* its particularity, which is not the case when the particular serves merely to indicate a historical 'trend'.
>
> (Beiner 1982: 127)

In judging beauty, Arendt suggests in her *Lectures*, following Kant, I am making a judgement that is not merely a subjective judgement of taste but is at once particular and universal. I am not simply recording what I myself like, but my belief and, indeed, the demand—based on reflection and comparison between myself and others—that my judgement is intersubjectively valid. For Arendt, the judgement of the beautiful is not simply that of an individual self, but neither is it simply that of Kant's idealised free and autonomous 'person' who stands outside the networks of space and time—and hence outside the political community—insofar as he is the locus of value. For Arendt, by contrast, the judgement is made by a person who is a member of a community—and 'community' here has to be read in terms of a public sphere that is through and through social: 'One judges always as a member of a community, guided by one's community sense, one's *sensus communis*' (Arendt 1970: 75).

Arendt's approach to the problem of political judgement is innovative and valuable; but in looking to Kant's analysis of our taste for beauty for a solution for political and historical judgement, she also simply disregarded Kant's account of the sublime—and those portions of Kant's aesthetics in which the consensual 'universals' of aesthetic judgement break down. As we have seen in Chapter 4, for Kant, the 'Orientals' were specifically denied the capacity to enjoy the sublime, and the Chinese were specifically denied public—as opposed to merely 'private'—taste. As such, they fall outside the *sensus communis* which is the aesthetic ideal on which Arendt seeks to build her politics. Furthermore, as I also demonstrated in Chapter 3, in the case of the sublime, deviation from a 'normal' response is not only tolerated but also even advocated for women who have a 'duty' to remain in touch with their fear. It seems that Kant could deal with an idealised 'common sense' which is evoked every time aesthetic judgement is employed, only because he also delimited the 'purely aesthetic' realm so as to exclude the sublime. This was, instead, described as being between the aesthetic and the moral. But since Kant did not allow all human beings to count as full moral agents or 'persons', it seems highly unlikely that Kant's account of judgement could provide Arendt with the sort of conceptual framework that she required as a bulwark against totalitarian terror. It was, after all, by excluding Jews, gypsies, homosexuals and other 'degenerate' types of humans from full (Aryan) personhood that the National Socialist 'solution' to cultural decay operated.

Troublingly, there are even aspects of Kant's aesthetics that could be used by the Nazis, and it is no accident that Alfred Bäumler, one of the most important Nazi philosophers, also started out by publishing a book on Kant's third *Critique* (Baeumler 1923) and played a significant role in politicising the Kant Society during the 1930s. I am not suggesting that Kant was the same type of racist as Bäumler, but he provides resources for racism when he differentiates between the status of judgements of the beautiful and of the sublime. Thus, in the case of the beautiful, Kant insists that we have to suppose that all humans *should* make the same judgement as me; in the case of the sublime Kant is clear that it is not *all*—but only *some*—human beings who have the appropriate moral and cultural education that will enable them to transcend the initial displeasure and derive delight from the terror and conceptual abyss of the sublime. Since Kant indicates that this mode of transcendent enjoyment is not even an *ideal* response for all humans (most notably women), where understanding comes up against its limits, Kant does, in the end, secure an objective standard of judgement only via his 'moral proof' for the existence of a theistic God who is omniscient, omnipotent, omnibenevolent, wise and at the same time just (*CPJ*: 444–47).

In recent political debate, there has often been an appeal to the 'Enlightenment' values of universal reason to solve the crisis in value judgements and interpretative frameworks that face us today. As we have seen, however, the paradigmatic 'Enlightenment' philosopher, Immanuel Kant, was singularly lacking when dealing with empirical human differences. And it was, curiously, the anti-rationalist philosopher, Friedrich Nietzsche, who provided a way to think difference afresh. Controversially, I have suggested that Arendt, Lyotard and Derrida have also provided more productive openings for re-imagining justice than we could hope to find in Kant.

There is, however, a real problem with Arendt's own 'return to Kant'. As we have seen, she deploys the language of the *sublime* (of terror, shock and a conceptual 'abyss') to outline the problem in understanding and judging history that confronts twentieth-century man; but, ironically enough, in her own response to modern dilemmas it is a development of Kant's aesthetic response to the *beautiful* that takes centre-stage. Insofar as *historical* problems are concerned, it seems to be the problems of the sublime—the 'abyss' of Auschwitz and of totalitarianism—that troubled her most. But that left her in a quandary. Perhaps Arendt would have found a way of solving this problem had she lived to complete the book on *Judging*; we cannot know. What we can be sure about, however, is that Kant cannot provide her with an adequate model for envisaging the new universals and community that her political project required. There is more than one type of embodied spectator or judging human, something that her deployment of Kafka's parable of the 'umpire' of the wrestling match conceals.

Arendt does, in fact, comment on the practical impossibility of ever finding oneself in the elevated position of Kafka's 'umpire'; but what she never adequately addresses is the problem of there being competing narratives which emerge from the 'small non-time-space in the very heart of time' in which the 'he' is located (Arendt 1961: 13). She notes that Kafka was right to call his 'umpire' a 'he'—and not a 'somebody'—but this means that, in her solution to the problem of political judgement, the problem of the *embodied* human (the '*somebody*') still remains unaddressed (12; 1978: i, 210). The 'event' has been rendered more human by adding in the man who judges at the fulcrum of the 'press' of the future and the past. But that man still lacks a specific mode of embodiment; Arendt has privileged *natality*, but she still downplays *physiological* birth.

Unfreezing the frame

Despite the puzzles and problems of Arendt's account of judgement and interpretation, her approach to the question of unimaginable evil in history seems relevant again today. To rewrite Arendt on totalitarian terror, we could say that 'the rise of terrorism is now the central event of our world', and also say, with her, that underlying the question of terror is a clash in values, and that this is what has generated the crisis of modernity (and also that of our post-'postmodern' world). Arendt seeks to make philosophy *political* as she criticises the categories of Western metaphysics, morality and theology, and instead looks to aesthetics for a guide as to where to start again in building our value system anew.

In *Part 1* of *Life of the Mind* Arendt wrote about the way that even an ordinary word—such as 'house'—'"*is something like a frozen thought that thinking must unfreeze*"' (1978 i: 171). She also quotes Wittgenstein on the task of philosophy as uncovering '"*bumps* that the intellect has got by running its head up against the limits of language"' (115). To think again about the ways in which life can *bump* against conceptual frameworks and 'unfreeze' our thoughts with respect to the sublime, I have argued in the last three chapters of this book that it is useful to look within the 'folds' of history and at Nietzsche's reconfigured '*sublim*'. To encounter the 'other' we do not need to be taken 'beyond' this space–time world, but into a different relation to the present and the future as the past is transformed. Via a series of 'bumps' and 'shocks' that can open up an 'abyss' in our conceptual understanding, our interpretative and value framework can be unfrozen, and perhaps even enriched. Often, for us, that encounter comes via the 'event' of an artwork; however historical events can also be transformative—but (and this is the opposite of what Arendt herself asserts), they are most likely to be so when the tricks of psychic and emotional 'distancing' are placed under strain.

Arendt's emphasis on the role of the narrator and the philosopher to interpret—and to construct a new framework for judgement—for *historical* events and for *human* agents is profoundly important; but for the ruptures in understanding brought about by twenty-first century 'terrorism', Arendt's model of psychic distance and imaginative understanding of an 'umpire'—based on Kant's analysis of the beautiful—does not seem enough. Instead it seems necessary to look again at the problematics of the sublime—but without writing out Western philosophy's failure to adequately register embodied differences and cultural, religious and ethnic diversity, and also without supposing that there are some things which can never be told.

Arendt's account of the ideal 'umpire' of history who judges the present and the past emphasises disinterestedness and psychic distance; but in the twenty-first century the Western 'consumer' of images and twenty-four-hour news bulletins has become too estranged from the 'actual'. We have learnt to tame and domesticate even the most appalling images of violence or of disaster, by viewing suffering 'as if it were a picture'—not in the manner of the sublime, but in the manner of the picturesque, in which all potential chaos or disorder is contained by the boxing and framing process that is imposed by the mind's eye.

Knowledge of the techniques of the digital manipulation of images and the editing of films has provided us with a set of temporal utilities that allow us to distance ourselves from registering images—and perhaps even the world that we negotiate in our everyday lives—as fully 'actual'. We are further distanced from our own reactions since we also know that there is no televisual or journalistic communication that does not involve a degree of manipulation. Not all narratives and images are equal, and many cannot even be registered either because of self censorship, or because of the prior censorship of the media, of books or other aspects of the 'public sphere' that consign racial, ethnic, cultural and also sexual difference to the waste-bin of the 'uninteresting', the journalistically 'dull' or as being of concern to merely 'minority interests'.

In practice, it would seem, it is only some (and not all) other human beings and entities that are seen as bound up with our identities in ways that might move us to terror or even to anxiety; but that does not mean that we should not multiply narratives and perspectival viewpoints as we set about registering the complexity and multifaceted complications of the past and also the 'now'. Indeed, the need for a *multiplicity* of historical narratives of the concept of the sublime remains urgent if the trauma and terror linked to twenty-first century representations of 'difference' and the 'other' are to be addressed. And these histories will need to be *politically* aware, and recognise the position of the *human* judge (the 'somebody', not just the 'he') who is located in the 'press' of the moment, where the temporalities of anticipation and remembrance intersect.

In Chapter 1 of this book I quoted Andreas Huyssen who argued for the importance of intensifying 'the productive tension between the political and the aesthetic, between history and the text, between engagement and the mission of art' (Huyssen 1984: 271). Huyssen did not focus on the sublime, in particular, as he described the 'landscape of the postmodern' that surrounded him in 1984. We are now faced with a much more tension-ridden environment than Huyssen might have expected when he wrote those words, and questions about multiculturalism, ethnic diversity and the need to respect difference(s) are more politically charged now than they were then.

The conceptual and imaginative 'freezing' of the language of 'terror' has also intensified, so that the hope that Derrida registered in October 2001 that a productive political transformation might emerge from the 'trauma' cf 'September 11' now also, in many ways, seems dated. The repetitive patterns of incomprehension have only increased as we find ourselves subjected to multiple visual and auditory rhetorics of terror. It has, after all, been profoundly disturbing to hear the American military appropriating the language of 'Shock and Awe' that has, traditionally, been associated with the aesthetics of the sublime. And it has been even more troubling to register the way that the endless repetitions and replays of gross acts of violence have made terror seem everyday—producing neither 'shock' nor 'awe', but a kind of numbness of response.

The swift changes in the political and cultural landscape during the time that I have spent writing this book have often made me wish that I could put the problems of the sublime to one side until the so-called 'war on terror' has gone away. But it is precisely Hannah Arendt's procedure of finding an implicit politics in aesthetic judgement that has made it impossible for me to shirk the task of keeping discussions of the sublime alive, and also alive to human differences. The problems of the politics of the sublime and of its links with terror have not been solved. As I indicated in Chapter 1, this was never the intention. But this book will have succeeded if it has shown how thinking the sublime and the event in terms of *human* differences and the blind spots of *history* provides a framework that makes questions of aesthetics—so often regarded as marginal to philosophy—integral to debates about intolerance, global justice and the 'clash in values' today.

NOTES

1 A terrible prospect

1 A list of in-text abbreviations and referencing conventions can be found in the 'Notes on the Texts and Abbreviations'.

3 Kant and the unfair sex

1 My quotations from the *Remarks* are indebted to Cooley and Frierson's valuable translation, but I have made substantial corrections. Their translation is ncw being revised for publication by Cambridge University Press.

BIBLIOGRAPHY

See also 'Notes on the Texts and Abbreviations'.

Abdullah, M. S. (1981) *Geschichte des Islams in Deutschland*, Verlag Styria.

Allen, Prudence (1985) *The Concept of Woman: Volume 1, The Aristotelian Revolution 750 BC–AD 1250*, The Eden Press.

Anidjar, Gil (2003) *The Jew, the Arab: a History of the Enemy*, Stanford University Press.

——(2004) 'The Jew, the Arab: An Interview with Gil Anidjar conducted by Nermeen Shaik', *Asia Source*, February 2004. Online. Available at: http: www.asiasource.org/news/special_reports/anidjar.cfm (accessed 17 August 2005).

Archer, Michael, Guy Brett and Catherine de Zegher (1997) *Mona Hatoum*, Phaidon.

Arendt, Hannah (1951) *The Origins of Totalitarianism*, Allen and Unwin, 3rd ed., 1967.

——(1953) 'Understanding and Politics', *Partisan Review*, 20: 377–92.

——(1958) *The Human Condition*, University of Chicago Press.

——(1961) *Between Past and Future*, Faber and Faber.

——(1964) '"What Remains? The Language Remains": a conversation with Günter Gaus', in *The Portable Hannah Arendt*, ed. Peter Baehr, Penguin Classics, 2000.

——(1970) *Lectures on Kant's Political Philosophy*, ed. Ronald Beiner, University of Chicago Press, 1992.

——(1978) *The Life of the Mind, Part 1: Thinking; Part 2, Willing*, Secker and Warburg, 2 vols.

Aristotle (c.350 BCE) *On Rhetoric: A Theory of Civic Discourse*, trans. George A. Kennedy, Oxford University Press, 1991.

Arnim, Bettine von (1835) *Goethe's Correspondence with a Child*, trans. Bettina von Arnim, Longman, Orme, Brown, Green & Longmans, 2 vols, 1837, with a Preface by Bruce G. Charlton (2004). Online. Available at: http://www.hedweb.com/bgcharlton/bettina-goethe.html (accessed 9 February 2006).

——(1839) *Die Günderode*, ed. Christa Wolf, Insel Verlag, 1983.

Ashfield, Andrew and Peter de Bolla (1996) *The Sublime: a Reader in British Eighteenth-Century Aesthetic Theory*, Cambridge University Press.

Assmann, Jan (1997) *Moses the Egyptian: The Memory of Egypt in Western Monotheism*, Harvard University Press, 1998.

——(1999) *Das verschleierte Bild zu Sais: Schillers Ballade und ihre griechischen und ägyptischen Hintergründe. Lectio Teubneriana VIII*, B. G. Teubner.

Bachofen, Johann Jakob (1861) *Das Mutterrecht*, Krais and Hoffmann.

Baeumler, Alfred (1923) *Kants Kritik der Urteilskraft: Ihre Geschichte und Systematik*, vol. 1, Max Niemeyer Verlag.

Bailly, Jean Christophe and Robert C. Morgan (1995) *Dorothea Tanning*, trans. Richard Howard, Braziller.

Barolini, Helen (1994) 'The Italian Side of Emily Dickinson', *The Virginia Quarterly Review*. Online. Available at: http://www.vqronline.org/viewmedia.php/prmMID/7433 (accessed 13 February 2006).

Battersby, Christine (1981) 'An Enquiry Concerning the Humean Woman', *Philosophy*, 56: 303–12.

——(1989) *Gender and Genius: Towards a Feminist Aesthetics*, The Women's Press; Indiana University Press.

——(1998) *The Phenomenal Woman: Feminist Metaphysics and the Patterns of Identity*, Polity Press; Routledge.

——(2005) 'The Man of Passion: Philosophy, Emotion and Sexual Difference', in *Representing Emotions: New Connections in the Histories of Art, Music and Medicine*, eds Penelope Gouk and Helen Hills, Ashgate, 139–54.

Beckley, Bill (ed.) (2001) *Sticky Sublime*, Allworth Press.

Beckley, Bill and David Shapiro (eds) (1998) *Uncontrollable Beauty; Toward a New Aesthetic*, Watson-Guptill Publications.

Beiner, Ronald (1982) 'Hannah Arendt on Judging: Interpretative Essay', in Hannah Arendt, *Lectures on Kant's Political Philosophy*, ed. Ronald Beiner, University of Chicago Press, 1992.

Beistegui, Miguel de (2005) *The New Heidegger*, Continuum.

Bernal, Martin (1987) *Black Athena: the Afroasiatic Roots of Classical Civilization: Volume 1, The Fabrication of Ancient Greece 1785–1985*, Free Association Books, 1988.

Blakemore, Steven (1997) *Intertextual War: Edmund Burke and the French Revolution in the Writings of Mary Wollstonecraft, Thomas Paine, and James Mackintosh*, Associated University Presses.

Bloom, Harold (1973) *The Anxiety of Influence*, Oxford University Press.

Borradori, Giovanna (2003) *Philosophy in a Time of Terror: Dialogues with Jürgen Habermas and Jacques Derrida*, University of Chicago Press.

Brand, Peggy Z. and Carolyn Korsmeyer (eds) (1995) *Feminism and Tradition in Aesthetics*, Pennsylvania State University Press.

Brown, Norman (1959) *Life Against Death: the Psychoanalytical Meaning of History*, Sphere Books, 1970.

Burke, Edmund (1757/59) *A Philosophical Enquiry into the Origin of our Ideas of the Sublime and Beautiful*, ed. James T. Boulton, Blackwell, 1987.

——(1790) *Reflections on the Revolution in France*, in *The Writings and Speeches of Edmund Burke*, eds L. G. Mitchell and William B. Todd, Oxford University Press, 1989, vol. 8.

Canovan, Margaret (2000) 'Arendt's Theory of Totalitarianism: a Reassessment', in *The Cambridge Companion to Hannah Arendt*, ed. Dana Villa, Cambridge University Press, 25–43.

Carter, Erica (2004) *Dietrich's Ghosts: the Sublime and the Beautiful in Third Reich Film*, British Film Institute; University of California Press.

Cassirer, Ernst (1918) *Kant's Life and Thought*, trans. James Haden, Yale University Press, 1981.

Caws, Mary Ann, Rudolf E. Kuenzli and Gwen Raaberg (eds) (1991) *Surrealism and Women*, MIT Press, 1993.

Chadwick, Whitney (1985) *Women Artists and the Surrealist Movement*, Thames and Hudson.

Chailley, Jacques (1971) *The Magic Flute: Masonic Opera*, trans. Herbert Weinstock, Knopf, 1972.

Chambers, Simone (2002) 'Can Procedural Democracy be Radical?', in *The Political*, ed. David Ingram, Blackwell, 168–88.

Cheetham, Mark (2001) *Kant, Art and Art History*, Cambridge University Press.

Clark, Kenneth (1956) *The Nude: the Study of Ideal Art*, Penguin, 1964.

Coleridge, Samuel Taylor (1817) *Biographia Literaria*, J. M. Dent, Everyman's Library, n.d.

——(1835) *Specimens of the Table Talk of Samuel Taylor Coleridge*, ed. Henry Nelson Coleridge, John Murray, new ed., n.d.

——(1845) *Anima Poetæ: From the Unpublished Note-Books of S. T. Coleridge*, ed. Ernest Hartley Coleridge, William Heinemann, 1895.

——(1991) *Coleridge Among the Lakes and Mountains*, The Folio Society.

Constable, Catherine (2005) *Thinking in Images: Film Theory, Feminist Philosophy and Marlene Dietrich*, British Film Institute.

Cooley, Matt and Patrick Frierson (trans.) (2005) 'Kant's Remarks on the Observations on the Feeling of the Beautiful and Sublime'. Online. Available at: http://people.whitman.edu/~frierspr/kants_bemerkungen2.htm (accessed 1 January 2007).

Curiger, Bice (1989) *Meret Oppenheim*, trans. Catherine Schelbert, Parkett; ICA.

Dennis, John (1701) *The Advancement and Reformation of Modern Poetry* excerpt in Ashfield and de Bolla (1996), *The Sublime*, Cambridge University Press, 32–34.

—— (1704) *The Grounds of Criticism in Poetry*, excerpt in Ashfield and de Bolla (1996), *The Sublime*, Cambridge University Press, 34–39.

Derrida, Jacques (1978a) 'The Parergon', excerpts from *The Truth in Painting*, trans. Geoff Bennington and Ian Mcleod, University of Chicago Press, 1987, in *The Continental Aesthetics Reader*, ed. Clive Cazeaux, Routledge, 2000, 412–28.

——(1978b) *The Truth in Painting*, trans. Geoff Bennington and Ian Mcleod, University of Chicago Press, 1987.

——(1997) *Adieu to Emmanuel Levinas*, trans. Pascale-Anne Brault and Michael Naas, Stanford University Press, 1999.

Dickinson, Emily (1975) *The Poems of Emily Dickinson*, ed. Thomas Johnson, Faber.

Duff, William (1767) *An Essay on Original Genius; and its Various Modes of Exertion in Philosophy and the Fine Arts, Particularly in Poetry*, Edward and Charles Dilly.

Eliot, George (1859) *The Lifted Veil*, in *Silas Marner, The Lifted Veil, Brother Jacob*, ed. Peter Mudford, Dent, Everyman, 1996.

——(1963) *Essays*, ed. T. Pinney, Routledge and Kegan Paul.

Felski, Rita (1989) *Beyond Feminist Aesthetics*, Hutchinson Radius.

Freeman, Barbara Claire (1995) *The Feminine Sublime: Gender and Excess in Women's Fiction*, University of California Press.

Freud, Sigmund (1912) 'Recommendations to Physicians Practising Psycho-Analysis', in *The Standard Edition of the Complete Psychological Works of Sigmund Freud*, vol. 12, trans. James Strachey, The Hogarth Press, 1953–.

——(1916–17) *Introductory Lectures on Psychoanalysis*, trans. James Strachey, Pelican Freud Library vol. 1, Penguin, 1974.

——(1920) *Beyond the Pleasure Principle*, in *The Essentials of Psychoanalysis*, trans. James Strachey, ed. Anna Freud, Penguin, 1986.

——(1925) 'Some Psychical Consequences of the Anatomical Distinction Between the Sexes', in *On Sexuality*, trans. James Strachey, Pelican Freud Library vol. 7, Penguin, 1977.

——(1933) 'Femininity', in *The Essentials of Psychoanalysis*, trans. James Strachey, ed. Anna Freud, Penguin, 1986.

Frierson, Patrick R. (2003) *Freedom and Anthropology in Kant's Moral Philosophy*, Cambridge University Press.

Gilbert-Rolfe, Jeremy (1999) *Beauty and the Contemporary Sublime*, Allworth Press.

Gilroy, Paul (1993) *The Black Atlantic: Modernity and Double Consciousness*, Verso.

Glassie, John (2002) 'Oldest Living Surrealist Tells All', salon.com, February 11 2002. Online. Available at: http://dir.salon.com/story/people/feature/2002/02/11/tanning/index.html (accessed 20 November 2006).

Goethe, Johann Wolfgang von (1833) *Faust, 2. Teil*, Stuttgart and Tübingen.

Golding, John (2002) *Paths to the Absolute*, Thames and Hudson.

Görtz, Franz Josef (ed.) (1991) *Die Liebe der Günderode: Ein Roman in Briefen*, R. Piper GmbH.

Gould, Timothy (1995) 'Intensity and its Audiences: Toward a Feminist Perspective on the Kantian Sublime', in *Feminism and Tradition in Aesthetics*, eds. Peggy Z. Brand and Carolyn Korsmeyer, Pennsylvania State University Press, 66–87.

Greene, John C. (1954) 'Some Early Speculations on the Origin of Human Races', *American Anthropologist*, 56: 31–41.

Grundlehner, Philip (1986) *The Poetry of Friedrich Nietzsche*, Oxford University Press.

Günderrode, Karoline von (1979) *Der Schatten eines Traumes*, ed. Christa Wolf, Sammlung Luchterhand, 1981.

——(1991) *Sämtliche Werke und ausgewählte Studien*, ed. Walter Morgenth, Strömfeld, Roter Stern, 3 vols.

Guilbaut, Serge (1983) *How New York Stole the Idea of Modern Art*, University of Chicago Press.

Haden-Guest, Anthony (2001) 'On the Track of the "S" Word: a Reporter's Notes', in *Sticky Sublime*, ed. Bill Beckley, Allworth Press, 49–56.

Harrison, Charles and Paul Wood (eds) (1992) *Art in Theory 1900–1990: An Anthology of Changing Ideas*, Blackwell, 2001.

Hegel, G. W. F. (1807) *Phenomenology of Spirit*, trans. A. V. Miller, ed. J. N. Findlay, Oxford University Press, 1977.

——(1835) *Aesthetics: Lectures on Fine Art*, trans. T. M. Knox, ed. J. N. Findlay, Clarendon Press, 1998, 2 vols.

Hertz, Neil (1973) 'A Reading of Longinus', in *The End of the Line: Essays on Psychoanalysis and the Sublime*, Columbia University Press, 1985, 1–20.

——(1978) 'The Notion of Blockage in the Literature of the Sublime', in *The End of the Line: Essays on Psychoanalysis and the Sublime*, Columbia University Press, 1985, 40–60.

——(1985) *The End of the Line: Essays on Psychoanalysis and the Sublime*, Columbia University Press.

Hitler, Adolf (1925–27) *Mein Kampf*, trans. Ralph Manheim, introd. D. C. Watt, Hutchinson, 1969.

Hume, David (1739–40) *A Treatise of Human Nature*, eds. L. A. Selby-Bigge and P. H. Nidditch, Oxford University Press, 2nd ed., 1978.

——(1751) *An Enquiry Concerning the Principles of Morals*, in *Enquiries Concerning the Human Understanding and Concerning the Principles of Morals*, eds. L. A. Selby-Bigge and P. H. Nidditch, Oxford University Press, 3rd ed., 1975.

Huson, David (2001) 'A Willful Misunderstanding?' (sic.), *Telepolis*, 19 September 2001 [author Hudson, David]. Online. Available at: http://www.heise.de/tp/english/inhalt/te/9594/1.html (accessed 17 April 2006).

Hussey, Christopher (1927) *The Picturesque: Studies in a Point of View*, G. P. Putnam's.

Huyssen, Andreas (1984) 'Mapping the Postmodern', in *Feminism/Postmodernism*, ed. Linda Nicholson, Routledge, 1990, 234–77.

Ijsseling, S. (1976) *Rhetoric and Philosophy in Conflict*, Nijhoff.

Ingram, David (1987) *Habermas and the Dialectic of Reason*, Yale University Press.

Irigaray, Luce (1974) *Speculum of the Other Woman*, trans. Gillian C. Gill, Cornell University Press, 1985.

——(1977) *This Sex Which is Not One*, trans. Catherine Porter and Carolyn Burke, Cornell University Press, 1985.

——(1980) *Marine Lover of Friedrich Nietzsche*, trans. Gillian C. Gill, Columbia University Press, 1991.

——(1984) 'Divine Women', in *Sexes and Genealogies*, trans. Gillian G. Gill, Columbia University Press, 1993, 57–72.

——(1985) 'A Natal Lacuna', trans. Margaret Whitford, *Women's Art Magazine*, 58 (1994): 11–13.

——(1990a) *Je, Tu, Nous*, trans. Alison Martin, Routledge, 1993.

——(1990b) 'Questions to Emmanuel Levinas', trans. in *The Irigaray Reader*, ed. Margaret Whitford, Basil Blackwell, 1991, 178–89.

——(2004) *Key Writings*, ed. Luce Irigaray, Continuum.

Jung, Carl Gustav (1929–54) trans. R. F. C. Hull, *Alchemical Studies, The Collected Works of Jung* vol. 13, Routledge and Kegan Paul, 1967.

——(1944) *Psychology and Alchemy*, trans. R. F. C. Hull, *The Collected Works of Jung* vol. 12, Routledge and Kegan Paul, revised ed. 1967.

Jauch, Ursula Pia (1988) *Immanuel Kant zur Geschlechterdifferenz*, Passagen Verlag.

Kafka, Franz (1920) 'HE' in 'Notes from the Year 1920', *The Great Wall of China*, trans. Willa Muir and Edwin Muir, Schocken, 1946.

Kant, Immanuel (1764) *Observations on the Feeling of the Beautiful and Sublime*, trans. John Goldthwait, University of California Press, 1960. Abbreviated to *Obs*.

——(1764–65) *Bemerkungen zu den 'Beobachtungen über das Gefühl des Schönen und Erhabenen'*, in Kant (1902–), *Gesammelte Schriften*, vol. 20 (III/7), 1–192. Available at: http://www.ikp.uni-bonn.de/kant/aa20/Inhalt20.html (accessed 30 April 2007).

——(1775/77) 'Of the Different Human Races', in *The Idea of Race*, eds Robert Bernasconi and Tommy L. Lott, Hackett Readings in Philosophy, Hackett, 2000, 8–22.

——(1781/87) *Critique of Pure Reason*, trans. and ed. Paul Guyer and Allen W. Wood, Cambridge University Press, 1998. Abbreviated as *CPR*. The 1781 page numbers are marked A; the 1787 page numbers are marked B. Published in Kant (1902–), *Gesammelte Schriften*, vols. 3 (B ed.) and 4 (A ed.).

——(1784) 'An Answer to the Question: What is Enlightenment?' in Immanuel Kant (1996a), *Practical Philosophy*, trans. and ed. Mary J. Gregor, Cambridge University Press, 1996.

——(1785) *Groundwork of the Metaphysics of Morals* in Kant (1996a), *Practical Philosophy*, trans. and ed. Mary J. Gregor, Cambridge University Press.

——(1786) 'Conjectural Beginning of Human History', in *Kant on History*, ed. Lewis White Beck, Bobbs-Merrill, Library of Liberal Arts, 1963.

——(1788) *Critique of Practical Reason* in Kant (1996a), *Practical Philosophy*, trans. and ed. Mary J. Gregor, Cambridge University Press.

——(1790) *Critique of the Power of Judgment*, trans. Paul Guyer and Eric Matthews, Cambridge University Press, 2000. Abbreviated to *CPJ*. Unless otherwise noted, numerals refer to the pagination of vol. 5 of the German Akademie edition.

——(1793) *On the Common Saying: That May be Correct in Theory but it is of no Use in Practice*, in Kant (1996a), *Practical Philosophy*, trans. and ed. Mary J. Gregor, Cambridge University Press.

——(1793/94) *Religion Within the Boundaries of Mere Reason*, trans. Mary J. Gregor and Robert Anchor in Kant (1996b), *Religion and Rational Theology*, trans. and ed. Allen W. Wood and George di Giovanni, Cambridge University Press. Abbreviated to *RWB*.

——(1795) *Toward Perpetual Peace* in Kant (1996a), *Practical Philosophy*, trans. and ed. Mary J. Gregor, Cambridge University Press.

——(1796) 'On a Recently Prominent Tone of Superiority in Philosophy', in Kant (2002), *Theoretical Philosophy after 1781*, ed. Henry Allison and Peter Heath, trans. Gary Hatfield, Michael Friedman, Henry Allison and Peter Heath, Cambridge University Press.

——(1797/98) *The Metaphysics of Morals*, in Kant (1996a), *Practical Philosophy*, trans. and ed. Mary J. Gregor, Cambridge University Press.

——(1798/1800) *Anthropology from a Pragmatic Point of View*, trans. Victor Lyle Dowdell, Southern Illinois University Press, 1996. Abbreviated to *Anth.*

——(1803) *Education*, trans. A. Churton, University of Michigan Press, Ann Arbor Paperbacks, 1960.

——(1817) *Lectures on the Philosophical Doctrine of Religion*, ed. Ludwig Pölitz, trans. Allen W. Wood, in Kant (1996b), *Religion and Rational Theology*, trans. and ed. Allen W. Wood and George di Giovanni, Cambridge University Press.

——(1902–) *Gesammelte Schriften*, ed. der Deutschen [formerly Königlich Preussischen] Akademie der Wissenschaften, Walter de Gruyter Verlag. Abbreviated in the text to *KGS*.

——(1930) *Lectures on Ethics*, trans. Louis Infield, Harper and Row, 1963.

——(1952) *Critique of Judgement*, trans. James Creed Meredith, Clarendon Press.

——(1991) *Bemerkungen in den 'Beobachtungen über das Gefühl des Schönen und Erhabenen'*, ed. Marie Rischmüller, Felix Meiner Verlag, Kant-Forschungen Bd. 3.

——(1996a) *Practical Philosophy*, trans. and ed. Mary J. Gregor, Cambridge University Press.

——(1996b) *Religion and Rational Theology*, trans. and ed. Allen W. Wood and George di Giovanni, Cambridge University Press.

——(2002) *Theoretical Philosophy after 1781*, ed. Henry Allison and Peter Heath, trans. Gary Hatfield, Michael Friedman, Henry Allison and Peter Heath, Cambridge University Press.

——(2005) *Notes and Fragments*, ed. Paul Guyer, trans. Curtis Bowman, Paul Guyer and Frederick Rauscher, Cambridge University Press.

Kelly, Michael (ed.) (1994) *Critique and Power: Recasting the Foucault/Habermas Debate*, MIT Press.

——(ed.) (1988) *Encyclopedia of Aesthetics*, Oxford University Press, 1998, 4 vols.

Kofman, Sarah (1970) *The Childhood of Art: an Interpretation of Freud's Aesthetics*, trans. Winifred Woodhull, Columbia University Press, 1988.

——(1980) *The Enigma of Woman: Woman in Freud's Writings*, trans. Catherine Porter, Cornell University Press, 1985.

——(1982) 'The Economy of Respect: Kant and Respect for Women', *Social Research*, 49: 383–404.

Krauss, Rosalind E. (1993) *The Optical Unconscious*, MIT Press.

Kuehn, Manfred (2001) *Kant: A Biography*, Cambridge University Press.

Lacan, Jacques (1959–60) *The Ethics of Psychoanalysis*, ed. Jacques-Alain Miller, trans. Dennis Porter; *The Seminar of Jacques Lacan, Book 7*, 1st pub. in French 1986, Routledge, 1992.

——(1972–73) *Feminine Sexuality: Jacques Lacan and the École freudienne*, eds Juliet Mitchell and Jacqueline Rose, trans. Jacqueline Rose; selections from *The Seminar of Jacques Lacan, Book 20*, 1st pub. in French 1975, Macmillan, 1982.

[L.C.S., pseudonym] (1752) *Hermaphroditisches Sonn-und Monds-Kind*, by Johann Friederich Krebs bookseller, Hof und Universität Buchdruckerei.

Laqueur, Thomas (1990) *Making Sex: Body and Gender From the Greeks to Freud*, Harvard University Press.

Ledger, Sally, Josephine McDonagh and Jane Spencer (eds) (1994) *Political Gender: Texts and Contexts*, Harvester Wheatsheaf.

Levi, Primo (1958) *If This is a Man* published together with *The Truce* (1963), trans. Stuart Woolf, Abacus, 2004.

Levinas, Emmanuel (1989) *The Levinas Reader*, ed. Sean Hand, Basil Blackwell.

Levinson, Jerrold (1998) 'Schopenhauer', in Michael Kelly (ed.) (1988), *Encyclopedia of Aesthetics*, Oxford University Press, vol. 4, 245–50.

Lewis, Bernard (1999) *Semites and Anti-Semites: an Inquiry into Conflict and Prejudice*, W. W. Norton, 3rd ed.

Longinus (1957) *On Great Writing (On the Sublime)*, trans. and ed. G. M. A. Grube, Bobbs-Merrill, The Library of Liberal Arts.

Lorraine, Renée (1995) 'A History of Music', in *Feminism and Tradition in Aesthetics*, eds Peggy Z. Brand and Carolyn Korsmeyer, Pennsylvania State University Press, 160–85.

Lyotard, Jean-François (1977) *Les TRANSformateurs DUchamp*, Galilée.

——(1979) *The Postmodern Condition: a Report on Knowledge*, trans. Geoff Bennington and Brian Massumi, Manchester University Press, 1984.

——(1982) 'Answering the Question: What is Postmodernism?', Appendix to *The Postmodern Condition: a Report on Knowledge* (1979), trans. Geoff Bennington and Brian Massumi, Manchester University Press, 1984, 71–82.

——(1983) *The Differend: Phrases in Dispute*, trans. George Van Den Abeele, University of Minnesota Press, 1988.

——(1985) 'Newman: the Instant', in *The Lyotard Reader*, ed. Andrew Benjamin, Basil Blackwell, 1989, 240–49.

——(1986) 'A Response to Philippe Lacoue-Labarthe', in *ICA Documents 4: Postmodernism*, Institute of Contemporary Arts.

——(1988a) *The Inhuman: Reflections on Time*, trans. Geoff Bennington and Rachel Bowlby, Polity Press, 1991.

——(1988b) *Peregrinations: Law, Form, Event*, Columbia University Press.

——(1988c) *The Postmodern Explained: Correspondence 1982–1985*, ed. Julian Pefanis and Morgan Thomas, trans. Don Barry, Bernadette Maher, Julian Pefanis, Virginia Spate and Morgan Thomas, University of Minnesota Press, 1993.

——(1989) *The Lyotard Reader*, ed. Andrew Benjamin, Basil Blackwell.

——(1991) *Lessons on the Analytic of the Sublime*, trans. Elizabeth Rottenberg, Stanford University Press, 1994.

Macksey, Richard (1997) 'Longinus', in *The John Hopkins Guide to Literary Theory and Criticism*, John Hopkins University Press, 1997. Online. Available at: http://www.press.jhu.edu/books/hopkins_guide_to_literary_theory/longinus.html (accessed 25 August 2005).

Maclean, Ian (1980) *The Renaissance Notion of Woman*, Cambridge University Press.

Mahowald, Mary Briody (ed.) (1978) *Philosophy of Woman: Classical to Current Concepts*, Hackett Publishing Co.

Martin, Wendy (ed.) (2002) 'Susan and Emily Dickinson: Their Lives in Letters', in *The Cambridge Companion to Emily Dickinson*, Cambridge University Press.

McEwen, John (1990) 'An Honest Vision', *The Independent Magazine*, 20 January 1990.

Mendus, Susan (1987) 'Kant: "an Honest but Narrow-Minded Bourgeois"?' in *Women in Western Political Philosophy*, eds Ellen Kennedy and S. Mendus, Harvester.

Moers, Ellen (1963) *Literary Women*, The Women's Press, 1986.

Montesquieu (Charles de Secondat, Baron de la Brède et de Montesquieu) (1721) *Persian Letters*, trans. C. J. Betts, Penguin Books, 1973.

——(1748) *The Spirit of the Laws*, trans. and ed. Anne M. Cohler, Basia Carolyn Miller and Harold Samuel Stone, Cambridge University Press, 2004.

Morris, Meaghan (1988) *The Pirate's Fiancée: Feminism, Reading, Postmodernism*, Verso.

Nancy, Jean-Luc (1993) 'The Sublime Offering', in *Of the Sublime: Presence in Question*, ed. and trans. Jeffrey S. Librett, State University of New York Press.

Newman, Barnett (1990) *Selected Writings and Interviews*, ed. John P. O'Neill, University of California Press, 1992.

Nietzsche, Friedrich (1854–61) *Frühe Schriften, Bd. 1, Jugendschriften 1854–61*, ed. Hans Joachim Mette, Verlag C. H. Beck, 1933–40, reprinted 1994.

——(1872/86) *The Birth of Tragedy*, prefaced by 'Attempt at Self Criticism', in *The Basic Nietzsche*, trans. and ed. Walter Kaufmann, The Modern Library, 2000. Abbreviated to *BT* and referenced by section.

——(1873) 'On Truth and Lies in a Nonmoral Sense', in *Philosophy and Truth: Selections from Nietzsche's Notebooks of the early 1870's*, trans. and ed. Daniel Breazeale, Humanities Press International, 1994, 77–97.

——(1881) *Daybreak: Thoughts on the Prejudices of Morality*, eds Maudemarie Clark and Brian Leiter, trans. R. J. Hollingdale, Cambridge University Press, 1997. Abbreviated to *D* and referenced by section.

——(1882/87) *The Gay Science*, trans. and ed. Walter Kaufmann, Vintage, 1974. Abbreviated to GS and referenced by section.

——(1883–85) *Thus Spoke Zarathustra*, in *The Portable Nietzsche*, trans. and ed. Walter Kaufmann, The Viking Press, 1968. Abbreviated to Z.

——(1886) *Beyond Good and Evil*, trans. Walter Kaufmann, Vintage, 1966. Abbreviated to *BGE* and referenced by section.

——(1887) *On the Genealogy of Morals*, trans. Walter Kaufmann and bound with Nietzsche, Friedrich (1908), *Ecce Homo*, Vintage, 1969. Abbreviated to GM and referenced by section.

——(1888) *Twilight of the Idols*, in *The Portable Nietzsche*, trans. and ed. Walter Kaufmann, The Viking Press, 1968. Abbreviated to *TI*.

——(1908) *Ecce Homo*, bound together with Nietzsche (1887), *On the Genealogy of Morals*, trans. Walter Kaufmann, Vintage, 1969.

Novalis (Friedrich von Hardenberg) (1800) *Hymns to the Night*, trans. Dick Higgins, revised ed., 1988.

——(1802) *Heinrich von Ofterdingen*. Available at: http://gutenberg.spiegel.de/novalis/ofterdng/ofterdng.htm (accessed 24 April 2006).

——(1978) *Werke, Tagebücher und Briefe Friedrich von Hardenbergs, Band 1 Das dichterische Werke, Tagebücher und Briefe*, ed. Richard Samuel, Wissenschaftliche Buchgesellschaft, 1999.

Padilla, Katherine Mary (1988) 'The Embodiment of the Absolute: Theories of the Feminine in the Works of Schleiermacher, Schlegel, and Novalis', unpublished PhD dissertation, Princeton University.

Pateman, Carole (1988) *The Sexual Contract*, Polity Press.

Pfefferkorn, Kristin (1988) *Novalis: A Romantic's Theory of Language and Poetry*, Yale University Press.

Plato (*c*.385 BCE) *Symposium*, trans. Walter Hamilton, Penguin, 1951.

Pollock, Griselda (1988) *Vision and Difference*, Routledge.

Price, Uvedale (1810) *Essays on the Picturesque*, Mawman, 3rd ed., 3 vols.

Rampley, Matthew (2000) *Nietzsche, Aesthetics and Modernity*, Cambridge University Press.

Reinhold, Karl Leonhard [Br. Decius] (1788) *Die Hebräische Mysterien oder die älteste religiöse Freymaurerey*, Georg Joachim Göschen.

Reresby, Tamworth (1721) *A Miscellany of Ingenious Thoughts and Reflections*, excerpt in Ashfield and de Bolla (1996), *The Sublime*, Cambridge University Press, 43–44.

Robin, Corey (2004) *Fear: the History of a Political Idea*, Oxford University Press.

Rommel, Gabriele (ed.) (1998) *Geheimnisvolle Zeichen: Alchemie, Magie, Mystik und Natur bei Novalis*, Peter Lang.

Rousseau, Jean-Jacques (1762) *Emile or On Education*, trans. B. Boxley, Everyman, 1956.

——(1782) *Reveries of a Solitary Walker*, trans. Peter France, Penguin, 1979.

Russell, Pamela (1993) 'The Palaeolithic Mother Goddess: Fact or Fiction?', in *Reader in Gender Archaeology*, eds Kelley Hays-Gilpin and David S. Whitney, Routledge, 1998, 261–68.

Said, Edward (1979) *Orientalism*, Vintage, 1994.

Saint Girons, Baldine (1998) 'The Sublime from Longinus to Montesquieu', trans. F. L. Rush, *Encyclopedia of Aesthetics*, ed. Michael Kelly, Oxford University Press, 1998, vol. 4, 322–26.

Salomon, Nicolas (1695) *Dictionaire hermetique, contenant l'explication des termes, fables, enigmes, emblemes et manières de parler des vrais philosophes*, Laurent d'Houry.

Sanborn, Frank B. (1909) *Recollections of Seventy Years*, Gorham Press, 2 vols. Online. Available at: http://www.walden.org/institute/thoreau/about2/S/FranklinSanborn/ (accessed 13 February 2006).

Sandel, Michael (1982) *Liberalism and the Limits of Justice*, Cambridge University Press.

Scharf, Aaron (1974) *Art and Photography*, Penguin, 1974.

Schelling, Friedrich Wilhelm Joseph (1801–4) *The Philosophy of Art*, ed. and trans. Douglas W. Stott, 1st pub. in German in 1859, University of Minnesota Press, 1989.

Schiller, Friedrich von (1790) 'Die Sendung Moses', *Thalia*, 10th Stück. Online. Available at: http://gutenberg.spiegel.de/schiller/moses/moses.htm (accessed 23 December 2005).

——(1795) 'Das verschleierte Bild zu Sais', *Die Horen* (1795): 9th Stück. Online. Available at: http://gutenberg.spiegel.de/schiller/gedichte/sais.htm (accessed 23 December 2005).

——(1801) 'On the Sublime', in *Naïve and Sentimental Poetry and On the Sublime*, trans. and introd. Julius A. Elias, Frederick Ungar Publishing Co., 1975.

Schopenhauer, Arthur (1809–18) *Manuscript Remains: volume 2, Critical Debates (1809–1818)*, ed. Arthur Hübscher, trans. E. F. J. Payne, Berg, 1988.

——(1819/59) *The World as Will and Representation*, trans. E. F. J. Payne, Dover Publications, 2 vols., 1966. Intext references abbreviated to *WWR*.

——(1851) 'On Women' from *Parerga and Paralipomena*, trans. in *The Essential Schopenhauer*, Unwin Books, 1962.

Schott, Robin May (1988) *Cognition and Eros: a Critique of the Kantian Paradigm*, Beacon Press.

Sedgwick, Eve Kosofsky (1986) *The Coherence of Gothic Conventions*, Methuen Press.

Şen, Faruk and Hayrettin Aydin (2002) *Islam in Deutschland*, Verlag C. H. Beck.

Shell, Susan Meld (2003) 'Kant's "True Economy of Human Nature": Rousseau, Count Verri and the Problem of Happiness', in *Essays on Kant's Anthropology*, eds Brian Jacobs and Patrick Kain, Cambridge University Press.

Spies, Werner (ed.) (1991) *Max Ernst: a Retrospective*, Tate Gallery.

Steinberg, Leo (1983) *The Sexuality of Christ in Renaissance Art and in Modern Oblivion*, University of Chicago Press, 2nd expanded ed., 1996.

Stone, Merlin (1974) *When God Was a Woman*, Dial Press.

Strauss, Jonathan (1998) *Subjects of Terror: Nerval, Hegel and the Modern Self*, Stanford University Press.

Tanning, Dorothea (2001) *Between Lives: an Artist and Her World*, W. W. Norton.

Voltaire, François Marie Arouet de (1753) *Essai sur les moeurs et l'esprit des nations*. Online. Available at: http://www.voltaire-integral.com/Html/00Table/11.html (accessed 1 May 2006).

Waithe, Mary Ellen (ed.) (1991) *A History of Women Philosophers, Volume 3: 1600–1900*, Kluwer Academic Publishers.

Weiskel, Thomas (1976) *The Romantic Sublime: Studies in the Structure and Psychology of Transcendence*, John Hopkins University Press.

Welton, Donn (1998) 'Biblical Bodies', *Body and Flesh*, ed. Donn Welton, Blackwell.

Williams, Evelyn (1994) 'Extracts from an Unpublished Workbook', in *Antinomies: Works by Evelyn Williams*, Catalogue on an Exhibition curated by Christine Battersby and Victoria Pomery, with an essay by Christine Battersby, The Mead Gallery, Coventry, 23 April–30 May 1994.

——(1998) *Works and Words*, eds Derek Birdsall and Bruce Bernard, Omnific.

Wolf, Christa (1979) *No Place on Earth*, trans. Jan van Heurck, Virago, 1995.

Wolff, Janet (1993) *Aesthetics and the Sociology of Art*, Macmillan, 2nd ed.

Wollstonecraft, Mary (1790) *A Vindication of the Rights of Men in a Letter to the Right Honourable Edmund Burke*, Woodstock Books, 1994.

——(1792) *A Vindication of the Rights of Woman*, Dent, Everyman, ed. 1929.

——(1796) *A Short Residence in Sweden, Norway and Denmark*, published together with William Godwin (ed.), *Memoirs of the Author of the Rights of Woman* (1798), ed. Richard Holmes, Penguin, 1987.

Wood, Marcus (2000) *Blind Memory: Visual Representations of Slavery in England and America 1780–1865*, Routledge.

Wood, Theodore E. B. (1972) *The Word 'Sublime' and its Context 1650–1750*, Mouton.

Wordsworth, William (1888) *The Complete Poetical Works*, Macmillan.

Yaeger, Patricia (1989) 'Toward a Female Sublime', in *Gender and Theory*, ed. Linda Kauffman, Blackwell, 191–212.

Yeats, William Butler (1937) *A Vision*, Macmillan, corrected ed., 1962.

Young, Edward (1759) 'Conjectures on Original Composition', *English Critical Essays: Sixteenth, Seventeenth and Eighteenth Centuries*, ed. Edmund D. Jones, Oxford University Press, 1947.

Young, Iris Marion (1990) *Throwing Like a Girl and Other Essays in Feminist Philosophy and Social Theory*, Indiana University Press.

Zammito, John H. (1992) *The Genesis of Kant's Critique of Judgment*, University of Chicago Press.

——(2002) *Kant, Herder and the Birth of Anthropology*, Chicago University Press.

Zylinska, Joanna (2001) *On Spiders, Cyborgs and Being Scared: the Feminine and the Sublime*, Manchester University Press.

INDEX

Related titles from Routledge

The Routledge Companion to Aesthetics
Second Edition

Edited by Dominic Lopes and Berys Gaut

'This is an immensely useful book that belongs in every college library and on the bookshelves of all serious students of aesthetics.'

Journal of Aesthetics and Art Criticism

'The succinctness and clarity of the essays will make this a source that individuals not familiar with aesthetics will find extremely helpful.'

The Philosophical Quarterly

The second edition of the acclaimed *Routledge Companion to Aesthetics* contains fifty-four chapters written by leading international scholars covering all aspects of aesthetics. The volume is structured in four parts: History, Aesthetic Theory, Issues and Challenges, and Individual Arts.

The new edition includes nine new entries: Creativity; Schopenhauer, Schiller and Schelling; Nelson Goodman; Style; Feminism; Ontology; Heidegger; Sartre and Merleau-Ponty. Many other entries have been revised and further reading brought up to date.

The Routledge Companion to Aesthetics is essential reading for anyone interested in aesthetics, art, literature, and visual studies.

ISBN 10: 0-415-32797-0 (hbk)
ISBN 10: 0-415-32798-9 (pbk)

ISBN 13: 978-0-415-32797-8 (hbk)
ISBN 13: 978-0-415-32798-5 (pbk)

Available at all good bookshops
For ordering and further information please visit:
www.routledge.com

Related titles from Routledge

Kant

Paul Guyer

'Kant is an absolutely first-rate general introduction to Kant's Critical Philosophy. Paul Guyer's interpretations are extremely well-supported, carefully and crisply argued, and highly insightful'

Robert Hanna, University of Colorado

'An impressive overview of the various strands of Kant's philosophy. With great skill Guyer manages to compress Kant's critical thought into a few hundred pages. This book will provide an excellent introduction to Kant's thought.'

Philip Stratton-Lake, University of Reading

'The book is impressive in very many ways. It demonstrates a mastery of the Kantian corpus and an ability to explain exceedingly complex arguments in a clear and accessible fashion. I think it will become essential reading for students wanting to grasp the broad sweep of Kant's thought without losing much by way of depth.'

Andrew Chignell, Cornell University

'That Guyer is able to cover this much material, clearly and without oversimplification, in a single, reasonably sized volume represents a unique accomplishment, which should prove to be extremely useful to a broad audience'

Eric Watkins, University of California, San Diego

ISBN 10: 0-415-28335-3 (hbk)
ISBN 10: 0-415-28336-1 (pbk)

ISBN 13: 978-0-415-28335-3 (hbk)
ISBN 13: 978-0-415-28336-6 (pbk)

Available at all good bookshops
For ordering and further information please visit:
www.routledge.com

Related titles from Routledge

Arguing about Art

Second Edition

Edited by Alex Neill and Aaron Ridley

'A most valuable supplement to any philosophical aesthetics course. one that would enliven and freshen it up, partly by deftly engaging students.'
Times Higher Education Supplement

'My first choice for a core text in an undergraduate course would be Neill and Ridley. On every topic their lively collection stimulates thought'
Peter Lamarque, European Journal of Philosophy

This acclaimed and accessible anthology is ideal for newcomers to aesthetics or philosophy. Neill and Ridley introduce a wide range of discussions including sentimentality, feminism and aesthetics, appreciation, understanding and nature. Each chapter is accompanied by a clear introduction and suggestions for further reading.

This new edition has been fully revised and updated. It includes five new sections on the art of food, rock music and culture, enjoying horror, art and morality and public art.

Arguing about Art will appeal to students of art history, literature, and cultural studies as well as philosophy.

ISBN 10: 0-415-23738-6 (hbk)
ISBN 10: 0-415-23739-4 (pbk)

ISBN 13: 978-0-415-23738-3 (hbk)
ISBN 13: 978-0-415-23739-0 (pbk)

Available at all good bookshops
For ordering and further information please visit:
www.routledge.com

Related titles from Routledge

Philosophy of the Arts
Third Edition
Gordon Graham

Praise for the previous editions:

'A textbook for students needs to satisfy many criteria ... These criteria are amply met by Gordon Graham's excellent book ... Graham's introduction to aesthetics informs, illuminates, and should elicit lively discussions in any courses that utilize it.' – *British Journal of Aesthetics*

'Graham's account is subtle and seductive ... attractive and readable.'
European Journal of Philosophy

'Graham's book rivals Dickie's [*Introduction to Aesthetics*, OUP, 1997] for its clarity and excellent organization, but Graham's more expansive style is more accessible to those who are new to philosophy.'
Journal of Aesthetics and Art Criticism

'Graham's discussion is thorough, authoritative, and accessible; one always feels in sure hands.' – *Philosophy in Review*

Philosophy of the Arts presents a comprehensive and accessible introduction to those coming to aesthetics and the philosophy of art for the first time. The third edition is greatly enhanced with new chapters on art and beauty, the performing arts and modern art, and there are new sections on Aristotle, Hegel and Nietzsche. The remaining chapters have been thoroughly revised and extended. This new edition:

- is jargon-free and will appeal to students of music, art history, literature and theatre studies as well as philosophy
- looks at a wide range of the arts from film, painting and architecture to literature, music, dance and drama
- discusses the philosophical theories of major thinkers including Aristotle, Hume, Hegel, Nietzsche, Croce, Collingwood, Gadamer and Derrida
- includes regular summaries and suggestions for further reading.

ISBN 10: 0-415-34978-8 (hbk)
ISBN 10: 0-415-34979-6 (pbk)
ISBN 13: 978-0-415-34978-9 (hbk)
ISBN 13: 978-0-415-34979-6 (pbk)

Available at all good bookshops
For ordering and further information please visit:
www.routledge.com